Growing Up Global

Growing Up Global

Raising Children to Be At

Home in the World

HOMA SABET TAVANGAR

BALLANTINE BOOKS · NEW YORK

A Ballantine Books Trade Paperback Original

Copyright © 2009 by Homa S. Tavangar

Line art on p. 111–112 by Anisa Tavangar

All rights reserved.

Published in the United States by Ballantine Books,
an imprint of The Random House Publishing Group,
a division of Random House, Inc., New York.

BALLANTINE and colophon are registered
trademarks of Random House, Inc.

LIBRARY OF CONGRESS CATALOGING-IN-PUBLICATION DATA
Tavangar, Homa Sabet.
Growing up global : raising children to be at home in the world /
Homa Sabet Tavangar.
p.   cm.
Includes bibliographical references and index.
ISBN 978-0-345-50654-2 (pbk.)
1. Child rearing. 2. Globalization—Social aspects.
3. Multiculturalism.
I. Title.
HQ769.T277 2009
305.23089'009051—dc22   2009021248

Printed in the United States of America

www.ballantinebooks.com

4   6   8   9   7   5   3

Book design by Debbie Glasserman

This book is dedicated to the memory and legacy
of my four beloved grandparents, who dared
to let their vision be world-embracing

Contents

Make Yourself at Home . . . in the World

Why I Wrote This Book and
Why You Need to Read It

My family and I spent the first three months of 2007 living in West Africa. As our days in The Gambia passed like a blur and the pace of our busy North American schedules acquiesced to life in a foreign land, it seemed that the reason for our long journey changed almost every day: to experience life in a different culture and environment during my eldest daughter's last year before high school; for the kids to attend an international school—so different from their homogenous, well-equipped American public school; to spend meaningful time with their cousins who have been raised in Africa; to be engaged in service where it was desperately needed; to get back in touch with my own heritage of pioneers and travelers to exotic lands; and so that I could write. Ultimately, though, I think it boiled down, for me, to a challenge I set up in my mind: It was to see "could we really do it; and what would *it* do to us?" A motivating principle in my life has revolved around belief in humanity's oneness. By exposing my children to such a different human experience, I was putting that belief to the test.

The unusual trip required a good deal of preparation and sacrifice—not the least of which was from my husband, who stayed home to work, visited us for one week, and returned at the height of winter to a quiet house. Once we got the idea into our heads that we could make adjustments in our lives to realize this dream, there seemed to be no reason important enough to prevent the trip. This was a precious window in our lives where we could take a sabbatical from our routine and be welcomed to experience firsthand a little-known corner of the world. The entire financial expenditure still amounted to less than a single year of private school tuition, I adjusted my work schedule, and the ordeal of putting my daughters through numerous vaccinations just made them stronger. After our public school administrators gave their support and our calendars were cleared for three months, the biggest challenge was what gifts to buy—mostly for people we had yet to meet—that would be both useful and fit within the strict forty-pound per person luggage limit.

Three things shaped my experience the most during our stay in The Gambia: volunteering in a local public school, where only about twenty percent of the sixth-graders were functionally literate; seeing what life in a relatively peaceful African country was like through the lens of my children; and condensing our experiences into a daily blog I wrote for the *Philadelphia Inquirer*.

As I helped my twelve-year-old daughter make sense of African children in frayed, American cast-off T-shirts approaching her shouting *"Two-bob, two-bob"* (white person, white person) to her face and then saying "Sponsor me" (for school fees or other expenses), while mansions stood nearby behind fortified gates and European tourists ambled the streets in a Muslim country wearing nothing but a bikini, I realized that our experience of traveling from suburban American life to a tiny African country could help inform other families about raising their children to become global citizens, too. So many people wanted us to share our experience with them. They didn't think they'd be going farther away than Disney World, but they did want to know what impact I'd seen on my kids and then share some of our stories with their own children. And, of course, we're not the only family with helpful experiences. There are millions out there from whom I—and my friends— would like to learn. Global social, political, and economic forces are crashing in around us and parents in my generation are grasping at straws to find ways to prepare our children for this unknown new world they will need to navigate.

If I ever doubted that it is possible for insulated American kids to feel "at home in the world," the reactions of my three children—who have lived in the same American suburb their entire lives—to their new environment, and particularly, the relationships with their new African friends, gave me hope. One of the highlights from our experience was how well my youngest daughter, just three-and-a-half at the time, adapted to her completely new environment. In her Gambian class, Sophia was the only light-skinned child (and she's the "darkest" one at her U.S. school). I talked with her about going to a new classroom, with new friends and teachers, but I didn't mention anything about how different she would be from her peers, trying to preserve her as a "blank slate." That first day, she sat still on my lap for thirty to forty minutes, intently watching the activity in the classroom. Then, when she became more comfortable, she walked over to the activity tables and explored. The next day—and each day after—the children hugged her when she walked in and made "birthday cakes" with bougainvillea and hibiscus flowers they picked for one another. I've never seen a more loving classroom environment, anywhere.

When we returned home, everyone who knew Sophia commented on how much she had changed. She was so comfortable going back to school, more ready to make friends, able to express more complex thoughts, and didn't display the same attachment anxiety to Mommy. The eagerness and openness with which her African friends welcomed Sophia affected her profoundly. Among these sweet children, differences of race and nationality became only points of interest when fixing one another's different textured hair. Circles of friendship were malleable and open. We were quickly invited into her friends' homes, where we ate foods that were novel to us, and the girls danced and played games or dress-ups in ways Sophia and I had never seen. By the end of our stay, she could switch in and out of speaking with a Gambian accent, became a fan of "football" (soccer), gained a new concept of physical beauty (preferring dark to fair complexions), and was undisturbed by going to a school without electricity. As she told her friends back at her American school, "It's okay, we had lots of sunshine."

The innocence of Sophia's age group demonstrates the impact that openness to new experiences can have. She had the fewest preconceived notions and thus took in the most. We already see the results: Her experience with these authentic friendships shaped her character in ways we are still uncovering. My other two daughters, ages twelve and fourteen at the time, also consider the friends they made from their international school, natives of The Gambia as well as Sierra Leone, Nigeria, Germany, and Lebanon—countries of which they had little or no prior knowledge, as the highlight of their "African experience."

THE OTHER SIDE OF THE STORY

The influence on my children of their direct exposure to such a different and loving cultural experience demonstrates how powerful feeling "at home in the world" can be for our children. That's the proactive reason to read this book: Simply put, positive experiences with the world's cultures enhance our lives.

I believe there is another very important, though less idealistic reason to read this book and put it to use. We live in a rapidly changing world, where we know that globalization shapes our daily lives and is a major determinant to one's financial and career success. At the same time, our borders seem more closed than they have ever been. The fears of terrorism, job outsourcing, and immigrants—legal or otherwise—along with less cultural and racial diversity in most American schools colors public policy and our exposure to the world.

This open-world, closed-world dichotomy became very clear to me when I spent the first anniversary of the September 11 terrorist attacks in Beijing, China. I was in an early morning business meeting with the executive team of the 2008 Olympic Games when I suddenly remembered that the date was 9/11/02. Back home in the United States, fear of another terrorist attack seemed to permeate all media and every conversation. But in bustling Beijing, the anniversary was barely acknowledged. The buzz in the air that day had more to do with moon cakes for the harvest festival and sealing the next deal in a booming economy.

More impressive than the deal-making and the ultramodern buildings going up at every corner were the children I met. On command, in city after city, they showed off their skills in martial arts, languages, and mathematics (granted, some of these were staged for the visitors, but other encounters were spontaneous and informal). Socially, they were charming and adept. These children had a destiny with the global economy—and they knew it. These three phenomena—witnessing this new global economic power, the focus with which children were educated and trained, and spending the first anniversary of the September 11 attacks away from home—showed me up close how much Americans need to learn about the rest of the world. Not everyone thinks like we do. Shifting economic, social, political, and even spiritual and psychological forces are colliding with our perceived *status quo*—whether we recognize them or not.

These issues took on a whole new light when I returned home from this first international business trip since having children, to discover I was pregnant with our third child. Once again, I needed to rearrange my life, and with images of 9/11 and of China's formidable economic engine fresh in my mind, I began to revisit my deepest parental concerns: How could we protect and care for this innocent life in a frenetic, confused, corrupt, angry, and at times, hostile world? I wondered how can we help our children feel at home in the world and give them the skills to think about complex issues on their own? Families can't simply isolate themselves and hope for the best. I had spent my career helping smart businesspeople make sense of global markets, and overcome their own deep-seated fears of the unknown foreign competition, but trying to navigate these issues for and with my kids perplexed me. It struck me that parents needed tools to help their children navigate the changing world, as much as businesspeople did. I wanted to move away from the defensive motivation that seemed to color our American perspective, with its yellow-orange-red Homeland Security alerts. Global competition or "flattening" should not become the next generation's "Red Scare."

I believe that gaining confidence and faith dissipates fear and anxiety. If my kids can relate to the world through a lens of hope and love and eagerness, then those children I met in China can be friends and helpmates, instead of enemies and competitors, and an African child can be so much more than someone you pity. If our children learn some stories, songs, or games of Arab children, perhaps the TV images of Palestinians or Iraqis would not seem as menacing and puzzling to them as they do to my contemporaries, today's generation of parents. Common sense, as well as empirical evidence, demonstrates that international consciousness in children leads to adults who can function more effectively in a global environment.

The election of Barack Obama, who declared to a crowd of hundreds of thousands of Berliners waving American flags, "I speak to you not as a candidate for President, but as a citizen—a proud citizen of the United States, and a fellow citizen of the world," attests to this new reality. He grew up traversing the gaps between multiple cultural milieus as did many of his advisors. We still have a long way to go. The end of a book review of *Putin's Russia* in the *Philadelphia Inquirer,* my local newspaper, summed up simply how we're doing:

> But as we wonder why the Iraqis react this way, and the French that way, and the Russians help the Iranians, and the Germans blithely lecture the United States on moral points only decades after incinerating millions, a common explanation coalesces. We don't know enough about other countries. We don't follow the rest of the world enough. Our newspapers and TV stations don't tell us enough. And we don't care enough.[1]

TAKING ACTION

The purpose of this book, then, is to offer practical steps for parents to incorporate the concept of international awareness and world citizenship as one of their family values. This book will attempt to provide perspective and solutions and to remove the trepidation about being at "one" with peoples of different cultures and beliefs. This is not about creating one amalgam of the world's cultures. Embracing the consciousness of world citizenship implies a more complex process of knowing one's self while appreciating others.

Treating world citizenship as a family value can help avoid the crisis mentality parents experienced after 9/11, when, on top of our own fears and insecurities, we suddenly needed to talk to our kids about the world. As with other difficult topics (like sexuality), one talk is not enough. Instead, we initiate a lifelong process of forming our deepest value systems: Parents offer guidance and a foundation; kids apply this knowledge along the way and incorporate it into their own actions and worldview. If the issues are ignored until a crisis comes along, then the moral compass likely will be confused. If the issues are addressed openly, today's children—tomorrow's leaders—will acquire a sense of confidence in approaching the difficult, often uncomfortable questions facing the world.

My aim is to encourage a proactive mindset, so that a family is not only reacting to world events that force the discussion—9/11, the Asian tsunami, war in Iraq, an interconnected global financial meltdown; the list keeps growing—but can connect genuinely with the people, circumstances, and challenges facing other human beings.

My own upbringing was like a laboratory for these ideas. My mother's family comes from a long line of Orthodox Jews and my mother was educated in Catholic schools. My father descends from devout Muslims. Both sets of my grandparents embraced the Baha'i Faith, which teaches the idea that there is one God, that all religions share a common spiritual foundation and that humanity is one. As a result of this choice, almost all of my relatives were both pushed and pulled out of their native land, Iran, in waves of emigration, from the 1940s through the 1990s. This resulted in our having family scattered to all corners of the earth. I have cousins that are Japanese, Malawian, and Austrian—a world family—so I have always considered myself connected with different people on the planet.

Not all families will have a direct link to disparate places and cultures in the world, or can get their kids on a plane to learn about other places and peoples first-hand, but you can expose them to the myriad cultures around the world, starting with the resources in your own communities. As you open your minds and your lives to other ways of doing things, you'll probably get to know yourselves and where you came from better; and possibly deepen the bonds within your own families along the way. Raising children to have a global mind-set could be the biggest step you and your family take toward building a more peaceful world—and it all starts at home.

GETTING FROM HERE TO THERE

This book is organized around the metaphor of making a new friend. The various chapters walk the reader through the elements of a lasting, fun, and interesting friendship. When I envision a "world citizen," I think of someone who has the capacity to be a friend to all. You don't have to start by trying to master all the world cultures—which is overwhelming for anyone. Instead, think of the process on the level of building individual friendships, learning about each other one step at a time, and having fun along the way.

Psychologists link friendship to an individual's health and ultimately, to one's survival.[2] While friendly interactions among children can spur learning, when your kids make a friend, the relationship is probably mostly fun and games. As parents, ideally, you get to know the families of your children's friends, and sometimes you need to supervise play. Extending the analogy, in each chapter I include fun, hands-on activities to do with children, along with some background for the parents, and information for further learning. To gauge the range of your knowledge on the subject or culture, in the first chapter I have developed an International Quiz, to test your *other* IQ. This gets you to ask yourself questions about your own experiences, assumptions, and patterns of behavior, which ultimately influence your children's worldview and formative experiences. I broke down the stages of forming a friendship in the following steps, which comprise subsequent chapters.

The first step is embracing the mind-set to make a friend and be a good friend. This calls for certain universal qualities, like empathy and respect, as embodied by the Golden Rule, which permeates all cultures and faith traditions. Subsequent chapters are more action-oriented and include lists of resources available for trying out with your family. Each chapter corresponds to things you would do with your friend, like greet them, play, go to school together, eat a meal, share a worship service, go to the movies, celebrate a birthday, and work on sustaining your friendship through service activities. Breaking down the elements of what makes diverse cultures similar as well as unique makes them easier to relate to, one of the goals of "growing up global." There is no need to attempt all the ideas contained in each chapter. Just start with two or three that appeal to you or your family members and have fun. Refer back to specific sections when you want to. Each chapter can stand alone as a reference for its particular topic.

If we remember that growing up with a global perspective is really a lifelong process and not one final destination—you don't just arrive—qualities of humility, curiosity, and compassion will be nurtured. These are the virtues of a true friend, and a world citizen.

Growing Up Global

Chapter 1

Be a Friend

Be a friend to the whole human race.

ABDUL-BAHA

My family's experience in Africa showed me that it is possible for our children to feel at home in the world and that nothing demonstrates this potential more clearly than the joys of friendship. The theme of friendship is universal, spanning age groups, cultures, incomes, and education levels. You don't have to go all the way to Africa to see this or to know that the social and emotional side of your child's development is at least as important to their happiness and future success as their academics.

To *"be a friend to the whole human race,"* a simple, yet profound process is launched. One doesn't need to feel the overwhelming burden of trying to teach their children about the whole world. The magic of one close friendship, and the many activities you experience together along the way, will yield its own lessons—naturally.

UNIVERSAL VIRTUES: THE FUNDAMENTALS

I believe it's the universal virtues—honesty, respect, patience, generosity, and empathy—that form the foundation for genuine communication in any cultural situation. More than knowing the quirks of each culture's acceptable table manners or how many kisses are required when greeting, people appreciate the sincere demonstration of universal virtues. You don't have to speak the same language to recognize when someone is afraid of you, or is being kind to you. In my young daughter Sophia's experience, she had no knowledge of racial prejudice or the many differences between African and U.S. life. Instead, she responded to the abundant love and kindness shown to her each day in her Gambian preschool.

Friends in unlikely places: Seeds of Peace

True friends can overcome the greatest barriers. Obstacles that seem insurmountable between warring ethnic groups can become inconsequential among friends or spouses of those same groups. At a minimum, true friends can confront the barriers. One nongovernmental organization, Seeds of Peace (seedsofpeace.org), makes an impact on the world by bringing youth from conflicting ethnic groups, like Palestinians and Israelis, or Indians and Pakistanis, together for programs like summer camp in Maine, where they learn leadership skills and share bunks, play, dance, and talk to one another. This enables them "to see the human face of their enemies." Testimonials from Seeds of Peace participants confirm that such intense personal contact has transformed the way they view and interact with the other group and has made a profound impact upon their worldview and lives well into adulthood.

Share examples like this with your children so they begin to see efforts that good people worldwide are making to build peace. The media exposes us to plenty of war, but how much do we know about actual peacemaking?

THE GOLDEN RULE

Sophia's experience at her African school embodied the Golden Rule, which every faith tradition and culture reaffirms. The idea of "Do unto others as you would have them do unto you" is probably enough to usher in world peace, if we could only take this principle to heart. It's a great starting point for teaching your children (and, of course, yourself) about connecting with the rest of the world.

The everyday life of adults as well as children—anywhere there is human interaction—puts this Rule to the test. From how we place our luggage in the overhead compartment of a crowded airplane, to sharing a favorite toy with a classmate, to who our preteen invites to his birthday party, we may be applying the Golden Rule. Without putting this principle into practice, you can't be a true friend; without the qualities of being a friend, seeing yourself at one with the world is limited to an intellectual exercise involving material differences.

The Golden Rule, taken to heart, helps to create a bridge between knowing about the differences (such as cultural practices, languages, and religious systems) and internalizing a profound empathy, or oneness with the rest of humanity. One

Expressions of the Golden Rule in the world's most widespread faiths

(IN ALPHABETICAL ORDER)

"Blessed is he who preferreth his brother before himself." Baha'i Faith

"Hurt not others in ways that you yourself would find hurtful." Buddhism

"Do unto others as you would have them do unto you." Christianity

*"This is the sum of duty: do not do to others what would cause pain
    if done to you."* Hinduism

*"None of you [truly] believes until he wishes for his brother what
    he wishes for himself."* Islam

"Thou shalt love thy neighbor as thyself." Judaism

of my favorite books for the whole family is *Children Just Like Me,* published in association with UNICEF. With each color spread of diverse children's lives, the reader sees how other children play, interact with their own families, what they eat, and where they live. After you and your children gain a greater understanding of the Golden Rule, look through these pages and ask questions that relate to the Golden Rule, like: Do you notice how Carlitos from Argentina or Erdene from Mongolia (or any other child in the book) is standing with his/her family, do they look like they respect one another? Love one another? Have fun together? How does the way they treat their siblings, friends, or even their animals show the Golden Rule? What part of your life is similar? If you met them, what could you do together? How would you show them that you understand the Golden Rule? Then, refer to the box above that illustrates the Golden Rule in the world's religions, and consider which one of the Golden Rule quotes would apply to their beliefs. How is that different from the one your family follows? How is it similar?

Of course, you don't have to own just that book to pose these questions and launch a meaningful discussion. You can use many other excellent resources that depict the lives of people around the world, starting with some of those listed following.

Start by practicing respect.

Raye Johnson, originally from St. Louis, Missouri, lived throughout the United States with her family while her husband moved up the corporate ranks. By all accounts, her children are successful, well-adjusted, and worldly people, having graduated from the country's top universities, then working both in the states and abroad, in business and in the arts. Raye had never traveled outside North America until her daughter, at age thirty-one, moved to London. And Raye's son had studied four foreign languages by his freshman year of college. How did the children become so cosmopolitan? Raye told me, "We encouraged them to explore and venture out, take risks; make new friends and be a friend—as we moved across the United States and experienced so many cultures that make up our country. My husband and I live by those principles ourselves so our children were able to follow our example. If they knew to respect their elders and their peers, and of course, themselves, they could do anything. I think it starts with that."

GO GLOBAL—RIGHT NOW! FIVE THINGS YOU CAN DO TODAY

If you are at all intimidated by the process, or the sheer number of possible ways to approach it, here is a short list of things you can do *right now,* likely without leaving the comfort of your zip code. Have fun helping your kids grow up global. It shouldn't be a chore and it shouldn't clutter your to-do list. Start by embracing even just a couple of the ideas for getting started here and you'll see that this can become a way of life for you and your family. Make subtle and easy changes *now* that will continue to pay dividends for years to come.

1. **Keep the world at your fingertips.** Purchase an up-to-date globe and keep it handy for easy reference. Cover a wall near the kitchen table or other central location with an oversized, laminated world map (there's nothing like munching on cereal in the morning and staring at the geography of Indonesia). Subscribe to a globally oriented magazine for kids and/or adults (or ask for a gift subscription); take time to read diverse perspectives and look at the photos with your kids. If they're not enthusiastic at the beginning, enjoy it for yourself. Your example is powerful and does influence them, as long as they're not feeling coerced. Keep old *National Geographic* (or other magazines) to cut up for future

arts and crafts projects or to donate to schools with limited resources in the United States or abroad.

Besides hanging a huge world map in their kitchen, our friends the Kitas, who live outside Allentown, Pennsylvania, framed collages of actual foreign currency they've collected from their travels abroad, with Moroccan rials next to old Italian lira, Grenadian East Caribbean dollars, and Japanese yen. The well-worn, multicolored paper money in a frame serves as a fun design element, while acquainting kids with diverse forms of currency, both current and obsolete.

2. **Surf the Internet.** For the past six years, almost every time I sit down to search the Internet I find a new series of sites that can contribute to this book's topic. Sorting out so many Internet resources remains daunting. A good start for global kids' resources is *National Geographic*'s My Wonderful World page (My wonderfulworld.org), and the American Library Association's "Great Websites for Kids" page (ala.org/greatsites), which can serve as a portal to other safe, updated, and high-quality sites. On the ALA site, under the heading Social Sciences, you will find links such as "Geography and Maps," "News and Current Events," "Cultures of the World," "Politics and Government," and "Religions of the World." The "News" section doesn't include many international perspectives, but the "Cultures of the World" section offers good diversity and exposure without being overwhelming. This section also includes links to some of the United Nations's websites for kids.

Another excellent launching point is the BBC (British Broadcasting Corporation) homepage: www.bbc.co.uk. (All websites based outside the United States have their country designation at the end of the site, like *.ca* for Canada, *.za* for South Africa, *.de* for Deutschland, or Germany.) See a wide range of news stories rarely carried by U.S. sources, whimsical as well as dramatic pictures from around the world, quick links to country profiles, and a link to "Society and Culture" that takes you to topics like "Religion and Ethics," "History," "Environmental Concerns," and "Parenting."

Take it a step further and set a foreign news source as one of your homepage tabs. Even if the source is British or Canadian you'll see a whole different angle to global news coverage and can share this (age-appropriately) with your children.

There is an abundance of resources on the Internet, from foreign films (and some Hollywood-produced ones, too), to organizations making a positive impact on the world, insightful blogs, music and books, some of which will be discussed in the following chapters and listed in the appendix.

3. **Find beautiful books.** I set off to write *Growing Up Global* with two favorite books by my side, *Children Just Like Me* by Barnabas and Anabel Kindersley,

mentioned earlier, and its companion, the 2002 UNICEF-released *A Life Like Mine: How Children Live Around the World. A Life Like Mine* is less whimsical, organized by the components of the UN's Convention on the Rights of the Child, but both take their readers on a global journey from a kids'-eye view.

Vibrant coffee-table and kids' picture books can bring diverse circumstances, people, and emotions to life, for all ages. Photographer Edward Steichen described his classic *The Family of Man* as "a mirror of the essential oneness of mankind throughout the world." I remember gazing into the faces of our family's copy while I was in elementary school, and then using it for high-school English essays, imagining one of the photographed subject's points of view. Other striking photo books include Peter Menzel's *Material World: A Global Family Portrait; A Day in the Life of . . .* series; and the *National Geographic* kids' books *A Little Peace, You and Me Together: Moms, Dads and Kids Around the World,* and *A Cool Drink of Water* by Barbara Kerley.

Find more great books at the end of each chapter. This list is updated periodically on the website *www.growingupglobal.net.*

4. **Enrich your playlists and music collection.** For my family and me, the more we stared at the faces looking at us from the pages of the UNICEF and other books, the more the children's situations became real to us. A great way to add to this sensorial experience is by listening to the music of the cultures depicted, music the children in the color pages might be listening to. Simplifying the task of tracking down such music, Putumayo World Music has built a reputation around introducing the best of world music to global audiences. With compilations ranging from lullabies to party music, women's voices, Arabic groove, and playground songs, you can get a taste of thematic global music almost as quickly as you turn the pages of the coffee-table books. Once you're introduced to flamenco or bossa nova, you can decide with which artists you'd like to spend more time. National Public Radio's website, *npr.org,* is another rich source for world music and the stories behind some of the songs. Click the Music tab and then the World Music tab. Don't miss their American folk and jazz music collections, also important cultural forces to introduce kids to. Share the global influence of some of your favorite musicians, like Harry Belafonte, Paul Simon, Peter Gabriel, David Byrne, Sinead O'Connor, and Yo-Yo Ma. Track down some of these icons' favorite international artists.

Revolutionizing the way we listen to music, iTunes and iPods make world music more accessible, too. Create a playlist of favorite world music you've heard on various websites and CDs, and don't just park them in the world music category. Include them with your favorites among dance and party mixes, mellow lists, inspirational music, and more. As kids become accustomed to so much musical diversity, they adjust naturally to the various sounds, making the genres feel less foreign and creating a bridge with new friends from all over the planet.

5. **Get passports.** Even if you have no intention or budget for international travel, possessing your own passports will put your family in the mind-set of the possible, as a very physical reminder of your world citizenship.

Regardless of how remote your foreign travel plans seem, with a passport that's valid for ten years for adults and five years for children fifteen and younger, you can be ready to go, without the added delay and expense of having one rushed to you. Your kids will see international travel within their realm of possibility and may take pride in having their very own passport. If you can afford a beach vacation nearby, an international trip might actually lie within reach, too.

If it's your first time getting a passport—don't worry, you're not alone. Even with a recent spike in passport applications, about 65 percent of Americans still don't own one. You can get information and forms from the U.S. State Department's website, at travel.state.gov. It's a simple process, but you'll need to apply in person. For minors under sixteen, both parents must be present during the passport application, or submit a notarized form. Do all of this conveniently at a designated local post office, library, or courthouse; there are thousands of local "acceptance facilities" set up to ease the process for taxpayers. Travel.state.gov lets you search for the closest facility. Get your official passport photos next time you're picking up a prescription or shampoo at your local pharmacy. If you forget, any post office with a passport service probably takes photos, too.

POLITICS VS. PEOPLE—REMEMBER TO MAKE A DISTINCTION

It would be hard to be a friend to the human race if we let the politics of governments or a vocal minority color our view of the people of that country or religion. Particularly with the news every day of terrorism, suicide bombers, and anti-American street protestors, distinguishing the rich cultures and the diverse perspectives of its people from the angry extremists on TV requires almost constant effort. I believe this forms a critical step to making peace on a large scale as well as on an individual level. There is a delicate balance to strike between recognizing the prejudice we might unknowingly carry against innocent people and the alertness to a tiny minority that might actually be so enraged that they would commit an act of violence.

During my last pregnancy, in 2003, I caught myself harboring exactly this prejudice while waiting for my monthly prenatal exam. In a large medical practice, each doctor sees expectant mothers during their pregnancy, so that the patient would know any doctor who might be on call during the time of delivery. A new doctor with a common Arabic name (I'll call him Dr. Muhammad Al-Husseini) had just joined the practice and was supposed to see me that day. As I waited on the cold examining table, wearing only a paper gown, I anxiously envisioned a dark, hairy-chested, garlic-breathed, heavily accented doctor who would check my privates and listen for my unborn baby. I tried to fight the image of the suicide-bomber terrorist in a white jacket with a stethoscope around his neck. I certainly knew better. Ironically, I also have been on the receiving end of the prejudice, from a young age.

When Dr. Al-Husseini walked in, I found myself breathing a sigh of relief. He had no beard or even mustache, he wore a closely cropped haircut, his eyes were blue, and he smelled like a fresh shower. I wasn't conscious of my prejudices (both before and after he arrived) until after my exam, which he conducted as a consummate professional and with a pleasant bedside manner. I felt ashamed to realize that I perpetuated exactly the kind of prejudice that I wanted to fight. This experience showed me that we each carry some prejudice; sometimes it is deep within our psyche and it is usually very hard to admit!

One of my earliest school memories is that of setting up the Iran table for the first-grade cultural heritage day at my school in Fort Wayne, Indiana. It was set alongside several tables showcasing Ireland and Italy. My schoolmates and I loved that our colors matched and that the countries all started with the letter "I": the Irish green and white next to two flags of red, white, and green for Italy and Iran. Our thrill was palpable when tasting the meatball in ragù alongside boiled potatoes and cabbage and my family's fluffy rice with dill, lima beans, saffron, and the favorite crispy potatoes from the bottom of the pot of rice. How proud I was to point to the map with the thumbtack on Tehran, knowing one fact that the adults clearly did not. In 1971, Midwest America, most Americans had never heard of Iran, and certainly couldn't find it on the map. The nation was a quaint mystery to the parents and teachers at Croninger Elementary, making us near-celebrities.

When I think back on that time, I am struck by the innocence of it. Not just my own innocence as a young child showing off my heritage, just learning to read and master the ride of a two-wheeler, but of the innocence of the world and the adults around me. Iran evoked little more than the image of an exotic land of flying Persian rugs and perhaps a glamorous king and queen—a Middle Eastern Camelot—to most of the Americans we knew. Today, more than a quarter century after the bloody Iranian revolution, at times I still hesitate to tell people that my family comes from that same country as the Ayatollahs and the hostage takers; and I am ready to clarify that "no, Iran is not Iraq. They are two separate countries, with different languages and cultures, but they are next door to each other, and yes, only one letter difference at the end of each country's name."

Some of those same children who enjoyed the saffron rice and trimmings in elementary school later taunted my sister and me with names like "hostage taker" and "sand Nigger" by the time we reached middle school. They were venting their anger over the flag-burning terrorists who took over the U.S. embassy and its 66 Americans for 444 days in "Eye-Ran," a country that suddenly everyone knew and despised. I hated that anyone would associate us with the bearded revolutionaries in Iran. My own extended family—with property confiscated and looted, cousins expelled from school and university, and a few members imprisoned randomly and even killed—was hurt more by the revolution than any of my tormentors could imagine. I stewed over these many injustices and misconceptions as we ushered in the first spring of the 1980s by scrubbing the yellow-and-white goo off our home's aluminum siding following the repeated pelting with eggs courtesy of the "patriots" from my school.

Showing me that children are probably more resilient than parents give them credit for, I had forgotten about this harassment of my junior high years until I began to write about my stronger memory of the first-grade cultural pageant. My memories of adolescence in Indiana are more about the anticipation of participating in my friends' Bat Mitzvah extravaganzas, trying out for the eighth-grade cheerleading squad, and slurping frothy Orange Juliuses during weekend mall excursions. The politics of my country of origin had little to do with my everyday experience growing up in Middle America. The friends who didn't let international politics get in the way of personal friendships looked forward to the crispy potatoes, or *ta-dig*, from the bottom of the pot of basmati rice and learned the art of *taarof*, in which insistence from the host calls for a little bit of insistence and graciousness back from the guest. Thanks in part to those friends who did not judge us by the anti-American flag-burners shown on the nightly news, I am able to share the positive aspects of Persian culture with my children, and I do recall my early teen years with fondness.

Today when I meet someone who has been friends with Iranians, we make a connection through the little things. I appreciate that they pronounce "Iran" (ẏ-rahn or ee-rahn) correctly; they know that we speak Persian or Farsi; they are acquainted with the subtleties of *taarof*, like not taking the last piece of golden *ta-dig*, even though they really want it; and they know that Persian culture is far removed from the relentless media image of angry street demonstrators shouting "death to America." Our lives are enriched on both sides by the ability to overcome the media images.

BEGIN TO MIX IT UP!

Raising my own children in largely homogenous suburbs, I know that making friends from different backgrounds takes effort. A conversation among women in my tennis group demonstrated how hard it could be for some people to break out of their self-imposed shell. Several women lamented that they wished they could meet new people. They socialize with a subset of their neighbors who also belong to their country club and attend the same church and, consequently, things just aren't that interesting anymore (ironically, it didn't occur to them that I was in the conversation and don't belong to their country club or their church and rarely see them off the tennis court). None of these people are powerless to grow their circle of friends, but they do need to step outside their same-old, same-old box to discover a "different" person standing right there in front of them.

Some of the ability to make diverse friends comes from innate qualities of curiosity, an outgoing personality, and self-confidence. But you don't need to be an extrovert to appreciate multicultural friendships. You do need to be willing to work to mix things up a bit. And the first time(s) you step outside your comfort zone, you may not yet have earned the trust of your neighbor.

In distilling the qualities of intercultural friendships, a key ingredient is trust. When there is trust, we don't doubt each other's motives, words, or actions. We

Host the world at your home.

Organizations like the National Council for International Visitors (www.nciv.org), active in ninety-one communities around the United States and AFS Intercultural Programs (www.afs.org) offer opportunities to host a professional or student from another country in your own home. NCIV provides cultural activities and home hospitality for foreign leaders, specialists, and scholars. Hosts serve as "citizen diplomats." Visitors may need a place to stay for a couple nights, or you could host a group for a meal. AFS offers intercultural exchanges in which a student or teacher from another country can stay in your home as a family member for a month, a semester, or a year while they study locally. If you're not ready to have someone live with you, you could offer to be in their network of "extended family," where they come to you for periodic meals, or to hang out, as an alternate home to their host family. Maybe you can't leave the country—let the world come to you.

feel safe, comfortable, and secure. We can express our thoughts and not feel like we will be scorned, laughed at, judged, or turned away from. We enjoy or at least attempt to understand cultural differences, and there is no fear of rejection because of them. A trust-imbued relationship is liberating and authentic.

These qualities—all learnable—can infuse and inform the atmosphere of the home. This point goes back to a central theme of this book: that becoming a world citizen calls for an appreciation of the essential oneness of people from so many different walks of life and that each individual family's culture can nurture this appreciation. The fact that you are reading this, itself a self-selection, shows your openness and interest in raising your children's global awareness.

On top of the effort needed to create trust and an open atmosphere in the home, it might simply be difficult to find people who are so different from you. I asked Justice St. Rain, from Heltonville, Indiana, population 1,232, how he could surround himself with so many diverse people and become so committed to global issues despite his rural Midwestern life. Mr. St. Rain owns InterfaithResources .com. He replied: "Every generation in my family did something that was new and different. My grandfather was the first person in town to have electricity on his farm. My grandmother joined the suffragists' movement for women's rights. My mother went out of her way to befriend people who were a bit different from everyone else. In our area, that was a big deal. They showed me that these differences make life more interesting and they're nothing to be afraid of. We weren't like all the other families from my school and I loved that. It made life more interesting. It made me curious; while the kids in my class were pretty bored with the same old stuff they were fed."

Recruit a "posse," or a diverse circle of friends to help your family connect globally. Think of the people in your neighborhood, at work, among your children's friends' parents, and old classmates—anyone you know from diverse ethnic, religious, professional, educational, economic backgrounds with whom you can talk honestly to make up your informal network for getting to know the world better. Your posse is a core group of people you can go to and ask what might seem like a silly or uninformed question, bounce off an idea for a charitable project or travel destination, or seek their thoughts on a political situation. They might invite you to a religious or cultural celebration. Between you there is trust and understanding— or you will build it—and they may offer you new perspectives and insights.

When starting out, extend this group to acquaintances, too, like the bus driver, dry cleaner, and pediatrician. Your community likely contains more diversity than you initially recognize. My friend Elizabeth learned a few Arabic words from her neighborhood's ice-cream truck driver who was Lebanese and who she

Honor the preferred name.

Particularly for women, do they prefer Mrs., Ms., Dr., or to be called by their first (given) name? Johnny Smith's mom can be called Ms. Jones, but her husband is Mr. Smith. Don't shield your kids from calling their friends' parents by two different surnames—they can handle it. Worldwide, women in cultures considered "traditional" often have not taken a married name. This is the case in places ranging from China and Malaysia to Iceland and Iran. Sometimes it indicates a feminist or professional preference, but it also might go back to longtime cultural traditions.

saw almost every summer day when her kids were little. Elizabeth, who is Jewish, described the first lesson after one of their conversations: "You say *'Shalom'* and we say *'Salaam.'* See how easy that is?!"

Know your friend's name—and say it right. The proper name to call a person from a culture you know little about can get tricky, particularly between generations and genders. When is it okay to use first names? Which of the names is actually the first name? Do they prefer to be called by their professional title, like Doctor or Professor or are they more informal?

Here are some general naming conventions in cultures whose practice is different from the standard in English.

- *In Spanish-speaking countries,* the person will have at least three names: the given or first name (which might actually be two names), the middle name, which is what North Americans consider the "last name," and the mother's maiden name, listed at the end. So, Juan Carlos Sanchez Paz is "Mr. Sanchez"; or "Señor (or Sr.) Sanchez"; to call him by his first name, use "Juan Carlos." In Brazil, where Portuguese is spoken, he would be "Mr. Paz."
- *In Chinese, Korean, and Japanese cultures,* the family surname comes first, the "middle" name is what we consider the "first" name, and if there is a third name it refers to the mother's family. Basketball star Yao Ming is "Mr. Yao," not "Mr. Ming." Chinese President Hu Jintao is President Hu. His wife does not take the family name, but their children are named Hu Haifeng and Hu Haiqing.

How do you say "John" in Russian?

The identical name might seem completely different in various languages. Here are a few common variations (but not an exhaustive list—there are too many to include!):

John = Ivan (Russian), Hans, Johann (German), Ian, Seon, or Sean (Gaelic), Evan (Anglo), Jan—pronounced Yân (Polish), Johannes or Sjon (Dutch), Juan (Spanish), Jean (French), Joao (Portuguese), Jukka, Juhani, or Johannes (Finnish), Yehia (referred to in the Quran), Yohanna (Arabic), Gianni, Giovanni (Italian)

George = Yuri (Russian), Joris (Dutch), Jorge (Spanish), Girgis (Arabic)

Paul = Pavel, can be abbreviated as Pasha (Russian), Pablo (Spanish), Paolo (Italian), Boulos (Arabic)

Peter = Piet or Petrus (Dutch), Boutros (Arabic), Patrick (Scotland), Kepa (Basque), Pierre (French), Pedro (Spanish)

Alexander = Alexandr, Alexei, or Sasha (Russian), Alastair (Gaelic)

Mary = Mariya (Russian), Maryam (Persian and Arabic), Mariama (West African dialects), Maria (Spanish, Italian, Finnish), Marie (French)

Catherine = Yekaterina—can be abbreviated as Katya or Katyusha (Russian), Katrina, Kaarina (Finnish), Catriona (Gaelic)

- *In Iceland and parts of South Asia,* members of the same family might all have different surnames, or they may not use them at all. Icelandic family surnames are created each generation by attaching the father's first name plus a suffix "-son" or "-dottir" (literally meaning son and daughter). So, the children of Jon Hanssen will be known as Stefan Jonsson and Eva Jonsdottir. If a wife does not adopt her husband's name upon marriage, and they have a boy and a girl, each member of the family will have a different "last" name or surname. Partly due to the ensuing confusion, Icelanders—like the Vietnamese and other Southeast Asians—refer to each other by first name, even in formal dealings. Calling the singer "Bjork" simply by one name follows the culture of her homeland and is not a stage name, like "Madonna" or "Cher." Even the prime minister is respectfully called by his or her first name, and the Reykjavik phone book alphabetizes lists by first, or given name, then includes the second name as well as the person's profession, to distinguish the individual. Phone books in Indonesia follow this format, too.

- *In Slavic languages (like Czech and Polish)*, surnames take different forms for masculine and feminine. A male member of Martina Navratilova's family could be "Navratil." In Polish, if a masculine surname ends in *-i* or *-y*, its feminine equivalent ends in *-a*. Immigrants who have settled outside Poland for several generations have largely dropped this practice, but those who have come more recently, and speak Polish, know the changed ending is good grammar. My daughter's classmate, Maya Jankowska, shares the surname spelling with her mother, Renata. But her little brother and father are Jankow*ski*. (And the "J" is pronounced as a "Y.") Renata told me, "When I fill out forms for my family members, officials assume that I have misspelled at least one of their names and always try to correct me!"

These examples point to the fact that the world is full of variations in how people are named and how names are passed on through generations. New Americans largely conform to accepted conventions in North American and European culture, and school children grow up learning stories of how their forefathers' and mothers' names were changed at Ellis Island. Immigrants continue to face these challenges with their "odd-sounding" or oddly structured names, but many are deciding to hold on to the distinctions that identify their homeland. The tapestry of names they bring to our neighborhoods can teach us much about where they came from, if we ask them respectfully. Teach your children to be willing to learn and say names properly, and address adults with an honorific (like Mr. or Mrs.)—this is an important step in showing respect and making new friends.

DO'S AND DON'TS OF MAKING FRIENDS FROM DIFFERENT BACKGROUNDS

In my conversations with a wide range of people about this subject, several ideas emerged as "do's and don'ts" in the effort to make a friend. The key, as common sense suggests, is sincerity and respect. When you show sincere interest in a person's differences, and respect for who they are, you learn so much and this will lead to a more authentic friendship. Some points may be more obvious than others and are not listed here in any particular order. Although most of this book contains advice for parents to pass along to their children or for families to engage in together, these do's and don'ts probably apply first to you, the adult. Your example in forming intercultural friendships will go a long way to creating comfort for your children to do the same.

- *Do* wait to get to know someone before asking about personal histories, like why they came to this country. There may be sensitivities behind this answer because of painful past experiences. As a friendship is nurtured, this story—mundane or dramatic—will probably naturally be told.

- *Don't* start with religion, politics, or even business. These topics may be the most interesting to you, but they might fall outside what's considered polite public conversation in the person's home country and be acceptable only after getting to know the person's circumstances or personality. Issues revolving around family are generally the safest icebreakers. Once you get to know your new friends you might realize they are even more forthcoming than American sensibilities you are used to—not only will you find variations among cultures, but also within one cultural group, just as we have in our own.

- *Do* invite parent and child for a play date at your home or in a neutral location (like a playground) for an initial get-together, if this is age-appropriate.

- *Do* strive to include children from diverse backgrounds in your children's birthday parties, even if this is not the inclination of your own children (i.e., your kids might not be closest friends with those children, but they are in the same class, team, or neighborhood). Expect that some of the parents will stay, not simply drop off and leave. Welcome them and take this as an opportunity to get to know one another, even if slightly.

- *Don't* start a conversation with general comments like "I love to have friends from different backgrounds." A couple years ago I was at a cocktail party where a person I had respected said this loudly to a group. (Actually, she said, "I love knowing different ethnic people.") It may be the case, but this comes across as ignorant and patronizing.

- *Do* be sensitive to dietary restrictions. You will hopefully share meals with friends from different cultures or belief systems. Knowing if (and how strict) your friends keep kosher or halal or vegetarian due to religious beliefs, as well as asking about allergies or aversions, could be the difference between a fascinating and enjoyable dinner and an awkward fiasco. You can ask them after offering the invitation.

- *Do* be aware if your friends don't drink alcohol and offer alternatives.

- *Do* make sure that your children have multicultural toys and storybooks and that the television programs and movies they watch are racially and culturally diverse. You might live in a community with virtually no diversity, but there are ways that you can supplement your family's experience so that diversity becomes part of your children's reality, regardless of the demographic composition of your community.

- *Do* pay attention to issues of racial diversity in addition to the "international" diversity emphasized in this book. As the images of the victims of Hurricane Katrina in New Orleans confirmed, racism still plagues America. Don't under-

HOW ARE YOU DOING SO FAR? TAKE THE INTERNATIONAL QUIZ SELF-TEST

The International Quiz included here gets you to ask yourself questions about your own experiences, assumptions, and patterns of behavior, which ultimately impact your children's worldview and formative experiences. It tests your *other* IQ. The questions can help you to think more concretely about what it takes to be at home in the world. There is no scoring or correct answer. If you really want to track how you're doing, write the answer in the margins, on the pages in the back of the book, or keep a journal, then you can refer back to them after you start implementing the steps in the chapters to come.

Friendships
1. Do you and your children have close friends who come from a culture or ethnic group that is different from yours? Where are they from?
2. Do you remember sharing different cultural experiences with your friends when you were growing up? Did your parents encourage this?
3. How do you and your friends share experiences reflecting your different backgrounds (i.e., through stories, foods, language, holidays, etc.)?
4. Have your children experienced a meal from a friend's different culture?
5. How many of your friends have a very different *economic* background/status from yours?
6. Do you have friends whose religious beliefs and experiences differ from yours? Have you or your children attended a religious service from a different faith?
7. How often do you socialize with friends from backgrounds (ethnic, economic, religious) different from yours?
8. Are you comfortable with such socializing? What is uncomfortable about this?

Travel Experience
1. Do you and your children possess a current passport?
2. Have you traveled outside of the United States?
3. If yes, to where have you traveled?
4. Are any of these countries considered "less developed"?
5. Have your children traveled outside of the United States?
6. If yes, what did they experience of the local culture?
7. In the case of both you and your children, how long did you stay abroad on each trip?
8. If you have not traveled abroad, can you reevaluate your travel budget and apply it to a trip outside the United States?

School and Education

1. Do you know the level or proportions of ethnic diversity at your children's school?
2. Do you know which teachers in your children's schools have firsthand knowledge of other cultures?
3. In your own education, what cultures and ethnic groups were part of your studies or social experience?
4. What are your children being taught about other cultures? Which ones? How in-depth? Is anyone with firsthand experience invited to share their perspective?
5. Have you looked at the texts and materials being used to teach foreign or minority cultures and experiences? Do these seem accurate and without bias?
6. Have you or your children studied or do you speak a foreign language(s)?
7. Which language(s) would you like them to learn? Why?
8. How can you supplement the language instruction they receive in school?

Media

1. Do you ever seek non-American sources for news and information (e.g., the BBC, Al Jazeera in English, other foreign press)?
2. If age-appropriate, do you discuss world events with your children? What kinds of events?
3. Have you watched a foreign film or TV show with your children?
4. If so, have you discussed what's different from the style and content of a U.S.-made program?
5. Do you own a globe or current world map?
6. Do you own or play any games about or from other world cultures?
7. Do you subscribe to any magazines depicting other cultures, such as *National Geographic Kids, Faces Magazine, Skipping Stones,* or *Discovery Kids*?
8. Have you visited any websites with your children that depict situations in other countries or educate on other cultures or lifestyles (e.g., United Nations websites, foreign country sites, etc.)?

Process the questions. Walking yourself through the questions helps you to assess where you and your family are in each part of the process of raising your children to be comfortable in the world. If you realize you would like to be more proactive in a particular area, future chapters will offer resources for doing so.

estimate the impact of media exposure on young children, particularly when it comes to negative racial stereotypes. Local news and crime shows offer a skewed presentation of our cities and I avoid watching these with my children. In another example, Kate Grant, who works from Northern California on women's health issues in Africa, told me that when she showed her then-six-year old-son pictures of life in a poor village in Ethiopia his first response was "Mommy, is that New Orleans?"

Reaching out to New Friends. With the trend of diverse immigrant families buying a home in the suburbs (contrasting with settling down in a particular ethnic neighborhood in or around a city), it's likely that eventually, if not already, your children will have friends at school that come from different cultural backgrounds. At the same time, you might find that you don't know the parents beyond a smile and a nod at school events, or that those parents are not included in outside social activities in which other families from school participate. Try to make an effort to get to know the family and include them in some social activities.

Annual events like a Fourth of July barbecue, Thanksgiving dinner, or Super Bowl party offer good opportunities for including new families, and in the end, both hosts and guests might have a better time than if the party took place with the same group they've always had. Celebrating July Fourth with new American citizens can offer a unique lens on the meaning of patriotism and of liberty, as well as on celebrations of similar national days in other countries. Thanksgiving with friends whose ethnic cooking differs from yours can enhance not only the side dish offerings, but also the dinner conversation. And a Super Bowl party that includes friends who grew up with totally different, fiercely competitive national sports, like "football" (a.k.a. soccer), rugby, and cricket can take the cheering to a whole new level, and possibly introduce great new snacks. The effort you make to reach out to new families will impact your children and send an important signal. When Junior's good friend from school is included, not only will he have more fun and be more engaged at the party, but his friendship can be a more authentic one: It's not restricted only to socializing at school with particular people, and he sees that the families are connected and share natural interests, becoming true friends.

———

"Being a friend" forms the foundation of becoming a world citizen, and the younger anyone starts out on this process, the less effort it takes to be effective and authentic. This effort is based on sincerity, common sense, and universal values like empathy and respect. The fact that each of the world's faith traditions teaches a form of the Golden Rule underscores how much we have in common with those whose customs and practices differ dramatically from our own. Helping our children to understand universal virtues and taking some simple actions to begin to gain a global perspective will make it that much easier for them to make friends from diverse backgrounds and to adjust to an everchanging global environment. It's these friendships across traditional boundaries that can ultimately contribute to a more just and peaceful world. Chances are your children already have exposure through their school environment to making diverse friends. Are they taking advantage of the opportunity? How do you facilitate this by your own example? With global trends toward fundamentalism and militancy even among children, I fear that the custom of teaching children the Golden Rule as one of their first lessons on morality in the family or in their house of worship may be supplanted by less peaceful or positive values. This makes the task of teaching our children to be a friend to all more urgent than ever.

Resource Books Cited in Chapter 1—That You May Find Helpful, Too

Children Just Like Me, Barnabas and Anabel Kindersley (New York: DK Publishing, 1995).

A Life Like Mine: How Children Live Around the World, UNICEF (New York: DK Publishing, 2002).

The Family of Man, Edward Steichen, editor (New York: The Metropolitan Museum of Art, 2002).

Material World: A Global Family Portrait, Peter Menzel (San Francisco: Sierra Club Books, 1995).

A Day in the Life of . . . series, which includes *A Day in the Life of India,* David Elliot Cohen and Raghu Rai (New York: HarperCollins, 1996); *A Day in the Life of Thailand,* David Elliot Cohen with Rick Browne and James Marshall (New York: HarperCollins, 1995); *A Day in the Life of Africa,* David Elliot Cohen (San Francisco: Tides Foundation, 2002); and more.

A Little Peace, Barbara Kerley (Washington, DC: National Geographic, 2007).

You and Me Together: Moms, Dads and Kids Around the World, Barbara Kerley (Washington, DC: National Geographic, 2005).

A Cool Drink of Water, Barbara Kerley (Washington, DC: National Geographic, 2002).

Additional Resource Books Related to Chapter 1

The Golden Rule, Ilene Cooper (author), Gabi Swiatkowska (illustrator) (New York: Abrams Books for Young Readers, 2007).

Do Unto Otters: A Book About Manners, Laurie Keller (New York: Henry Holt & Company, 2007).

Global Babies, The Global Fund for Children (Watertown, MA: Charlesbridge Publishing, 2007). Also from The Global Fund for Children and Maya Ajmera: *To Be a Kid* (1999) and *Be My Neighbor* (2004).

Who Belongs Here? An American Story, Margy Burns Knight (Gardiner, ME: Tilbury House Publishers, 1993).

Chapter 2

Greet Your Friend

When you bow, bow low.
CHINESE PROVERB

If you want to make a friend, start by greeting them. The Chinese proverb above indicates how simple, elegant, and brief a proper greeting can be; that greetings vary across cultures; and that they are indispensable, all the same. The greeting can serve as a portal, opening the door to a new friendship.

During our family's stay in West Africa, one of my favorite children was a four-year-old neighbor, Josephine. In the custom of that culture, as she walked into a room, she had been trained to go around and shake hands with everyone there, regardless of age. When I consider this issue of polite greeting, the image of this little girl, with her right hand out, endearing everyone she met, stands out to me. For my children, observing this petite child connect with everyone in her midst served as a valuable lesson and example. For a while we used a code word, *Josephine*, as a reminder to shake hands and properly greet someone.

GETTING USED TO SAYING HELLO

American children—and even adults—often don't offer a basic "hello" or acknowledgment of presence to someone they meet. Parents, often weary from so many other battles they must wage with their children, are starting to accept this, but for visitors from other countries—or Americans from older generations—this is an unacceptable rebuff. Experiencing some of the fun aspects of different cultures' greetings can help our children to be more aware of their own greetings in day-to-day interactions among their peers and elders. And this actually could be a pleasurable experience. It brings happiness to the person being greeted and breaks the ice. It shows you are open to getting to know that person.

Practice on the go. If I have the presence of mind to remember, sometimes while driving in the car with my children—particularly when they were younger, around age ten and under—I talk through what the proper greeting should look like (e.g., "Look the person in the eye, smile, say 'hello' or 'nice to meet you' " and show them how to shake hands). It could take five, ten, or a hundred times for it to be instilled as a habit. Sometimes my children would say that they were embarrassed to greet someone (usually the people to whom the greeting is most important, like an elderly family friend). My response was that it is more embarrassing to be considered rude or snobbish, and if you just say "hello" and smile, you get it over with—politely! So, while there are subtleties to getting the greetings right in diverse cultural environments, it's important to simply start at home, offering a polite greeting in your own comfort zone. When this element of polite manners becomes an automatic part of our children's everyday interactions, they can build from there to learn the greetings of cultures different from their own.

THE POWER OF AUTHENTIC GREETINGS

Once your children feel comfortable offering a simple greeting, it will be easier for them to learn some greetings outside of their own culture. Many people have conveyed to me that if they learn to greet someone in a foreign language, it has the effect of "reaching out" to meet the person in a new place. Even if the person they are meeting understands an English "hello," the effort made to say a few words in the other person's native language can introduce a level of warmth and closeness that even a heartfelt "hello" could not have done. This can open doors when traveling, but it also can create bonds at home—with a new classmate, neighbor, shopkeeper, or the family of a colleague from another country.

Getting started. If you don't know the particulars of a culture's greeting, start by trying to convey respect in the best way you know how. This goes back to the previous chapter and the Golden Rule: Focus on what you consider would show a sincere salutation. How would you like to be treated? This breaks down into a few simple steps.

- *Be yourself.*
- *Be sincere.*
- *Show respect.*
- *Then pay attention to cues from the other person.* Are they putting their hand out to shake yours, or to kiss you on the cheek, or are they starting to bow their head to you? Do they look you in the eye or avert their gaze?

As you try this, walk through the process with your child and convey that while you might not know the details or subtleties, you try your best and you pay attention to the other person and any lead they might take. Your kids may not get the greeting right for a long time, but when they see you try, they know it is worth the effort and will eventually emulate your attempts.

The basics for greeting the world. When you keep a globe or world atlas handy, your children will be more likely to start visualizing the range of countries, their locations, and your home in relation to so many others. Gaining familiarity with the continents can relate back to learning the greetings, as there are some general principles about greeting among different cultural backgrounds:

- With *Europeans,* shaking hands is a safe opening greeting throughout the continent. The southern parts of Europe tend to have warmer, more intimate greetings. In France, for example, two polite air kisses are exchanged between friends—men and women or two women—in Paris, but in the southern parts of France, it can be three or even four kisses, between two women, two men, or a man and a woman.
- With *Latinos,* initial greetings among friends come with a quick air kiss. How many kisses depends on the particular country and possibly your relationship (e.g., business or good friends). During conversation, Latin Americans may stand closer to you; they need less personal space, reflecting the warmth of their cultures. When one friend's mother first visited the United States from Peru, she repeatedly needed to remind her mother not to kiss everyone she met.
- With *Middle Easterners,* a cheek kiss or two or three is common among members of the same sex, but not between members of the opposite sex. It's normal for men in Arab (and African) countries to walk holding each other's hands. Avoid offering something with your left hand as it is considered unclean among traditional Arabs.
- With *Far Easterners* (e.g., Japanese, Chinese, Korean), bow, with hands on thighs. The deeper the bow, the greater the respect. Eyes look down while bowing.
- Among *South Asians,* cultural practices vary widely. Those from Hindu and Buddhist backgrounds might offer a "namaste" bow (palms pressed together with fingers below chin and nodding the head) while the large population of Muslims' greetings resemble Middle Eastern customs. More modern professionals reflect European greeting practices, like handshaking, but rarely kissing.
- *Africa* varies widely, but my experience in different regions usually is to shake hands, often placing the left hand on top of the right to show sincerity. An opening greeting can last for many minutes, to indicate your care for that person and their family.

Just as my children like to give an Eskimo kiss (rubbing noses) or a butterfly kiss (fluttering eyelashes on the recipient's cheek), these different types of opening greetings can be practiced as a fun and affectionate novelty. You also can try them as part of role-playing and imagination games, or rotating weekly or monthly with other cultural activities recommended in this book. When the gestures are practiced for fun in the comfort of your own home and with your own family members, they'll be less awkward to try when meeting someone new.

Generation gaps and cultural gaps. In order to better relate to what seems formal or foreign in other cultures' greetings, you can point out some of the practices experienced by your grandparents' generations. Emily Post's classic 1922 *Book of Etiquette* set the bar for polite manners for most of the twentieth century. In it, the rules for polite gentlemen are very different from those for respectable ladies, and as far as greetings, she thinks saying "hello" is a generally "vulgar" beginning, while saying "hi" doesn't even make it on her radar. Emily Post's view of America illustrates how manners and greetings evolve all over the world: Sometimes they blend together and seem similar and at other moments in time they are literally "worlds apart." But none of this is static—just like when you get to know an individual from a culture about which you might hold some bias, your view of their culture and customs might adjust drastically after you understand them better. This demonstrates how important it is to get to know people as individuals; that's when you realize that deep down inside we may not be so different.

The growing informality of greetings is common among youth all over the world—literally creating a "youth culture." My cousin's wife, Johanna Jochumsdottir, described to me the generation gap between her grandparents and teenage sisters in Iceland. "My grandparents are so offended—even traumatized—when young people walk into a room and say 'hi' like an American. But this has become the common greeting of Icelandic youth. Our traditional greeting is *Komdu sæll og blessaôur*/*blessuô* (male/female). This literally means 'May you be blessed and healthy.' 'Hi' is becoming a universal word among young people, but that doesn't make most elders happy."

What to do with a difficult name. When you are introduced to someone with a name you have never heard and can't even picture how it's spelled, how do you respond? Younger kids usually are much better at reacting to unusual names than adults, because to them, most names are new, without history or expectations—from Samantha to Siddharth. As kids hit late elementary and middle school they can be downright mean about what others are called, especially if they haven't been exposed to a spectrum of names. The first day of school or the presence of a substitute teacher can instill dread for the kid with a "difficult" name because they have learned to anticipate its butchering by a new teacher, followed by the snickering of children around them. Teachers can easily remedy this by getting the class list in advance and checking name pronunciations—with other teachers, administrators, on the Internet, or even subtly with the student herself—before roll call on Day 1.

A tough situation with names got worse after 9/11. Names like Muhammad, Hussein, Ahmed, and Ali happen to be among the most common in the world, including millions who carry these as first or last names in the United States, among whom are many American children. Kavita Ramdas, CEO of the Global Fund for Women in San Francisco, is Indian from a Hindu background and her husband is Pakistani and Muslim. Their daughter's name is Mira Husnara Ahmad. Kavita recalled to me that Mira, only eight at the time, saw a newspaper sometime after the attack and noticed that, like her, at least two of the hijackers had the surname Ahmad, which prompted Mira to ask her mother, "Is my name a bad name?" And not long after, kids at school made fun of Mira's middle name, too, associating her with Saddam Hussein. Adding to this, for about three years after 9/11, Mira and her father were pulled out of the security line each time they flew because their last name was on a "watch list."

With the election of Barack Hussein Obama to the U.S. presidency, the nation witnessed another side to the name *Hussein*. It fascinated me during the 2008 campaign that so many Obama supporters with familiar names like Sally Miller or John Smith changed their Facebook identity to "Sally Hussein Miller" and "John Hussein Smith" in solidarity with the American politician who has had to carry around a name loaded with so many connotations of a perceived enemy.

In my own case I have watched so many people's faces contort, conveying "What?!" when they hear my name for the first time. Some begin to speak very slowly to me after reading my name on a name tag or in a school directory, assuming that I cannot speak English because of my foreign name. I was once at a benefit event with my mother, where the first thing a woman introduced to us said, while staring disbelievingly at our name tags, was "What kind of names are those?" I answered, "Persian. What kind of name is yours?" She looked at me, again disbelievingly, and said, "I'm American." I said, "So am I." In order to model for your children how to respond to diverse names and avoid an awkward exchange like that, remember:

• Don't ask about the origin of their name as soon as you are introduced. Imagine the person had a name you are familiar with—would you start by asking them where they are from and what their family background is? You would probably make some pleasant small talk about the day, the event, and so on. If you're curious about their name and where they are from, remember they probably get asked about that all the time and it gets tiring. It's okay to ask, but not immediately.

- Once you do ask about their name, you can inquire about its origins to an adult or older child. And it's even nicer if you say—with sincerity—"That is a beautiful name, what is its origin (or where is it from)?" or "That is a lovely name, what does it mean?"

- Do try to read the person's body language. Some people may seem very outgoing at the introduction. After breaking the ice with some pleasantries, if you can't remember how to say their name, you can ask them to spell it for you. On the flip side, when I notice someone is perplexed by my name (90+ percent of the time!), I immediately spell it for them and sometimes give them an easy association for remembering it (e.g., I say "Homa, it's like Okla . . ." and I see the lightbulb go off in their heads when they complete the phrase with "Homa!").

- You don't have to know everyone's nationality at the outset. Particularly if the person seems shy or not willing to offer that information, wait, get to know her a bit, and detach yourself from knowing where she comes from. Just get to know her as an individual first.

- When you play with your kids and need to name yourself or a character in your game, suggest names that are different from what you normally hear. If the dolls or pets are given names like Masako, Usha, Elodie, Xanthe, or Khadijah, then your children become accustomed to think outside the box of "typical" names and will probably adapt more easily during introductions with names they have never heard. In Sophia's Gambian preschool, her three- and four-year-old classmates' names ranged from Abdul-Rahman and Fatoumata (a form of Fatima, the Prophet Muhammad's revered daughter), to John and RuthAnne. This became her new normal.

What NOT to name your doll

In late 2007, a British volunteer teacher in Sudan was slapped with a death sentence that got ratcheted down to two weeks' imprisonment—all because she allowed her Sudanese students to name their class teddy bear Muhammad. From her Western perspective she thought it would be nice to give the bear a familiar name. But from an extreme Islamic view, human images and likenesses are shunned, and for an animal to take the name of the Prophet is heresy. In even more extreme environments, children cannot play with dolls. This goes back to teachings that abolish pre-Islamic idolatry, and dolls may be thought to fall within that category. Further, just as the Quran, the Holy Book, is to be handled with extreme care, so is the image and name of Muhammad, and to a lesser degree, that of other Prophets.

LEARN TO GREET IN ONE—OR MANY!—FOREIGN LANGUAGE(S)

Becoming accustomed to diverse names is a step in the right direction of learning a few words in a new language. It's great to speak English—by far the most widely studied *second* language in the world. But if you step off the urban grid in most places in the world, or even in some ethnic neighborhoods in the states, you might not be understood if you speak only English. Make the effort to learn a few words in a foreign language with your kids, even if it's learning how to say "toilet" in five languages. This could be one of the best investments of your time; it's a great ice-breaker and your kids will probably do a great job of it.

How will you choose the language you want to learn? There are more than 6,800 known languages in the world and some countries have hundreds of native languages. To say the least, it's ambitious to try to learn a greeting in each language. But there are some simple ways to narrow down your list. You could start with your ethnic heritage. You could look around and see where your neighbors, colleagues, or community members come from. Or you could determine it by taking the top spoken languages on the planet and going down the list.

The list of the top twenty languages is fluid. Population sizes fluctuate and counting methods vary. You might find a list with some variations, like changing the order of the "top 20" (e.g., English is sometimes the second most spoken) or having a language like Wu Chinese in place of Punjabi. But overall, I found the list in the following table to be the most consistent.

Did You Know?

Papua New Guinea (can you find it on a globe?), with less than six million people, has the most languages—832—and Mexico is home to 295 native languages.

TOP 20 LANGUAGES BY NUMBER OF NATIVE SPEAKERS[1]

LANGUAGE	APPROXIMATE # OF SPEAKERS	WHERE IS IT SPOKEN AS AN OFFICIAL LANGUAGE?
1. Mandarin Chinese	NATIVE: 873 million 2nd: 178 million TOTAL: 1.051 billion	People's Republic of China, Republic of China (Taiwan), Singapore
2. Hindi	NATIVE: 370 million 2nd: 120 million TOTAL: 490 million	India, Fiji
3. Spanish	NATIVE: 350 million 2nd: 70 million TOTAL: 420 million	Argentina, Bolivia, Chile, Colombia, Costa Rica, Cuba, Dominican Republic, Ecuador, El Salvador, Equatorial Guinea, Guatemala, Honduras, Mexico, Nicaragua, Panama, Paraguay, Peru, Spain, United States (New Mexico, Puerto Rico), Uruguay, Venezuela
4. English	NATIVE: 340 million 2nd: 70 million TOTAL: 410 million	Antigua and Barbuda, Australia, The Bahamas, Bangladesh, Barbados, Belize, Botswana, Brunei, Cameroon, Canada, Dominica, Eritrea, Ethiopia, Fiji, The Gambia, Ghana, Grenada, Guyana, Hong Kong (People's Republic of China), India, Ireland, Jamaica, Kenya, Kiribati, Lesotho, Liberia, Malawi, Maldives, Malta, Marshall Islands, Mauritius, Micronesia, Namibia, Nauru, New Zealand, Nigeria, Pakistan, Palau, Papua New Guinea, Philippines, Rwanda, Saint Kitts and Nevs, Saint Lucia, Saint Vincent and the Grenadines, Samoa, Seychelles, Sierra Leone, Singapore, Solomon Islands, Somalia, South Africa, Sri Lanka, Swaziland, Tanzania, Tonga, Trinidad and Tobago, Tuvalu, Uganda, United Kingdom, United States, Vanuatu, Zambia, Zimbabwe
5. Arabic	NATIVE: 206 million 2nd: 24 million TOTAL: 230 million [World Almanac est. total 255 million]	Modern Standard Arabic: Algeria, Bahrain, Chad, Comoros, Djibouti, Egypt, Eritrea, Iraq, Israel, Jordan, Kuwait, Lebanon, Libya, Morocco, Niger, Oman, Palestinian Territories, Qatar, Saudi Arabia, Somalia, Sudan, Syria, Tunisia, United Arab Emirates, Western Sahara, Yemen. Hasaniya Arabic: Mauritania, Senegal Note: These figures combine all the varieties of Arabic. Some data sources, e.g. CIA World Fact Book, World Almanac, Ethnologue, treat these varieties as separate languages.
6. Portuguese	NATIVE: 203 million 2nd: 10 million TOTAL: 213 million	Angola, Brazil, Cape Verde, East Timor, Guinea-Bissau, Macau (People's Republic of China), Mozambique, Portugal, São Tomé e Príncipe
7. Bengali	NATIVE: 196 million TOTAL: 215 million	Bangladesh, India (Tripura, West Bengal)
8. Russian	NATIVE: 145 million 2nd: 110 million TOTAL: 255 million	Abkhazia (part of Georgia), Belarus, Kazakhstan, Kyrgyzstan, Russia, Transnistria (part of Moldova)

LANGUAGE	APPROXIMATE # OF SPEAKERS	WHERE IS IT SPOKEN AS AN OFFICIAL LANGUAGE?
9. Japanese	NATIVE: 126 million 2nd: 1 million TOTAL: 127 million	Japan, Palau
10. German	NATIVE: 101 million 2nd: 128 million TOTAL: 129 million	Austria, Belgium, Germany, Italy (South Tyrol), Liechtenstein, Luxembourg, Poland, Switzerland
11. Panjabi	Western: 60 million Eastern: 28 million TOTAL: 88 million	India (Punjab)
12. Javanese	76 million	Indonesia (esp. Java)
13. Korean	71 million	North Korea, South Korea
14. Vietnamese	NATIVE: 70 million 2nd: 16 million TOTAL: 86 million	Vietnam
15. Telugu	NATIVE: 70 million 2nd: 5 million TOTAL: 75 million	India (Andhra Pradesh)
16. Marathi	NATIVE: 68 million 2nd: 3 million TOTAL: 71 million	India (Daman and Diu, Goa, Maharashtra)
17. Tamil	NATIVE: 68 million 2nd: 9 million TOTAL: 77 million	India (Tamil Nadu), Singapore, Sri Lanka
18. French	NATIVE: 67 million 2nd: 63 million TOTAL: 130 million	Belgium, Benin, Burkina Faso, Burundi, Cameroon, Canada, Central African Republic, Chad, Comoros, Congo-Brazzaville, Congo-Kinshasa, Côte d'Ivoire, Djibouti, Equatorial Guinea, France, French Polynesia, Gabon, Guernsey, Guinea, Haiti, India (Karikal, Pondicherry), Italy, Jersey, Lebanon, Luxembourg, Madagascar, Mali, Martinique, Mauritius, Mayotte, Monaco, New Caledonia, Niger, Rwanda, Senegal, Seychelles, Switzerland, Togo, United States (Louisiana), Vanuatu
19. Urdu	NATIVE: 61 million 2nd: 43 million TOTAL: 104 million	India (Jammu and Kashmir), Pakistan
20. Italian	61 million	Croatia (Istria Country), Italy, San Marino, Slovenia, Switzerland

CHALLENGE YOURSELVES—SO MANY THINGS TO DO WITH THE TOP 20 LANGUAGES LIST

Quiz each other. Look at facts on the chart, then ask questions like "Guess what are the top five (ten, twenty) languages spoken in the world?" or "Which language is spoken by more people, Bengali or French?" and so on.

Learn about your community or neighborhood. How many people can you find who speak two of the top twenty languages? If you have an Indian grocer or restaurant in your area, do you know which is their native language? When you go into their store, after politely greeting them, it would probably make them very happy to talk to you and your children about their language and which part of India they come from. This informed interest is very different from an abrupt quizzing upon introduction such as the one I mentioned previously, in connection with "Greeting Someone with a Difficult Name."

Play some games. How many languages of the world can you think of? Fifteen? Fifty? Five hundred? This game can be played in multiple settings: as bouncing a ball on a playground or driveway or as an icebreaker (e.g., write the name of a language on a sticker, guests wear it on their backs and need to go around the room to get clues on what the language could be—this is best with preteens and up); on a long car ride (take turns, each person says a new language, no repeats allowed). Challenge yourselves by trying to go in alphabetical order (first person names a language starting with "A," next person with "B," and so on). Or you can play the reverse: Get a list of foreign languages (www.word2word.com is a good source) and see if you can figure out in which countries various languages are spoken (e.g., Maori—New Zealand, Mapuche—Chile, Zulu—South Africa). Try to make up your own variations on the game.

PUTTING THINGS IN PERSPECTIVE FOR OLDER KIDS

Look at the following map of U.S. states labeled with the names of different foreign countries whose economies shared a similar size, or Gross Domestic Product (GDP), based on 2006 World Bank data. My daughters and I started to think about how different the states are (e.g., in terms of climate, geography, lifestyles, languages, foods) from the countries on the map. Italy, Philippines, and Saudi Arabia are neighbors along the West Coast and Sweden, Morocco, and South Africa are adjacent on the East. There is no connection between overall economic size and population size of the country or the state—the *per capita* GDP, and big countries like England, Japan, Germany, France, India, and China aren't on the map, as their economies are larger than any single U.S. state. Nonetheless, this great tool can stretch the imagination. Anything that takes the name of a country you don't often hear and puts it in a context you weren't expecting, forcing you to think about that place, can be a good thing.

The map makes us think about where we live in relation to other economies. What's GDP? Very simply put, it's the total value of all the stuff (goods) and the services (like an electrician's, a babysitter's, or an accountant's work) in a nation or state. In many countries—especially developing ones—young people are very aware of the economic influences on their lives. Terms like *tariffs, quotas, foreign exchange, inflation, subsidy, underground economy, foreign aid,* and *policies of the World Bank and IMF* are considered every day, even in elementary school. As residents of the wealthiest country on the planet, I notice these concepts don't even make it on my kids' radar.

Other extensions of activities from this map: Look at the country labeled on your home state (or the neighboring states, or where Grandma lives, or where you used to live): How does the population of your state compare to the country labeled on it? Do you know what are considered the primary and secondary languages in that country? Learn the greeting in their language. Make a favorite dish from that country. Find some similarities with the country and the state it's labeled on.

("U.S. STATES RENAMED FOR COUNTRIES WITH SIMILAR GDP'S"

MAP USED WITH PERMISSION FROM THE YORK GROUP, THEYORKGROUP.COM)

Basic greetings in the ten most widely spoken languages. If you decided to learn a greeting in several of the most widely spoken languages, some expressions are listed on the next table. The best way to learn the greetings, of course, is to find a native speaker of that language to teach you. It is difficult to learn the pronunciation by reading it, and even hearing it from a nonnative speaker or on a website might result in inaccuracies. But the list offers a valuable starting point.

Some of the languages might be particularly hard to get right. For example, in Mandarin Chinese—the world's undisputed most-spoken language—words are distinguished by four tones. For someone who is not familiar with the language, the sounds are very difficult to differentiate (or pronounce) when strung together in words in a sentence. I have tried sharing a word I learned in Chinese with various native speakers and the conversation usually goes like this (but please, try anyway—at a minimum, it might evoke a good laugh!):

Me: "I learned a word in Chinese! It's 'díng hǎo.' "
Chinese friend: Blank stare, followed by a puzzled expression, then "What did you say?"
Me: " 'Díng hǎo,' it means 'awesome.' "
Chinese friend: Look of recognition, then "Oh, you mean *díng hǎo*!"
Me: "Yes, that's what I've been saying!"

My experience pronouncing the Chinese words contrasts sharply from my youngest daughter's. We've been taking her to a Saturday morning Chinese class at a local high school where parents are learning with their young children (starting around age two and a half). Since she was about four, Sophia could hear and pronounce the subtle tonal distinctions much better than Mommy and Daddy.

Games and activities to help practice the greetings. There are lots of activities you can try with your family around the Greetings in the Top Ten Languages. For example, you could share the top ten languages list over dinner with your family; each person could choose one language and spend the next week or two with that designation. So, Mom could take Mandarin Chinese, Dad Spanish, brother Arabic, and sister Hindi. Each person commits to learning the greeting in that language and it's their responsibility to greet the other members of the family in their language. By the end of one or two weeks, count how many times each person did (or didn't) use the designated greeting. Extra points can be given if additional words in that language are found and used appropriately (you might want to record new words on the tally sheet you use for the individual points), if you've found someone who speaks the language to practice the greetings with, or if they are used in play (especially for children younger than age ten). Give a special prize to the winner to make the contest more exciting. Games like this can create the effect of an inside joke or an ongoing bet or contest—family members vie with one another to do better and better.

HOW TO START DABBLING IN A NEW LANGUAGE

You enjoy testing some of the new greetings and notice your kids pronounce them much better than you do. If you are accustomed to enrolling your child in extracurricular activities like karate, soccer, or ballet, try one of these to gain more language exposure.

1. *Enroll in a nearby class through your local night school, a company like Berlitz, or a local college, or hire a tutor.* Private tutoring might be more difficult to sustain, as it is easier to cancel class when it's just your family and the tutor, but the attention will be exactly on your interests. Websites like www.local.com help you find local instruction all around the United States. Companies like Berlitz have moved beyond instructing only adults to offer an arsenal of resources for children's language development, in many different languages. Sometimes families opt to hire a tutor to teach by age groups in the family, or to teach the whole family simultaneously. Based on the studies showing different language learning styles for children versus teens and adults, the all-together strategy might pose challenges. But the powerful example of young and old learning together and the benefits from supporting one anothers' learning may outweigh the different learning styles.

2. *Purchase language instruction CDs and DVDs* through a company like Rosetta Stone, the MUZZY series from the BBC, or others through major booksellers or online. Many local public libraries also carry collections of language tapes, videos, and book/tape combinations in foreign languages or for language instruction if you want to find out how well they work and how well you respond to them. Library resources can help you decide if the language "speaks to you." You can also rent movies and music in that language to decide if you enjoy the culture and listening to the language. If you spend a lot of time driving your children around, getting CDs or tapes for the car—from language instruction to foreign-language music—will be a good way to gain exposure while you have a captive audience.

GREETINGS IN THE TOP TEN LANGUAGES

RANK + LANGUAGE	OPENING GREETING + ONE POLITE PHRASE	ADDITIONAL COMMENTS
1. Chinese, Mandarin	Hello [and how are you] = N ǐ hǎo. My name is = "Woh teh ming tsuh." Thank you = Xie Xie ("Shi-e Shi-e").	You need to know 1,500–2,000 characters to be considered literate in Mandarin.
2. Hindi	Hello (and Good-bye) = Namaste ("Nah-mah-STAY"). (*Namaste literally means: "the divine in me salutes the divine in you"*) My name is = Mehranam ("MEH-ra nahm"). How are you = Aap kaisi hai. Thank you = Sukria ("Shoo-kree-a").	Of the 22 national languages and 1,000+ dialects in India, Hindi, known as the "Latin of the East," is the "link-language" of the region.
3. Spanish	Hello, how are you? = Hola (silent "h"), como está? My name is = Me llamo ("May YAH-moh"). Thank you very much = Muchas gracias.	The second most spoken language in the United States—and growing every day.
4. English	You know this one!	The most commonly studied "second language." The large English-speaking countries are all considered "melting pots" where many different languages are spoken.
5. Arabic	Hi = Salaam. [More polite] Good day = Al Salaam a aleikum ("Ahl sah-LAHM ah ah-LAY-koom"). How are you? = Kayf Halaak/ Haaleek (female). Thank you = Shokran.	These terms are useful in any country with a large Muslim population, not only an "Arabic" country (e.g., Indonesia, West Africa).
6. Portuguese	Hello = Ola. How are you? = Tudo bom? Como vai ("vie")? Thank you = Obrigado/a (masculine/feminine).	More people speak Portuguese in South America than Spanish.
7. Bengali	Hello = Namaskar ("Nah-mah-SCAR") [also used in Hindi for more formal greeting]. How are you? = Tumi kamon aacho. I am fine = Aami bhalo aachi. Thank you = Dhannyabad.	Also known as Bangla, the vocabulary is based in ancient Sanskrit.
8. Russian	Hi = Privet. How are you? = Kak dela? My name is = Menia zovut ("Men-YAH zoh-VOOT"). Thank you = Spasiba.	The Russian alphabet is called Cyrillic. From 1917–90, Russian language was mandatory in Soviet bloc countries.
9. Japanese	Hello and good afternoon = Konnichiwa. Good morning = Ohayou (pronounced like "Ohio"). How are you? = Oganke-desu-ka. Thank you = Arigato. [All in the familiar form]	Japanese is an "honorific" language. Verbs, nouns, and prefixes are divided into three forms: polite, humble, and respectful.

RANK + LANGUAGE	OPENING GREETING + ONE POLITE PHRASE	ADDITIONAL COMMENTS
10. German	Hello, Hi = Guten Tag. How are you? = Wie geht es ihnen? Fine, thanks = Danke, gut.	Germans tend to use the formal "you" and the corresponding verb tense more frequently—until they know someone very well. The letter "ß" makes the sound "ss."

3. *Internet sites can offer an introduction to language instruction and some translation for free.* Hundreds of websites—from electronic greeting cards in various languages to foreign language instruction sites—offer words, expressions, and greetings in many, many tongues. Some of the sites include audio pronunciations, and some are simply text based, so the effectiveness will be limited. Trying to use the Internet sites for learning will require the most discipline, as there is no set schedule, financial investment, or accountability. So, if you're serious, you need to find a way to measure your progress. See www.word2word.com for a clearinghouse of links to online language courses for languages ranging from Abenaki to Xhosa. While this is an excellent one-stop resource, it still needs to be supplemented by finding a live person with whom to practice the words.

Sweden's World Children's Prize for the Rights of the Child, at www.childrensworld.org, teaches the greetings in the context of "meeting" children from different countries. Their "language school" in ten languages features greetings and videos of kids counting to ten in their native tongue. Like your children, these kids like to play and have fun. But they happen to live in conditions ranging from orphanages and refugee camps to war zones.

Another creative site for hearing different languages' greetings is the website for NASA's *Voyager* spacecraft, the agency's most successful planetary mission. It carries on board the "golden record"—"a kind of time capsule, intended to communicate a story of our world to extraterrestrials . . . containing sounds and images selected to portray the diversity of life and culture on earth," with "greetings from earth" to the universe in fifty-five languages. This powerful image, of the rich tapestry of the earth's cultures assembled by some of our greatest scientific minds, and going out to anyone in the universe who might find it, can teach what a small planet we share with speakers of many languages. It's also a fun way to envision universality, particularly for the child who is more oriented toward science fiction or science reality.

Start a conversation with an elder.

Almost every country in the world has changed dramatically over the past two generations. From growing up during the height of Communism in the Eastern bloc, or apartheid in South Africa, to living without our technological conveniences, the experiences that today's senior citizens had during their youth can present a precious memento of bygone eras, both good and bad, to young people today. Particularly for older kids, engaging in conversation with their friends' grandparents, or a resident at a local nursing home, or even through a house of worship (you don't have to join it to get to know some of its members) are wonderful ways to try out some words in another person's native language while global history comes alive. Older community members also can get involved with your after-school language club. Trying to envision a world without computers, where TV was a novelty, and today's brand of globalization has not yet taken hold—from Prague to Hanoi to Beirut—will provide plenty of fodder for some good discussions. This also offers kids great practice for polite greetings and for speaking the words they are learning in a foreign language. You make the call of how involved in the conversation you should be, depending on your child's maturity and comfort level for having you around.

4. *Start an after-school language club at your children's school.* Even if your school district is open to the idea of starting a language immersion program, it may take years to get off the ground. You can start a weekly or twice weekly after-school language club more easily. Recruit one to two parent volunteers who speak the particular language of interest and begin a basic program that lasts about one hour per session. If possible, ask other interested parents—no language knowledge necessary—to be classroom helpers.

WHEN YOU'RE READY TO SPEAK A NEW LANGUAGE

Ultimately, to move beyond the initial greeting, you will learn your friend's spoken language(s). Most people think of a citizen of the world as one who is multilingual. This implies significant effort, and fluency requires immersing oneself in a different culture. Although living in a new country is probably the best way to learn the language, it's not the only way. Children all over the world begin at a very early age to learn a second (or sometimes third and fourth) language. With the mix of so many

Did You Know?

More Americans than ever before—about one in five—speak a language other than English in their homes. In large cities like New York, almost half the population over the age of five speaks a language other than English at home.[2]

nationalities in the United States and newer immigrants renouncing the idea that their children must speak only English in order to be American, more U.S. children are speaking their "heritage language" at home. This makes conversing in a foreign language easier from your home community, without having to travel abroad.

'Alim's experience: lessons for growing up multilingual: My second cousin 'Alim Beveridge is fluent in four languages (English, Persian, German, and Spanish) and conversant in four more (French, Arabic, Hebrew, and Albanian). This is highly unusual, but in some ways, he reflects the modern experience of a family with a mixed cultural background. His father was American and his mother Iranian. They lived in Austria when he was young, so as he says, learning the first three languages was "something I just went through without choosing to do so." When he was eight years old the family moved to Israel, where his parents chose a school that simultaneously taught Hebrew, Arabic, and French. As a youth he spent a summer of service in Albania where, for the first time on his own, he chose to learn the language; and after graduating from Stanford University he worked in Bolivia, where he mastered Spanish in a few months. He is now married to a Bolivian and they are raising their two young sons trilingually.

'Alim's experience highlights several important lessons for parents:

1. His parents (and now he, as a parent) made language a priority in their home. Each of the parents spoke their native tongue with their child and were consistent in speaking only that language to the child, particularly from birth to age five (e.g., his father spoke only English to him, Mom only Persian, and he picked up German when he went out, went to school, or watched TV). This calls for a great deal of discipline and commitment by the parents.
2. By instilling multiple languages in their young child (even two languages would not be shabby!), the parents ensure that the brain becomes more receptive to

language acquisition, the ear becomes attuned to the distinct sounds of languages, and even various accents roll more easily off the tongue. 'Alim's accent in his more recently acquired Spanish sounds almost as "native" as his American English or his German accents.

3. Speaking or teaching multiple languages to a child makes learning another new language or communicating with someone speaking an entirely different language a much less daunting task. 'Alim described his then-five-year-old son's experience in trying to play with kids who didn't understand him during a trip to Israel: "He didn't let the language barrier deter him. He gestured, jumped up and down, drew pictures, and did whatever it took to play with those kids. Not understanding each other was not an option in my son's mind."

4. 'Alim is not a linguist or a language scholar. But the initial, deliberate exposure his parents gave him has developed into a love of languages and world cultures that he is passing on to his own children. He adds: "To really understand a culture, to access it, you must know its language. It encapsulates a new way of looking at the world. . . . It puts you in their shoes."

SUREFIRE STRATEGIES FOR LEARNING A NEW LANGUAGE

Young children absorb a new language more easily than adults do[3] and learning a foreign language helps in the acquisition of other subjects, like science and math. Consequently, an increasing number of U.S. public school districts are starting foreign language instruction earlier. Recognizing global social and political shifts, more are including non-European languages in their offerings for grades K–12.

Aim high to gain fluency: One huge challenge in school settings is to figure out how to leap from the snail's pace of language classes (even at excellent schools) with periodic instruction to carrying on a conversation in that language. While my own children learned Spanish beginning in first grade in their public elementary

"Effective language teaching is age appropriate. Young children need full immersion that imitates growing up with that language. Older students require grammar and structure along with meaning and conversation."

—Findings from the American Educational Research Association school, by middle school they still couldn't speak it in whole sentences. That next step requires using verbs in the correct conjugation, connecting words through proper prepositions, and other grammatical rules that a forty-minute session once or twice per week with twenty-five other kids would not allow. In other words, something more like 'Alim's experience growing up, or a "full immersion," is required in order to gain proficiency. To simulate an immersion environment, the American Educational Research Association (AERA) recommends:

- *Integrate the second language with instruction in other subjects* [i.e., teach math in French or Chinese].
- *Give learners ample opportunities to engage in meaningful discourse with other students and teachers using the foreign language* [i.e., have real conversations on meaningful topics].
- *Expose learners to a variety of native speakers of the target language* [i.e., meet plenty of people who speak the new language].
- *Focus instruction on attaining the language skills needed for communicating about and understanding academic subject matter, not on mastering a foreign language for its own sake* [i.e., teach what they need to know, and can and will actually use— not fluff].[4]

Trying language immersion at home: Internet resources like www.multilingualchildren.org, founded by a San Francisco mom who wanted her own children to grow up multilingual, offers a growing list of resources, playgroups, discussion boards, nanny lists, and other support for parents who want to focus on language immersion in the home. Another individual initiative comes from www.omniglot.com, about all things multilingual, with a special section on raising bilingual/multilingual children, go to www.bilingualbabies.com for discussion boards, a directory of bilingual playgroups, and other resources for parents. All sites contain lists of quality books and articles for more information on raising children multilingually.

Language immersion programs in U.S. school districts: Conditions of full immersion are not easy to create or maintain, but a growing number of American communities and school districts—from the Boston suburbs to Chicago and Portland—are trying them out. If your school district does not offer any language immersion programs, find out if its strategic plan might call for one. Among the better endowed districts, it could make a difference for them to know that families they serve are interested in such programs and that other top school districts around the country are implementing these programs. Be ready to get involved and for some hard work to see such a program to fruition—even the best school districts need to comply with numerous political and bureaucratic procedures, so it could take a long time and much convincing to start, especially when it involves funding something new. Alternatively, see if one of a growing number of publicly funded charter schools with an international focus might be accessible for your children.

Proof of immersion's success is found with years of French immersion in English-speaking Canada and English immersion at international schools around the world. Children in those school immersion environments graduate with fluency or near-fluency in the second language.

MORE TOOLS TO HELP ACQUIRE FOREIGN LANGUAGE SKILLS

When I was growing up, my parents wanted me to learn to read and write in the language of our heritage, Persian (known by many as Farsi, but saying "I speak Farsi" is like "I speak Español"—the word *Farsi* is used when speaking Persian), imposing a one-hour lesson on me most days after school during my tween years. I might have cried and protested every torturous day we had a lesson. Today I can read and write at a second-grade level in Persian. I'm glad that my parents didn't give in—parents always know best! We used Iran's national regulation 1960s-era textbook with a brown paper bag–looking cover, reading stories that I neither related to nor was interested in. There were no fun or interactive resources to help learn the language, and while living in Indiana, we were isolated from people I could take the class with.

I realized even then that my parents did their best, and just as they warned me, I'm happy about it now. My Persian language skills, though modest, served as a springboard for learning other languages and being open to other cultures. I share the (now funny) stories of my protestations with my own children, who derive great amusement from imagining me in such a state. When I insist they practice piano, or work on their own Persian lesson or other academic work they aren't excited about, it helps them to know I had similar struggles. Fortunately, today, there are so many fun resources for language exposure and learning—and the choices keep changing and improving. Here are a few good places to get started.

FOR KIDS UNDER TEN

Product websites: Marketers have caught on to the high demand for interactive and multicultural toys and tools, so this age group probably has the widest selection of products for learning and exposure to a new language. Check out magel lanstoyshop.com and languagelizard.com; both are good one-stop resources on the Internet for multilingual toys, books, CDs, and DVDs, and they are organized for sale by language of interest or age range. For multicultural toys and baby gifts see dollslikeme.com.

A worldwide favorite for language teaching (mentioned earlier) for ages one to twelve is MUZZY, the BBC Language Course for Children, available at early-ad vantage.com. This is one of the most expensive resources listed in this book, so you might try to lobby your local library to invest in the course or partner with another family or two to purchase a set. Overall, the selection of multimedia resources for learning languages like Spanish and Chinese is immense, but quality varies, especially if you are not a native speaker. *Beth Manners' Fun Spanish (and French) for Kids* ages two to six (audio CD) and items in the China Sprout catalog are a good start.

CDs: Songs by children's artists like Red Grammer, Ella Jenkins, and Raffi expose little ones to different cultures and to saying hello in various languages. Also, so many CDs carry song translations, including "Head, Shoulders, Knees, and Toes," "Happy Birthday," "Itsy, Bitsy, Spider," and other standards in various languages. These help younger children to 1) realize that the same thing can be conveyed through different languages; 2) get a feel for what it sounds like; and 3) begin to break down the process of translation. For a more sophisticated sound (for all ages), Putumayo and Ellipsis Arts' lullaby compilations from around the world offer a peaceful and pleasant alternative to many of the materials that aim for high stimulation to keep your attention and try so hard to make language learning fun! effortless! for hours! My older daughters also enjoy the less babyish sounding choices in these compilations.

Toys: Among the many toy offerings for this age group, Language Littles's smart soft dolls for girls and boys come from various cultures. Squeeze the hand of the doll and they speak either Korean, Greek, Spanish, Hebrew, French, Russian, Mandarin, German, or Italian. Littler ones might enjoy the "Friends Say Hello" multicultural puzzle by Eeboo. Dora the Explorer has become *the* brand for bilingual English-Spanish products, from her Talking Dollhouse (the bestselling dollhouse in Fisher-Price history) to her Talking Cash Register to computer games. On amazon.com, parents and teachers have compiled their favorite resources on Listmania! for everything from "Teaching Pre-K—Grade 2 Spanish" to "Father and Son's Social Justice Picture Books for Children" with numerous high-quality multicultural or multilingual books. Lezlie Evans's *Can You Greet the Whole Wide World?: 12 Common Phrases in 12 Different Languages* and *Can You Count Ten Toes?: Count to 10 in 10 Different Languages* and Karen Katz's *Can You Say Peace?* nicely juxtapose different languages.

For free: Kids over age four can play imagination games with dolls they pretend are from different countries or role-play that they themselves are from different countries and practice saying hello in the languages of the countries they are playing. My daughter Sophia sees me say hello to friends in Spanish or Persian or Portuguese and sometimes will spontaneously start pretending she's a grown-up that I should greet. She comes up to me with the exuberance of some of the people she's seen, imitates their accents, kisses me on both cheeks, and then we start to play tea party or "Mommy." No need to buy stuff to play pure imagination games.

FOR AGES TEN AND OLDER

Websites: For this age range, there are far fewer products to buy and more interactive websites that might make the language exploration and learning process more enjoyable. MUZZY products might still be relevant, but be careful the material doesn't feel too juvenile for this increasingly savvy age group, or else you might encounter resistance to the whole process. Just as this age group enjoys computer games, I found that safe, interactive sites online, like those found at www.languagegames.org or the websites put together by language teachers at various schools contain fun activities. Look up the sites of respected school districts for foreign language tools their teachers like. The Council on Europe has a game on eylgame.org to match the word meaning "hello" with one of the forty-five European languages it comes from. This is not easy, and it gives a sense of the wide range of languages concentrated on the European continent.

Watch TV or videos: Another fun way to get your middle-school-aged child more involved and exposed to a new language is to watch TV. Foreign language TV is available on basic cable across the United States, and some language channels might be available on premium channels or through a satellite dish. At a minimum, there is a wide selection of Spanish language TV, but also look for other languages of the large minorities in your community—even if they share an international TV station (e.g., two hours for Greek, two for Korean, two for Hindi, two for Arabic programming, and so on). Watching a sports game is a great entrée for the sports enthusiast—you see what's going on, so listening to commentary in the background can reinforce your comprehension. Most movie DVDs come with a language selection on the main menu. This usually is confined to Spanish, and possibly French. Other popular movies might be available on dubbed DVD by special order, but make sure you approve of the subject matter and content. Also, look for excellent global programming on PBS, Travel Channel, Food Network, BBC America, Discovery Channel, National Geographic, IFC, Sundance, and more.

Try YouTube: You don't actually need a cable TV subscription to watch some of the best international TV programs. You can see most of them on YouTube. Many of the videos that don't make it to our cable channels, posted by professionals and amateurs, might show a hilarious or witty side of a foreign culture that is rarely seen outside their country. To find good stuff on YouTube it helps to research other websites for suggestions of popular media from a country you are interested in before wandering aimlessly around a virtually infinite number of videos. Look for international film festival award–winning short films, check the YouTube channels in the nonprofits category, watch children's TV shows from other countries (e.g., search "children's TV show Japan"), experience Arabic or Cuban music, and see efforts like an entire channel from Queen Rania of Jordan dedicated to dispelling myths about Arabs. Of course, not everything posted on YouTube is uplifting, funny, or innocent, so parents should supervise, or even prescreen.

Listen to pop music: If your tween likes pop and hip-hop music, find CDs that suit their style (and your values) in the language you are trying to learn. Many artists already have Spanish language collaborations. Just as a form of hip-hop youth culture dominates globally, similar music styles are being recorded in virtually any language you're interested in. My husband downloads techno and pop hits from Tajikistan (in the former USSR) with Persian lyrics. Reading the liner notes and singing along not only helps teach vocabulary and pronunciation, it might also make children, tweens, and teens more excited about their own or a new culture. Remember to mix in world music playlists on your MP3 player.

FOR ADULTS

Play with your kids' toys: If my kids sense I have gotten them an educational toy (or computer game), they might stay away from it. But if my husband or I start playing around with it, trying to figure out how it works, they can't wait to get started, too. You'll learn what your kids are inclined to do and create more interest in the activity.

Join a conversation group: Many area Newcomers Clubs have foreign language conversation groups that regularly meet. You don't have to be new in your area to participate in one of these clubs. (Google "newcomers club" and you can go to the link of a national website with a state-by-state directory, or look for your specific area on the Google page.) By indicating your interest in learning that culture and language, you can participate in any of the activities of a particular language group even if you're not a "newcomer." (Languages spoken by foreign professionals working in the United States or their spouses are the easiest to connect with; in my area

Speaking Spanglish and other polyglots

In Southern California, the mixing of Hispanic, American, and other immigrant cultures is nothing new. Today, Spanglish is finding its way into the mainstream, particularly among young people. Blending languages (e.g., half a sentence in English and half in Spanish) takes place during recess and lunch breaks in schools in polyglot communities, in popular music and on radio programs, and is even catching on with bilingual television programming. The blending is not confined to the Spanish and English combination. In cities like Los Angeles, English is not the second language of choice for all immigrants. The presence of Hispanic workers in Korean markets and Persian restaurants or of Filippinos in Arab businesses, dictates which languages these new Americans will learn. Depending on demographic trends, unlikely languages show up on "official" documents, like Persian on the 2007 ballot for Beverly Hills's municipal election. You might soon hear the blending of languages wherever you live. By learning a popular second language you can join in on that conversation.

that's still Spanish, French, and German, but increasingly it's Mandarin, Hindi, and Portuguese.) This is a great way for your entire family to socialize with families from different countries.

Tap into university resources and students: Most universities have a foreign student population. Contact the local university's Office of or Dean of International Students. Invite one or more students over for dinner periodically, not only to help your family practice a language and learn about another culture, but so that the students can feel more at home in a new country. Many families develop close friendships with these students and stay in touch with them throughout their careers, often in leadership positions in their home countries. I also have had some good (but not always good) experiences with foreign students as babysitters or for odd jobs around the house. (NB: You need to be aware of immigration restrictions if hiring them.)

Hire a nanny: If you need to hire a nanny or an au pair, consider the benefit of the foreign language they might be able to teach your children. Seek out someone who speaks the language you're particularly interested in. If the nanny is a native Russian or Italian speaker, the chances are high that your children will pick up words in their language and learn about their culture. Ask around for an agency with a good reputation in your town, and see Nanny.org.

———

A world citizen is comfortable with diverse people, and new associations begin, simply, with the opening greeting. Start by making sure you and your children make a habit of greeting the people you regularly meet—slow down and be conscious of this simple act. With this courtesy as a building block, try to learn the greetings or gestures of the different cultures with which you come into contact. And from there, you can learn a few polite phrases together. If you don't regularly have contact with people speaking other languages, choose a culture or language based on your heritage, personal interests, travel goals, or other criterion and make the effort to associate with speakers of that language. Ultimately, the goal is to learn a new language. Almost every country in the world—with the exception of the United States—begins immersing their children in a second (or third or fourth) language from a very young age. This not only shows that multiple language mastery is possible, but that it is a necessity in a globalized world. It takes a great deal of effort, so the best way to encourage your child is to serve as an example and make it a natural activity for the whole family to engage in. There are more age-appropriate resources than ever before to encourage the process of language acquisition. On top of this, in U.S. "polyglot" communities, where many cultures are living and working side-by-side, young people are speaking a blend of languages, forming cultural models that never existed before, and setting trends— picked up in popular media—that the rest of the country will emulate.

Everyone might not have the benefit of shaking hands with a little girl like Josephine, but her example reminds my family that learning to offer a polite greeting can open the doors to new friendships from all over the world. After a warm greeting, we can do so much with our new friends—eat! play! watch a movie! celebrate!

RESOURCE BOOKS CITED IN CHAPTER 2—THAT YOU MAY FIND HELPFUL, TOO

I cite Emily Post's classic 1922 *Book of Etiquette*. More useful and accessible for the reader will be *Emily Post's Etiquette* (17th Edition), Peggy Post (New York: Collins Living, 2004) or *Miss Manners' Guide to Rearing Perfect Children*, Judith Martin (New York: Scribner's, 2002).

Can You Greet the Whole Wide World?: 12 Common Phrases in 12 Different Languages, Lezlie Evans (author), Denis Roche (illustrator) (New York: Houghton Mifflin, 2006).

Can You Count Ten Toes?: Count to 10 in 10 Different Languages, Lezlie Evans (author), Denis Roche (illustrator) (New York: Houghton Mifflin Harcourt, 2004).

Can You Say Peace?, Karen Katz (New York: Henry Holt and Company, 2006).

ADDITIONAL RESOURCE BOOKS RELATED TO CHAPTER 2

Whoever You Are, Mem Fox (author), Leslie Staub (illustrator) (Orlando, FL: Harcourt Inc., 2007).

Imagine a House: A Journey to Fascinating Houses Around the World, Angela Gustafson (Minneapolis: Out of the Box, 2003).

Chapter 3

Play!

You can discover more about a person in an hour of play

than in a year of conversation.

PLATO

You've greeted your friend, now it's time to play! Most children naturally get the wisdom of Plato's quote about play. They get to the business of play and don't need much discussion to begin a friendship. A ball can do more to bring people together than hours of talk, even among warring (or Cold Warring) nations and groups.

Through play, parents can immediately achieve three objectives of "growing up global" with their children: First, playing together provides unpreachy, quality, interactive time with our children (not to mention, it gets them away from the TV and computer); second, it can help to show so many common traits among different cultures; and third—the flip side—it can demonstrate some of the qualities that make various cultures stand apart from one another.

By simply playing new or unusual games together or pointing out ways in which the same game is played in other countries, our children can start to grasp the idea of "unity in diversity." This means that we are comfortable with approaches that are very different from our own and that these differences can make life more interesting. In cultures with a weaker tradition of democracy (or in subcultures within a highly democratic country), there might be discomfort around accepting people or practices that stray from the norm. Through the introduction of diverse games and unusual ways to play, parents can instill an appreciation of diversity and democracy in their children while simply playing with them.

THE GAMES THAT UNITE US

When my family was living in West Africa, we became accustomed to seeing almost anything that had been thoroughly exhausted as a source of food or fuel get kicked toward a goal. Bottle caps, tin cans that could no longer be reused as containers, rotted cashew shells, abundant unripe mangoes—all got kicked around on the dusty streets and trails during the dry season to mimic a soccer game. An organized soccer game (called "football" everywhere except the United States) between rival neighborhoods at the sandy open field of the local elementary school on a Friday afternoon (after the noonday prayer, marking the start of the weekend) would draw hundreds of people of varying ages to cheer on their teams. Many of the excellent players had no shoes to wear, let alone fancy shin guards or matching jerseys. My girls saw that determination was all it took to get the game going.

As we drove through different neighborhoods of Banjul and its environs, we would watch for chalkboards displayed by enterprising TV owners who wrote the schedule of upcoming professional football games on the boards they'd prop against their mud and tin homes or storefronts so that anyone could pay a small fee to come watch Manchester United play Barcelona or Nigeria versus Zambia on their eighteen-inch, Taiwanese TV screen. These cottage industries form a vital connection between people who are too poor to own a TV or have electricity in their homes, and the international sports superstars, advertising sponsors, and the passion that revolves around the sport worldwide. As a result, children who are considered the "poorest of the poor" have heroes from Brazil or France or Nigeria who they aspire to be like, and thanks to thriving used-clothing markets, they proudly wear the team jerseys of their favorite athletes.

We witnessed how the same game that parents in our U.S. home community rush their kids around for on Saturdays is passionately played where people can't imagine owning a car. It's the *game* we have in common. There is much more that we share, but the game serves as a starting point. When we wanted to buy a departing gift for the kids we got to know at our Gambian Sunday School class, the only thing they asked for was a decent soccer ball—they had just one that had to be shared by about fifty kids.

TEN WAYS SOCCER CAN HELP YOU GROW UP GLOBAL

A quick search on amazon.com reveals there is a whole genre dedicated to exploring how soccer explains the world, or "soccer sociology." In many ways, soccer acts like the universal language. Tuning in with your children to the worldwide devotion to soccer provides an excellent springboard for learning about other cultures and worldviews. Use soccer to grow up global.

Here are a few ways to begin:

1. *Tap in to the global game through FIFA* (pronounced "FEE-fa"), the International Football Association, which sponsors the World Cup games (see www .fifa.com). FIFA is the world's largest sports association. Navigate this website for a great window to the world. In addition to seeing game highlights and scores, kids can learn about developments in the sport, about what fans in the various countries are concerned about, about how soccer teams and players are giving back in their respective countries, and even learn about the countries themselves. In 2007, the year we were in The Gambia, there was no professional World Cup contest (it's held once every four years), but the Under-20s age group (U-20s) had their own World Cup and the Gambian U-20 team (almost miraculously) made it to the final sixteen round. The whole nation rallied around fundraising to get the boys to the matches in Toronto. Once we were back in the states, my family followed the team's performance on the FIFA site and watched their bittersweet return home.

2. *Start to follow a few international teams.* Pick favorites. You can start narrowing down which teams to pick based on your favorite countries (choose these based on your heritage, your friend's, your favorite type of food, the language

Go all out during the World Cup games.

Dan and Susan Harasty live in central New Jersey with their four children, ranging in age from six to fifteen. They met in Swaziland while Susan was with the Peace Corps and Dan volunteered nearby for six months. It's too costly for all six of them to travel internationally, but Dan and Susan consciously try to instill a sense of belonging in the world for their children. When the World Cup soccer games are played once every four years, Dan prints out a schedule and each member of the family picks one to two different countries whose games they try to follow. Dan says, "The youngest pick first, and take Italy and France; I pick last and usually get the countries they hear the least about, like Albania. By the end of the series, my country is cool." Everyone finds where "their" country is located on the globe. If they can, they make the flag of their country to wave during their game.

you want to learn to speak, your favorite jersey, or hundreds of other reasons—get creative!). The FIFA site includes an interactive world map. Hitting the Teams tab brings up a map of the world with country abbreviations and flags for all those teams playing. Click on the flag and learn about the team.

3. *Learn about the lives of your favorite players.* "Football" players abroad are the biggest celebrities in many countries. Some of the top players came up through hard circumstances, possibly playing the game in the streets of their tough neighborhoods. For school biography projects, or just for general interest, kids can choose an international player to learn about.

4. *Cheer for the U.S.A.* There's no reason you can't be a patriot and still grow up global. Track the travels of the U.S. team. Look for links with the local immigrant population (e.g., Polish and Eastern European influence on the Chicago pro team, or Central Americans on DC United). Where are your favorite U.S. players and coaches from? Join the fans at a pro soccer game near you.

5. *How are the women and girls doing?* Which countries have professional women players? Does the foreign country you chose to follow have a women's team? Are their teams supported by the public at large? What might be some of the obstacles faced by the girls in other countries as they get serious about sports? Did you know the world's number one team of women has long come from the United States but our men's team struggles to make qualifying rounds? Why might this be? Proudly wear a jersey of a women's team. Tickets to the games usually cost less than the men's, so invite a small group to join you in cheering on a women's team, or celebrate a birthday with friends by going to a women's game.

6. *Get to know players or their parents with a different worldview.* In communities all across America, the children of immigrants are more likely to join a soccer team than any other sport. And those parents might make the best coaches—some have known and loved the sport with a level of intensity that simply didn't exist when we were growing up in the United States. For lots of kids, playing on a team is largely a social experience, so it can open a door to meeting families from different cultures. Among parents, conversations start spontaneously in between cheering on the sidelines. I recall learning tips for staying warm at my daughter's games one blustery November from Canadian parents. The following week a family from India brewed a spicy chai tea and transported it in a large carafe to share with us, providing a much-needed change of pace early on a Saturday morning. The act of serving us hot paper cups of tea at the game created a simple but lasting connection—a memorable "icebreaker."

7. *Adults can play, too.* If you're an adult and want to play, find one of the numerous leagues in towns across America. These are largely made up of international residents, who grew up with "football," and a few enthusiastic Americans. When my cousin Ramin, who grew up in Iran and Australia, started working on Wall Street, he found a league nearby in Chinatown, organized by a Chinese restaurant owner. Now he plays on a northern New Jersey men's league at least twice a week with friends from Nigeria, South Africa, Brazil, Central America, Turkey, and more. His teammates might be cab drivers, doctors, or CEOs, but those distinctions fade away on the turf. Over the years, these are among his best "American" friends.

8. *If you get to travel abroad, try to attend a local football/soccer game.* There are few events that will demonstrate local culture and passions more than a football match. You don't have to attend a professional game; a youth league will provide plenty of entertainment. If you don't know where to begin to find a game, ask someone at your hotel—they might even invite you to join their family at a game.

9. *Watch a soccer movie. Bend It Like Beckham* has become the classic soccer movie. It provides both a lens into a girl's struggle as well as a look at life in an Indian household in England, with the clash of cultures taking place between generations of an immigrant family. The American film *Gracie* follows the classic sports movie formula, of overcoming a tragedy and the odds, but delivers a good soccer flick and family drama. Like *Bend It,* this also got a PG-13 rating; unfortunately, it's not suitable for kids just starting soccer in elementary school.

   The predicament of women in Iran who must dress like men to get into the World Cup qualifying match is portrayed in *Offside.* Ages thirteen and up can see how the absurdities of barring women from watching sports matches are circumvented by young fans. *The Cup,* from Burma, follows younger Tibetan monks who try to watch the World Cup final from their monastery in exile. The devotion to the sport of fans from actual, remote tribal villages in Mongolia, Niger, and Brazil plays out in their quest to get TV reception for the 2002 World Cup final in *The Great Match,* made by a crew from Spain. Soccer documentaries *The Boys from Brazil* and *The History of Soccer* (a seven-DVD set) also show the passion of the game outside the United States.

10. *Help all kids access soccer and sports.* Organizations like the U.S. Soccer Foundation, BallforAll, Velletri Soccer Group, Grassroot Soccer, UNICEF, in partnership with FIFA at unicef.org/football, and many more can connect your family with global soccer programs that positively impact struggling local

communities. These charities work through organized sports to help advance kids' academics, their community's development, and keep them healthy and out of trouble. America SCORES, the U.S. Soccer Foundation, and organizations within various metropolitan areas (like DC United and Dallas Scores) all support opportunities for disadvantaged kids in the United States to pursue the sport as a door to other opportunities.

OLYMPIC GAMES AS A PORTAL TO GROWING UP GLOBAL

Soccer might not be your (or your kids') thing. You can try activities similar to the ten previously listed for various Olympic sports, like archery, track, volleyball, and kayaking in the summer, or luge and curling in the winter. There are thirty-five official Olympic sports listed at Olympic.org. Learn about top athletes from different countries, about countries competing at various levels, and locations where qualifying rounds are taking place. The site is rich in information about the Olympic movement and embracing a worldview.

Introducing your children to lesser-known sports like fencing might pique their interest to try an unusual pastime. Children who grow up pursuing a non-mainstream sport often display qualities of independence and discipline. They might also attract college recruiters—either because university teams need to fill slots in that sport, or they might believe such an unusual skill makes for an interesting candidate for their school.

If you'd like to travel to Olympic venues but can't make it to the actual games (or want to avoid the crowds), visit the sites of past games. In North America, see Montreal's Olympic structures as part of a larger trip to Canada's French-speaking province—and it's cheaper than a trip to Europe. Go skating, skiing, or snowboarding, or watch competitions like bobsled and figure skating at one of the sites of past winter games, in Lake Placid, New York; Salt Lake City, Utah; Calgary, Alberta, and the 2010 Winter Games outside Vancouver, British Columbia. Attend a summer event at Atlanta's Centennial Olympic Park.

SIT-DOWN GAMES FROM AROUND THE WORLD—ROOTED IN ANCIENT CULTURES, SPANNING GENERATIONS

Many of the most popular board or "table" games have long histories from rich and ancient cultures. As with soccer, playing these can create a bridge with friends from other cultures. Most don't require that you speak the same language, and with these games there is no physical barrier to entry, so young and old, athletic and physically challenged can play together.

Chess is estimated to be the second-most popular game in the world after soccer, played by hundreds of millions of people. Tens of thousands of people play round-the-clock on the Internet, ensuring the game's legacy among a new generation.

In Atlanta, chess's growing popularity reflects the expansion of the region's immigrant population.[1] Colombian and Venezuelan players along with South Asian, former Soviet bloc, and African immigrants comprise some of the city's most competitive players. Summer camps in Atlanta and other cities help kids master the game, and community centers are vibrant with chess tournaments that attract the elderly and the young, new and longtime residents in a healthy environment united for the love of the game.

If you're interested in history, research the origins of the game, as it spread from ancient Sanskrit India to Persia and then Arabia. After it became popular among the Arabs around the time of the appearance of Muhammad, it traveled to Europe and took hold to become the game we see today. Chess is one of the many innovations of society that spread from the Arabian Peninsula to the west.

If you don't know how to play, ask a friend or maybe an elderly neighbor to teach you and your child. See if your school offers a chess club before or after school. Like a soccer team, this can serve as a bridge between children of diverse backgrounds. If your school does not offer a chess club, then start one. School administrators like it for the intellectual and positive social benefits offered by the game. Host an end-of-year chess club potluck, which will probably become an international dinner. It offers a chance for the various families to share foods from their home culture and socialize outside of the confines of school.

Backgammon and its many variations of table games were played by ancient Romans, Egyptians, Mesopotamians, and Persians for thousands of years and, like chess, later spread to become popular throughout Europe. When we have lively family dinners or even at a picnic, a game of backgammon usually breaks out. Often the grandfathers or uncles challenge each other and children stand over their shoulders, strategize, and cheer. Future sons-in-law who want to bond with the patriarchs have done well to accept the challenge of a backgammon game— and graciously lose. This simple and fun game also creates a bridge between cultures and generations. It takes less concentration and intensity to play than chess, so it is more accessible for more people. You can play it online in order to learn the game if it's not possible to play at home.

Mancala, an African game (known by many different names throughout Africa), spread to South and East Asia centuries ago and has been popular in the United States for decades. It might be the oldest game known to man, with boards carved into ancient Egyptian temple roofs dating before 1400 B.C. As with chess and backgammon, artisans worldwide have crafted elaborate game boards that collectors prize. Buy the wooden board with about forty-eight smooth stones in almost any toy store, or you can make your own, with an empty egg carton and marbles, shells, or stones. Kids might research and adorn it with ancient Egyptian or African symbols. Many Internet sites teach the rules if you need them. We started playing this game with our girls when they were very little, around three or four, on a simple wooden board with colorful stones. They loved to play this rhythmic, uncomplicated game and we welcomed an alternative to CandyLand.

Checkers, known as "Draughts" (pronounced *drafts*) in England, traces its roots back to an archaeological dig in Iraq, dating to 3000 B.C. The modern version was designed around the year 1100 in France. It's another great language-and culture-bridging game played by young and old around the world.

Parcheesi was a popular board game when I was growing up in the 1970s, but it came from a centuries-old game, *Pachisi,* still known as the national game of India. Related "cross and circle" games were found to be played by Montezuma's subjects among precolonial Mayans in Mexico and other Native American cultures. Hasbro's Sorry! is a popular variation on this theme. Start a family game night and revive this universal game.

Risk has gotten older kids and their parents or family members to think about the world for almost a century. It's another board game that's gained popularity online. Warning: It's bellicose—"attack, defend, and take over the world!" The game board is a map of the world, divided into forty-two territories, spanning six continents. Players control opposing armies and fight for power over territories. The ultimate goal is to gain control of the world by eliminating all of the other players. You don't want to teach your children war, but you can learn from war. You can offer teachable moments relating to the strategy, discuss how real world conflicts over the accession of territory created national borders of today, and what price people have paid over the war games of their leaders. This gives an opportunity to think about the number of wars that continue to rage today. Find out how many there are and what they are fighting over. The Nobelprize.org website includes essays about wars over the past century, profiles of peacemakers, as well as electronic games for high-school-aged kids on serious topics like prisoners of war, the map of world conflicts, and nuclear proliferation.

Playground games to help you "visit" a new country (no purchase necessary). In addition to soccer and many of the Olympic sports, there are so many other universal games to play on the playground or in your neighborhood, from tag to rock-paper-scissors (known as *Jan Ken Po* in Japanese), sometimes with slight variations. Monkey-in-the-middle in Thailand is called *Ling Ching Bon* or "monkey snatches ball." Hide-and-go-seek in Iraq is known as *Suk Suk,* meaning "home home," and when a hider is found, they race back to home base to avoid being "it," just like the Welsh game "Danny one-two-three" (*Danny un, dau, tri* in Welsh).

Tag probably has the most variations. We used to play snake tag, TV tag, and freeze tag when I was growing up. Variations on snake tag—where the person tagged joins the "it" by hand and the snake or chain grows bigger with each person caught—include *l'aranya peluda* ("hairy spider" in Catalonia), *Kettenfangen* ("chain tag" in German), and *Mamba* ("snake" in southern Africa).

The games stay fresh when you discover variations from other cultures—both in how to play it and how to say it. It's exciting to learn words in a new language and everyone gains a little confidence that they can say something familiar but totally new. Instant translation programs online can fill in words from a particular language. Search the game in that culture, or ask a friend about variations they may remember on the playground in the country where they grew up. Words are more easily remembered in a foreign language during a game because they are being used in a fun context.

If you have a particular country you'd like to learn about with your children, are traveling to, or where a new friend is from, you can try a game from that country as a means to get to know its culture better, and the games can be taken together as a sort of "journey around the world." With elementary-school-aged kids, you can pretend you are going on a trip to the country whose game you are going to play. What do you need to prepare for your trip? Look at each of the games listed following as a "visit" to that country. The original name of the game in its native language is listed after the English translation—try using the original name as part of your "travels."

***Visit the Netherlands! Play Conquer New Lands* (Landje veroveren *in Dutch*):** This is sort of like a physical version of the game Risk, with four to eight players. Object of the game: Remain a free country. Draw a big circle with chalk on the ground, divided into pieces like a pie or a pizza. Each child will be a country. Write the name of each country on one of the pie pieces. To start the game each child stands with one foot in their own country. In the original version, one designated person says, "I declare war on . . . (name of one of the countries)." Then all the children run away from the circle. Only the child/country that war has been declared on (the new "warrior") stays in the circle, then calls "STOP!" At this call, all the children stop running. Then, all must try to get back into their own country by walking slowly to the circle when the warrior calls, "WALK." When one or more children get close to the circle the warrior again can call "STOP." Remaining with at least one foot in their country, the warrior needs to try to tap a child (this also can be done by lying on the ground to extend the reach—the warrior can move around, but only within their own country). Once a child has been tapped, they have conquered the other country. Try to get as many new lands as possible. Children who reach their pie piece without being tapped are free. The last country to be conquered will be the next warrior.

(You can vary the concept of war by saying instead: "I will UNITE with . . ." Instead of being a warrior, the "it" person can be the UNITER, the UN secretary general, a monarch, or the president.)

Visit Thailand! Play Crow Sits on Eggs (**E-Gar Fuk Khai** *in Thai*)**:** Two circles are drawn, one within the other. The outer circle should be about four feet in diameter and the inner circle just one foot. Small rocks or other similar-sized objects are then placed inside the smaller circle. One of the players is chosen to be the "crow." That player has to remain within the circle and guard the eggs. The others have to try and steal the eggs from the crow. They can do anything they like to trick and tease the crow. However, they mustn't enter the circle or be touched by the crow. When all of the eggs have been stolen the crow is then blindfolded. The players then have to hide the eggs that they have stolen. When they are ready, the blindfold is taken off and the crow has to search for its missing eggs. The owner of the first egg to be found then takes over the role as the "crow." (This and other Thai playground games can be found at: Thaistudents.com; search for games.)

Visit Ireland and Wales! Play QUEENIE-I-O: Whoever's "on" has a tennis ball. He or she turns around and throws the ball backward over their head. Everyone else tries to catch the ball, and if they do, they shout out, "Caught the ball," and now that person "on." But if they don't catch it, someone in the circle puts the ball behind his or her back and everyone else puts their hands behind their backs as well. The person who is "on" tries to guess who has the ball. If they guess wrong, whoever really has the ball is now "on."

Visit Nigeria! Play Catch the Tail: This is a variation on Snake Tag. Kids form two teams; each is a snake. Each team has a tail (handkerchief or scarf) in the pocket of the last person in the chain. The other team tries to capture the tail in order to win.

Visit Korea! Play The Line Between South Korea and North Korea (**Sam Pal Sun**)**:** Children in South Korea usually play this game in a parking area (this reflects how crowded and urbanized their country is). There are four or more people on each team. One team is the defender and blocks the other team to prevent them from going past the area that is marked with a flag. If all the offense team passes the border, they win. This is a variation on a game of tag, and cooperation among team members is the key to winning.

Learn about more global games.

With good resource books that diagram the game boards, provide detailed instructions, and tell about the origin of various activities from around the world. You can start with: *Kids Around the World Play! The Best Fun and Games from Many Lands,* by Arlette N. Braman; *The Multicultural Game Book: More Than 70 Traditional Games from 30 Countries,* by Louise Orlando; and *Hands Around the World: 365 Creative Ways to Encourage Cultural Awareness and Global Respect,* by Susan Milford.

Visit Mexico! Play Sea Serpent **(La Vibora):** Each player in a line puts his hands on the shoulders of the person in front of him. Two players make a bridge with their hands that everyone else marches under. They sing: *"La vibora, vibora del mar, todos quieren pasar."* ("The sea serpent, sea serpent of the sea, everyone wants to pass.") On the last word, the bridge comes down and anyone captured is out of the game. This is similar to the game London Bridge.[2]

Visit the world! Play Hopscotch with different numerals: If you can count from one to ten in another language, try writing the numerals. Get two for the price of one: Chinese numbers are written the same as Japanese, and Arabic the same as Persian, though the words and pronunciations are completely different. It's sort of like writing the same numerals in English and French, but saying them in the two languages.

LEARN GLOBAL GAMES—FOR A CAR RIDE, A PARTY, OR A PLAYDATE

Beyond playing the games that are popular in other countries, learning games that utilize knowledge of global geography, culture, language, environment, and trends also helps to start feeling at home in the world. These are great for passing the time on long car rides, for make-believe in the backyard, or for older kids, to test knowledge of international issues and places.

The places game: I can't remember a long car ride from my childhood when we didn't play the "places game" at least once on the trip. We'd start with the name of our current location, and the next person had to name a place that started with the last letter of the previous place named. For example, I would start with New York.

The next person would say Kalamazoo, next is Oklahoma, then Arizona, then An-tioch, then Haverford, and so on, with no repeats. Kids who are starting to read can play this. It gets more interesting if you try to play variations, like only cities and towns, or only places outside the United States.

For a real challenge, try replacing places with languages. For example, start with English, then you can say Hebrew, then Welsh, then Hawaiian, and so on. When our youngest was three or four, she'd hear the game being played, pick up on names of exotic locations, and this helped her own vocabulary and knowledge of the world, without much effort. When she wanted to play, we'd give her a turn—she could say the name of anywhere she wanted.

Games using new names: When playing any imagination or role-playing game, try mixing up the names, away from the more common Tommy, Annie, and Mary. Try Boutros, Bronwen, Kofi, Olga, Fariba, and other "foreign" names. If you don't know where to begin, you can look up top athletes from various foreign countries, or the names of famous authors or actors abroad, or just search online for "most popular names in (name a country or language)." Variations for different ages can include playing ABCs using different cultures' names (like A is for Aixa, B is for Bayan, and so on); naming dolls differently; or even thinking outside the box for naming pets. By acquiring a comfort level with a wide range of names, the tongue and brain-map become more limber.

Games using the globe: Keeping a globe handy can lead to lots of creative thought and play. During their elementary school years, my kids would spontaneously spin the nearby globe and wherever their finger landed when the globe stopped spinning would become their new home. Sometimes the game would repeat with one turn after another: "Now I live in Tuvalu." "You live in Amsterdam." "Daddy lives in Windhoek," and on and on. It took many spins before they tired of this. You can take the game further, by giving them three spins and then they choose where they would like to live. Ask them why they chose that place, then talk about what kind of job they could do there; what kind of things they would need to bring with them (e.g., warm clothes or cool? any animals? what kind of food and home supplies will they need?). If you know the languages or want to look them up, you can talk about what language they need to learn to live in that place.

When we were staying in Africa, some nights after dinner the older kids would play "country capitals." Spin the globe or open a world atlas; pick a random country and challenge the players to name the country's capital city. I thought this would be easy for me, but then my nephew challenged me with capitals of countries like Kazakhstan, Turkmenistan, Estonia, and Fiji—making me realize how much I didn't know. Even knowing the capital of Canada and Germany might be a challenge, so this is a good game for all ages over seven (or so).

Talking and interactive globes make fun gifts for kids and encourage discovery of geography, topography, demographics, and other information. Look into LeapFrog's Explorer Smart Globe and the Talking Odyssey III Interactive Globe.

Visit a foreign market (pick your own country). One person or team is the shopkeeper and the other person or team is the shopper. The shopper has a list of items they would like to purchase but the two sides don't speak the same language. Try to buy what's on your shopping list without using words. For older kids, you also can take it to the next level by trying to bargain over the price. This gives kids a glimpse into how body language and charades can help overcome language barriers and what travelers might experience abroad, or how visitors to our country may feel when they don't speak English.

Take a virtual journey around the world on mywonderfulworld.org. *National Geographic* leads this campaign for global learning for kids, spurred after the results of the Roper-National Geographic 2006 study revealed a poor knowledge of geography among young people in the United States. There's a tab for Games & Cool Stuff that links to many interactive sites from around the world.

Leave them alone to play. As we saw with the kids who used just about anything to kick toward a goal, it doesn't take an arsenal of toys to "play globally." Children who are left alone to play long enough and often enough to use their imaginations are playing more like their peers abroad, and thus may connect best with them.

My friend Maryam, who grew up in Germany, recalls coming home from school by midafternoon and spending most of the rest of the day playing outside. The boys' play was not so different from the girls' and she notices the same when she returns to Germany for long visits with her children. In the United States, her children, especially when they were under ten, played with many more toys indoors and these seemed to follow gender lines: dolls, play kitchens, and makeup kits for her daughter; cars, science kits, and dinosaurs for her son. Getting them away from the TV was always a struggle. These same kids who still liked to play or watch TV in the basement on a nice day at home seemed to go into a totally different mode at their grandparents': Despite the presence of new toys and poorer weather in Germany, they loved to join the kids from the neighborhood and spend much of the day outside. "It's like they flipped a switch and all of a sudden my kids changed into having German kids' play mentality. When they were a little older (around eleven and fourteen) they went to summer camp in Germany, which was double the fun for them: They got to spend every day immersed in active and creative play, and they were the most popular kids there because they had come from America."

One factor that might contribute to this mind-set of play that she recalls is the practice of taking babies outside, even in cold weather. This is thought to build their strength and get them accustomed to the temperature changes. Cold temperatures called for warm coats and hats, but didn't mean that kids couldn't be outdoors. Giving children the freedom to play on their own is a priceless luxury.

Get involved in the global movement to promote sport and play in poor communities around the world. Along with FIFA and the Olympics, which were mentioned previously, organizations like Right to Play (righttoplay.com), "creating a healthier and safer world for children through the power of sport and play," Peace Players International (peaceplayersintl.org), Sports Sans Frontieres (sportsansfrontieres .org), WomenSport International (sportsbiz.bz/womensportinternational), and many others promote play as a means to peace and development. To weave something serious into your discovery of games and the world, these organizations offer a unique window to the world of play and the opportunity to play. If your child plays a sport, their team could "adopt" a partner team through one of these organizations. Every time your team wins or loses a game they can commit to doing or getting something special for the partner team, as a motivation to win more games and to be of service to the other team.

Look for video games that are fun but nonviolent (or create your own!). *A Force More Powerful,* available through the website of the same name, defeats dictators and corruption and defends human rights through nonviolent strategies used successfully in real conflicts around the world. It was created for adults, but is appropriate for ages fourteen and up. *Karma Tycoon,* available through karmatycoon.com and dosomething.org, offers "a thrilling ride through the world of social entrepreneurship." Instead of trying to make a million dollars for themselves, players in target grades seven to twelve are making the world a better place—and finding out how complicated the task can be. At gamesforchange.org you can find more electronic games that address a wide range of global issues.

Video games with online capability know no boundaries. Realistically, if your kids played video games before, they'll continue. Instead of banning them altogether, look for those that offer positive experiences. The Nintendo Wii Sports and Rock

Band games are conducive to multiple generations in our family playing together, from my five-year-old nephew to my high-schooler, college-aged niece and nephews, and sometimes my parents.

If you have a wireless Internet system in your home, the Wii's capabilities go global. This means that you can play with friends anywhere in the world with the same system and can browse the Internet. I like the interactive world map capability. It allows users to navigate around the TV with their wireless controller and zoom in on anywhere in the world. News features, from serious to absurd, pop up for any spot on the planet you select. Pick up factoids on geography and current events while relaxing between games. Sony PlayStation and Microsoft Xbox newer generations also go online. They carry intense (and often violent, like the immensely popular Halo, Grand Theft Auto, Call of Duty—World at War) games that millions worldwide play together from remote locations.

My nephew Peymon was an avid online gamer during his senior year of high school, where he'd schedule game times with players from Japan, Mexico, India, and throughout the United States. He described "chat" taking place in multiple languages. However, when I asked if any of those people could actually be a friend of his or if he would visit them in their country, he replied, "No, that would just be weird if anyone wanted to meet me from playing Warcraft or Halo." So in this case, the game goes global, but this is not likely a path to creating lasting connections from afar.

Get your kids active with strategies to combat couch potatoes. Active video games like the Wii help get kids moving, but systematic effort—at home, at school, from advertisers, and by government—is needed to stem the rise of "couch potatoes" worldwide. Globalization of children's consumption is almost complete, and so far it's not pretty. More kids are sitting watching TV, playing video games, or on the computer (and eating junk food) everywhere. This contributes to the rise in childhood obesity, ADHD diagnosis, diabetes, heart disease, aggressive behaviors, and passivity globally. In 2006, one out of ten children worldwide was considered overweight or obese.[3] In the United States, the number of overweight children and adolescents doubled in the last two to three decades, and similar doubling rates are being observed in Europe and even in developing countries where children prefer Western behavior and diets.[4]

Alarmed, countries ranging from England to Norway and China are implementing nationwide strategies for "reactivating" kids. For example, the European Union invested one hundred million euro (about $140 million) behind an "active commuting" program in several test cities, advocating walking, riding a bike, or taking public transport; and private European companies have committed to stop marketing junk food like soft drinks to children under twelve. These "macro" policies will have little impact without awareness and effort by parents. Here are ten ideas parents can try that have worked with kids across the world.

1. *Walk your child to school, if possible.* This is so important that test cities in England reward parents for doing this. It creates an opportunity to talk and relax with your child with clear physical and environmental benefits.

2. *Insist on outdoor play.* Be like kids in northern Europe and many other cultures, where cold weather doesn't keep them indoors. In those traditional cultures, getting fresh air is as important as eating a balanced diet. This practice can't start out of the blue, so parents will have to make getting outside in cooler weather an attractive option: Have games in mind and good accessories to help bundle up. Once kids get into the habit, parents won't need to coax or encourage so much.

3. *Look for a preschool with well-thought-out physical education and games programs.* In Chinese preschools and kindergartens, activities on the playground are strategically placed, so children choose their favorites while also developing a range of muscles, skills, and coordination. A growing number of preschools worldwide incorporate yoga into physical exercise.

4. *Keep quality physical education in elementary school and beyond.* The Chinese sound mind–sound body philosophy permeates the school system. Every public school in China conducts morning exercises—a fifteen-minute drill each day, with coordination and timing improving as children progress over the years. Most elementary-aged kids do a total of two hours of physical activity (adding together the early morning, midmorning, afternoon, and P.E. classes) and secondary do about one hour.

5. *Kids should dress comfortably for school.* In parts of Latin America and China, a typical school uniform is a track suit, so this makes it easier to go right to physical activity—no need to use valuable class time changing, and kids stay comfortable, modest, and active.

6. *Be an example.* Exercise with your child. All over China, everyone from the teachers to elderly grandparents take part in public exercising, like *wu shu* martial arts and *tai chi*. Karate and other martial arts classes may be attended by parents and kids together; this is also true of swimming, skating, tennis, and golf.

7. *Make TV inconvenient.* If you can, avoid putting the TV in a convenient place, like the family room or near the kitchen. After setting up our big, new TV in the center of family activity, where turning it off presents a struggle, I learned from several Indian, Russian, and Iranian families whose children were star

Try yoga.

The growing practice of yoga links the East and the West. For children to enjoy yoga, especially when starting young, treat it like play and stimulate their imaginations. When kids practice the ancient poses—stretch like a dog, balance like a flamingo, breathe like a bunny, or stand strong and tall like a tree—they are making a connection between the universe and their own bodies. Benefits from a sustained practice of yoga can lead to a more profound experience of stillness, balance, flexibility, focus, peace, connection, health, grace, and well-being—qualities that many children living in our fast-paced, immediate-gratification environment lack.

Lots of books and videos have been produced for kids' yoga. For the littlest ones, see the *Itsy Bitsy Yoga* books by Helen Garabedian. Sydney Solis's *Storytime Yoga* shares multicultural stories, songs, and exercises. SmartFun Activity Books' *Yoga Games for Children: Fun and Fitness with Postures, Movement and Breath* is a good source for group activities and games. I like the *Yoga Pretzels* deck of cards from Yoga Ed.—they're instructive, attractive and easy to follow.

pupils throughout their school careers that they kept their nice set in the parents' room or in the basement, so TV never served as their kids' default activity. Last but not least, no TVs in kids' bedrooms.

8. *Place computers in full view.* Do put the computer in a convenient, open space, so you can monitor how much time and which activities your child engages in. By putting it in the open, they will be more aware of it, too. You may want your child to embrace the world figuratively, but beware of having the whole world at their fingertips.

9. *Set clear rules for TV watching and computer use time. Be aware of the pitfalls.* For example, a friend stopped her rule of "Video games only after homework is finished" because she noticed her son's work got sloppier in order to get it over with quickly and play. You also might consider the rule of "no TV at all during weekdays." Just make sure your child isn't going to friends' homes to watch after school and the rule doesn't overshadow the spirit of why you established it in the first place (i.e., it shouldn't turn into a constant and bitter battle).

10. *Find a sport older kids can play independently of school schedules.* Particularly as kids grow up and their schoolwork gets more demanding, make sure their routine is balanced with regular exercise or sport. In Finland, considered one of the most sports-oriented countries in the world, it's estimated that two out of three citizens are involved in a sports organization. Their program targeting six to twelve-year-olds entails two hours per day of exercise, and eighty percent of under-eighteens practice some sort of organized sports, requiring at least five days per week of practice.[5]

————

Throughout recent history, playing together has united people. Examples of North and South Korea merging their teams for the 2000 Olympic Games, of Palestinian and Israeli children playing soccer and basketball in adjacent neighborhoods, and even the thawing of relations between the United States and China in 1971 through Ping-Pong[6] attest to the power of play to overcome deep divisions. Awareness of these powerful examples can reinforce the commitment to "be a friend to the whole human race" by playing all kinds of games with all kinds of people. Learn about other cultures through their games. Use games entailing geography and culture to teach, test, and reinforce global knowledge. Play classic board games to stimulate the mind and get in touch with ancient cultures. Engage in physical activities to stay healthy—for the body, soul, and mind. Most of all, allow games to instill fun in the process of "growing up global."

RESOURCE BOOKS CITED IN CHAPTER 3—THAT YOU MAY FIND HELPFUL, TOO

Kids Around the World Play! The Best Fun and Games from Many Lands, Arlette N. Braman (author), Michele Nidenoff (illustrator) (New York: John Wiley & Sons, 2002).

The Multicultural Game Book: More Than 70 Traditional Games from 30 Countries, Louise Orlando (New York: Scholastic Professional Books, 1993).

Hands Around the World: 365 Creative Ways to Encourage Cultural Awareness and Global Respect, Susan Milford (Charlotte, VT: Williamson Publishing, 1992).

Mexico and Central America: A Fiesta of Cultures, Crafts and Activities for Ages 8–12, Mary C. Turck (Chicago: Chicago Review Press, 2004).

Itsy Bitsy Yoga: Poses to Help Your Baby Sleep Longer, Digest Better, and Grow Stronger, Helen Garabedian (New York: Fireside, 2004).

Itsy Bitsy Yoga for Toddlers and Preschoolers: 8-Minute Routines to Help Your Child Grow Smarter, Be Happier, and Behave Better, Helen Garabedian (Cambridge, MA: DaCapo Lifelong Books, 2008).

Storytime Yoga: Teaching Yoga to Children Through Story, Sydney Solis (Chicago: The Mythic Yoga Studio, 2006).

Yoga Games for Children: Fun and Fitness with Postures, Movement and Breath (SmartFun Activity Books), Danielle Bersma and Marjoke Visscher (Alameda, CA: Hunter House, 2003).

Yoga Pretzels: 50 Fun Yoga Activities for Kids and Grown-Ups, Tara Kuber and Leah Kalish (Cambridge, MA: Barefoot Books, 2005).

ADDITIONAL RESOURCE BOOKS RELATED TO CHAPTER 3

How Soccer Explains the World, Franklin Foer (New York: Harper Perennial, 2005).

Play with Us: 100 Games from Around the World, Oriol Ripoll (Chicago: Chicago Review Press, 2005).

Chapter 4

Go to School

Education is the most powerful weapon which
you can use to change the world.
NELSON MANDELA

For generations, the experience of teaching and learning all over the world changed very little: Children assembled in a central building, sat together as a group facing one adult, and somehow soaked up the information she offered—which might have very little relevance to the lives they led outside the schoolhouse. But that has changed dramatically. My memories of school sometimes seem to have more in common with *Little House on the Prairie* than my own children's experience. We are in the midst of possibly the most significant revolution in what it means to go to school. Technology breakthroughs create virtual schools and virtual students, regardless of location, language, and social status; and children from Texas to Norway to Korea to Argentina are being judged by the same academic standards and may possibly be competing for the same jobs.

This chapter explores how our American schools, as well as schools around the world, can help (or hinder) kids to "grow up global," and ways that parents can assist schools or supplement the curriculum at home to provide a global perspective. Utilizing the school environment to gain a global perspective helps our children tap into the learning revolution that's underway and also helps them compete—and make friends—across every form of boundary.

WAYS TO HELP OUR SCHOOLS COMPETE BETTER

U.S. students' rankings fell toward the bottom of wealthy nations in education scores at the turn of the millennium, even as we stood as the world's superpower. Singapore, number one globally in math for fourth and eighth graders for the past decade, had a standard of living comparable to many African countries just forty

A new type of three Rs

The Gates Foundation asserts globally competitive schools need a new Three Rs: *rigor, relevance, and relationships.* Schools should engage all students with a rigorous curriculum, offer course work that is relevant to their lives and aspirations, and foster strong relationships between students and adults. The foundation has invested about one billion dollars to promote the new three Rs and the redesign of American high schools. Learn more at gates foundation.org.

years ago. Singapore's focus on its people as its greatest resource and its priority of sustaining its multiculturalism comprised some of the building blocks of the island-nation's success. Its example also shows that these international rankings are like moving targets, and nothing is out of reach. Ambitious schools worldwide compete with—and learn from—the best in any country, not just on the other side of town.

Our American education system needs to offer a curriculum and a community that allows children from all economic backgrounds to gain the skills of a competent global citizen. As *New York Times* columnist Bob Herbert wrote about American education: "[We] need something better than a post–World War II system in a post-9/11 world."[1] But how does this begin? Here are a few steps schools can take to start on the path toward enhancing their ability to compete globally.

Integrate international awareness in the general curriculum. Research confirms that for international awareness to take hold in schools it should not be treated as an add-on topic taught separately from the core subjects. For example, given the predominance of testing in reading, literature by non-American authors, or stories about life in different cultures, can be used for any grade level. Story problems in math can contain diverse cultural situations; some of the origins of that field of math can be introduced (this will often involve the presentation of Arabs in an intellectual light, contrasting with the media images); and so on. Organizations like the Asia Society and some curriculum development companies have created useful materials for integrating international understanding in lesson plans.

In Sydney, Australia, the High Resolves Initiative, www.highresolves.org, interactively engages thousands of high-school students to become purposeful global citizens, seeking to transform the way youth see their place in the world and to envision a future where leaders think and act in the collective interest. Its curriculum is designed to "provoke teen-agers to reflect on the following questions: 1) What is my role as a global citizen? 2) In 50–100 years will my actions and choices be on the 'right' side of history? and 3) How can I make a difference?" In the United Kingdom, Oxfam's Education for Global Citizenship offers a guide for primary and middle school curricula, with materials available at www.oxfam.org.uk/educa tion/gc/ so that anyone can learn from their model. Even if these initiatives are not implemented in your school, the issues they raise can be discussed in the classroom, in a youth group, or at the dinner table.

Examine how learning is organized. For example, in most U.S. states, social studies lessons from grades one through twelve almost exclusively focus on the United States, with at least one year in elementary school and again in middle school devoted to studying the home state. In ninth grade, a World Cultures class might be introduced, and in tenth, it may be European history, but it goes back to American history in eleventh and twelfth grades. So, the signal our schools send to the kids is that our intellectual focus is primarily on ourselves. Most learning about other countries, cultures, and beliefs, until the age of eighteen, comes in the form

Scouting can raise global awareness.

Today's Girl and Boy Scout programs offer many choices for discovery, beyond crafts, cookies, and camping, to building awareness of diverse cultures and faiths. In my recent experience with Girl Scouts, I have watched independence and self-esteem nurtured, along with a bigger sense of the world. Connections can be made with active troops in virtually every country on earth and quite a few badge activities incorporate international awareness. Area troops might band together to celebrate World Thinking Day, each representing a different country. In some communities, Girl Scouts have helped some Muslim girls integrate while still maintaining their identity. They can use "Allah" for "God" if they wish in the pledge, and some wear their sash daily, along with their *hijab,* in part to gain the trust of suburban neighbors.

This all helps reinforce the idea that something "all-American" also can be global and inclusive. Where classrooms might be set in their curricula and demands, the Scout troop might offer flexibility and creativity to dive deeper into a few world cultures or gain a general knowledge of the planet.

of the wars fought by the United States, or a "fun" multicultural program one day per year.

Curricula in many other countries contain much more material about the rest of the world. This might have become standard because of geographic proximity (e.g., a country within a continent—Europe, Africa, Asia, Latin America—needs to know its neighbors), or colonization (e.g., the fifty-three member countries in the British Commonwealth, ranging from New Zealand to Ghana to Pakistan, all learn about one another), or even intimidation (the United States, Japan, and Russia are widely studied in the countries and territories they once dominated economically or politically), instead of a broader high-mindedness, but the outcome is a general knowledge about many cultures and countries beyond one's own.

Look at how you treat your teachers. Teachers are under tremendous pressure at all kinds of schools to produce across-the-board outstanding scores on national- or state-administered standardized tests, regardless of academic background or the language proficiency of their students. For example, a student who does not yet speak English but is enrolled at the school needs to take the same academic performance test as everyone else, as does a child in special education with a learning disability—all of these factors will affect the overall grade (and funding) given to a school. The multinational rankings that place Singapore at the top for elementary and middle schoolers and Finland number one for older kids point to stark differences with the United States in teacher training (both before and during their careers), relative pay, the amount of classroom time allotted to work with pupils to allow depth in a subject, and possibly at the root of all this, the level of respect for teachers.

An exchange between a friend's twelve-year-old daughter, Julia, and the mother of one of Julia's friends, who is a successful professional, brought this issue to light:

> THE ADULT: "Julia, you are so talented, what would you like to be when you grow up?"
> JULIA: "Well, I love working with children, I am thinking that I would like to be a teacher."
> THE ADULT: "Oh, you can do so much better than that!"

We all probably know people with this attitude. A teacher's salary is nowhere near the top tier of professional salaries in the United States; it has been like that for generations and has traditionally been a profession relegated to women's work. A *Strong American Schools* report cites the fact that the world's best education sys-

Teacher Gifts

Next time you're deciding what to get your children's teacher for the holidays or end-of-year gift, try something with a global flavor. This demonstrates your family's values and helps your teacher gain a more global perspective that can be passed to his or her students. There are lots of possibilities:

• *A book:* Every year my friend Liz gets her sons' teachers her favorite book: *Material World: A Global Family Portrait.* This 1995 coffee-table-worthy book gives a rich illustration of the varied lives of "statistically average" families in thirty countries. This gift is beautiful, dignified, and grown-up—so it's a personal gift, not like giving them a book explicitly for the classroom. It also informs and enlightens, like an added training resource. Alternately, if you know the teacher enjoys reading, you can get novels or memoirs that introduce life in different cultures.

• *A donation:* For the teacher who has everything, or seems to get everything from her students, I donate to a cause in their name. This is like a double gift: They'll get a card and description of the donation from me and, usually, another acknowledgment from the organization a few weeks later. I like to act locally *and* globally by giving on behalf of the teacher to local and international causes, especially those that support education, to resonate with the teacher's interests. This shows them we don't have to choose between either local or global, and also gets my kids excited about the cause we are sharing with their teacher.

• *A handicraft:* Ten Thousand Villages and others (Google "fair trade gifts") carry attractive items—decorative and useful—that make a difference in the world. Supporting craftspeople in needy communities while finding a unique gift for your teacher is a win-win-win. In England, Oxfam stores are found in just about every commercial district, making shopping for products that make a difference widely accessible and accepted.

tems select their teachers from the top third of their college graduates, whereas most U.S. teachers graduate in the bottom third of their class.[2] In order to stop losing ground over other advanced countries, the U.S. education system must seriously address how to recruit talented people into teaching. In the meantime, the biases of our culture toward the noble profession of teaching need to be closely examined. It's not just the polite thing, it's the smart thing.

In the countries of northern Europe, teachers are widely known to have greater prestige than businessmen. As a result, talented men and women are attracted to this profession, they can demand more rigor from their students, and this is reflected in higher exam scores on international comparisons. In China, where the Confucian tradition still reigns, teachers earn a far higher *relative* salary and respect than in the states, though this seems to be changing with the astounding growth rate of Chinese business and respect for capitalism. And at the bottom extreme, in many of the poorest countries, teachers' pay barely covers the basic expenses required for survival, so the resulting respect paid to teachers—especially from those in more privileged classes near the city—is almost zero. With the dignity afforded to these workers so low, they cannot demand much from their pupils, nor do they expect top materials or support from their administrators, resulting in a fragile educational system. When we returned to the United States, I remember my girls commenting on how amazing it was that their teachers all drove their own cars to work. This was unheard-of in West Africa, as that could cost the equivalent of several years' salary, and was totally out of reach to an honest teacher.

Equip teachers with adequate training. We expect a good portion of our kids' learning about the world to come from their schooling. But few classroom teachers have received adequate training in crosscultural communication, sensitization to cultural nuances, how to teach about global issues, or even how to identify if classmates are reaching out across various boundaries and becoming friends. Opportunities might arise all the time within the classroom, but the teacher needs to be equipped in how to use those teachable moments.

I was involved in a book and school supplies drive to benefit a school in Ethiopia when I realized this can even be an issue at the "best" suburban schools. As we were loading boxes into a truck, the kindergarteners walked by on their way to recess. They were impressed with the boxes of books piled high and the colorful Mac computers ready to load into the truck. I told some of the animated kids, "These are going to a school in Ethiopia" or "These are going to help kids in Africa who don't have computers in their classrooms." Their accompanying teachers responded by saying, "Wowww" or "Ohhhhh." But that was it. This was a great opportunity that could have gone in many directions with the kids, even as they walked to the playground. The adults in charge could have said things like "Can you say *Ethiopia*?" "When we get back in our classroom let's look for it on the map." "Why do you think we're sending our old books and computers to them?" "How do you think these will benefit those kids?" "How will the supplies get there?" or any host of questions to spur discussion and learning. This was a golden opportunity for the youngest in the school to gain an instant connection with a group of children in a faraway country, but it was essentially dissipated because the adults closely interacting with them had no way to make a connection with the "beneficiaries" in Ethiopia.

Some simple training and awareness-raising could remedy that, without burdening the teachers. In this case, the school administrators possessed an enlightened sense of the world, setting aside supplies (instead of letting them go in a dumpster) that could benefit needier schools, learning from some of the lessons of the foreign school administrators, and even researching possible exchange programs and funding sources. Most schools reserve in-service days for teacher training, but this may be dedicated to administrative matters rather than continuing education. Even just a couple days per year of solid, targeted training for teachers of all grades on some of these basic global awareness issues can make a big difference. Principals can assign a book for all the staff to read at a leisurely pace and discuss in groups over the course of a semester. As parents concerned about this matter, ask your school's principal or superintendent, or attend a school board meeting to ensure that the global awareness mandates are matched with action, and that action is workable for busy teachers.

Utilize resources created for homeschooling. Early homeschoolers chose this path largely due to strong moral and religious convictions; but more parents today are homeschooling to allow the depth of examination of a single topic. For a growing number of families who opt their kids out of traditional school for extended world travels, homeschooling material helps keep their kids on track with academic topics at school.[3]

A veritable bank of resources for homeschoolers has become available to anyone wanting to offer more to their children than the basic school curriculum allows. Some of the websites specifically describe categories either for "homeschool curriculum" or for "enrichment"—acknowledging the growing need for supplementing traditional schoolwork. Websites of companies like Saxon Homeschool, Sheppard Software, Jiskha, Online Learning Haven, and organizations like Global Village School or individual family initiatives like Virtual Homeschool International (VHI) have a wealth of information available free or for a low cost, for parents wishing to supplement their children's school curriculum. VHI's subscription rate is just $20 per year for all the materials they have assembled.

These independent curricula educate about the world, but they also can teach core subjects the way high achievers abroad learn. For example, Singapore's winning math technique is packaged for homeschoolers through singaporemath.com. The thousands of families as well as some American states that use this method want to emulate the island-nation's success in producing the world's top math achievers. Like scientists who collaborate across borders to create innovation, we can teach our kids by utilizing the best models.

Tap into the arts. One of the best windows to the world and to education about the world is through the various arts that have flourished in every culture on earth. Your children's schools might have a strong program that introduces them to the arts globally, but many schools do not, and there is always more that can be supplemented from home, through after-school clubs or special programs inserted into the school year with the help of parent volunteers.

Find out if your children's school includes a Cultural Arts component or similar enrichment program. Usually organized by volunteers and paid for by parent fundraisers, Cultural Arts programs bring artistic talents from diverse genres (like theater, live music, dance, writing, puppetry, and spoken word) and cultures for special schoolwide assemblies, workshops, or artist residencies for longer-term visits and in-depth coverage of a topic. These opportunities give kids a chance to experience dynamic art forms and live performances, and watch new cultures come to life. In addition to assisting with the considerable logistical requirements, parent volunteers can help to make sure programs represent the diversity of cultures and art forms and possibly pass along the wealth of their school: If your school books an arts assembly, you might be able to negotiate a favorable fee with the artists to visit a partner school in a needier community. Additionally, visiting artists often prepare curricular materials to enhance classroom learning and prepare their audience in advance of their own show. Volunteers can help circulate this information for the enrichment of the children as well as the teachers—it might offer ideas for future lessons or deepen the teachers' understanding of a cultural issue.

Along with school enrichment opportunities, knowledge of the arts can begin at home. Starting with preschoolers through elementary ages, you can get ABC and picture books that introduce them to great painters and art forms from around the world. Popular children's art books like *Frida* by Jonah Winters, the *Katie* series by James Mayhew, and *Dinner at Magritte's* by Michael Garland are available at most public libraries and each opens a window to a different artist.

One of my favorite places to get a sense of books on art for kids is at a museum gift shop. There, all in one area, I get an overview of new art books in all genres and for all ages. Of course, I can purchase them—and they make great birthday party gifts. But I also jot down the names of some of the books and authors, and offer these titles to our school library or for teacher wish lists. If I want to keep them at home I might look up the titles on our public library's website, or I can buy them with a discount (or even used) online.

A visit to the art museum can revolve around a particular culture. For example, at the Philadelphia Museum of Art we might dedicate a trip to Japan, China, Arabia, Holland, Italy, or France and map out several parts of the museum featuring paintings, housewares, and sculpture from that country. By focusing on a particular culture we feel like we're on an adventure or scavenger hunt, which most kids prefer to a generic visit to a vast museum. By the end of a focused visit, they feel like experts on the topic or style. Purchasing an annual family membership to the museum allows us to target each visit. We don't feel like we need to cover the whole place in a day, we can take advantage of member activities, my children learn from the example of supporting the arts in the community, and we get a "deal" with unlimited access to the museum for a good price (along with discounts at the museum shop and restaurant, and other cultural venues in town). Because our time is limited and we can't make too many museum trips in a year, I usually limit annual family membership to one major museum per year. This year it could be the art museum, last year the natural history, next year the science museum, and so on.

When I was little, I loved the nicely framed reproduction Renoir painting of a little girl hung in my bedroom. As I grew up I realized how close I felt to this painting and the artist, just by having a copy on my wall. It was "my painting." You can go a step further by decorating children's bedrooms with a few posters or prints by artists from different countries depicting a variety of scenes that appeal to them. The pictures don't need to be similar to one another. Through the juxtaposition of these diverse images, your child will become more comfortable with different styles—naturally. I am amazed by how well children as young as age three recognize artistic styles from different cultures or the works of various artists—just because they've had exposure to their work.

Appreciate music. Make music. Listening to great music from all genres from many countries, as offered by various world music CD compilations, is one excellent way to expose children to the world. Another is through learning a musical instrument. If your child wants to play a string instrument, contrast it to the sitar, oud, lute, or mandolin. Drums have so many variations in Latin America, Africa, the Middle East, and Asia. How do they sound different? How are they made and how do different cultures adorn their drums? For piano players, expose them to a hammered dulcimer, which is dear to everyone from the Appalachians to the Persians. Woodwind variations from the Inca pan flute to the Chinese *dizi* bamboo flute

The Suzuki method unites music students globally.

Started as a means of helping children in war-torn Japan after WWII, the "Suzuki method" has become one of the most popular ways to learn music, guiding private lessons worldwide. Dr. Suzuki observed that healthy, hearing children learn to speak their native tongue perfectly using the dialect and accent of their native environment. Children hear words repeated thousands of times before they speak, and when they do, they don't fear failure. If something as complex as language can be absorbed so naturally by children, then music and other skills could be learned in a more natural and simple way, too, with lots of repetition and parental involvement.

Find Suzuki method teachers at suzukiassociation.org and other sites online.

and Arabic reed *nay* create haunting melodies. And the methods of learning an instrument vary widely across cultures. The Japanese Suzuki method has become almost universal. The traditional Russian method assumes a single-minded focus on the classics and rigor. The Indian method customarily passed knowledge from a master instrumentalist to an apprentice-student. Some exposure to the rigors of music learning in these various cultures might help in the often difficult process of kids' learning an instrument.

Few American children are exposed to the world's various musical styles from a young age, and their classroom teachers rarely are, either. We try to play some of this music at home while cooking dinner or cleaning up. The CDs make nice gifts for teachers, school libraries, or administrators (and can be used by the whole school). As mentioned in previous sections of this book, you can start with compilation CDs to give a taste of various styles and artists.

Learn from the great schools of the world. Exposing children as well as school professionals to realities in places like Hong Kong, Switzerland, Singapore, Finland, or countless other places that might improve the way we do things provides a fresh view of one's local circumstances. This is not to create an inferiority complex, but to realize that the American way isn't the only way, and in fact, there are numerous innovations flourishing all over the world. This sort of realization fights complacency, instills curiosity in the positive attributes of other countries, and can even

Teaching Japanese math techniques at the strip mall

Like the transformation of the "Made in Japan" product label to denote top quality, the image of education in Asia today connotes excellence.

Hoping to learn from those successes, parents around the United States have enrolled by the thousands in the Japanese-originated Ku-Mon program (www.kumon.com), which provides after-school enrichment and drilling in math and reading. The idea behind Ku-Mon is that in order for children to master a subject (not just get it for a test, but to learn it for good) they need significantly more practice on each concept than schools offer. So, kids meet twice a week with a tutor at the Ku-Mon center (often located in a church or unassuming strip mall) and then worksheets are taken home so the child does hundreds more problems during that week, devoting at least twenty minutes every day to the worksheets. It takes a particular motivation to succeed in the classes, so this is not for every child—but this does give a sense of the dedication some students show for academic success.

contribute to enhancing the positive competitive spirit in your child or your school. The ability to balance images of suffering and deprivation in some countries' schools with those of schools that are highly organized, materially endowed, and scholastically excellent in other countries is part of being able to put global realities into context and grasp the bigger picture of the world's diversity. This is a skill that will serve our children well for their entire lives.

Watch the documentary *Two Million Minutes* with your teen or interested middle schooler, available at 2mminutes.com. The film tracks the way time is spent by high-school students in three countries—the United States, China, and India—over the four years (or two million minutes) of high school, and offers an interesting contrast of preparations for the global economy.

DON'T WAIT—START YOUNG FOR EDUCATING GLOBALLY

The United States spends more per pupil enrolled at the preprimary level (about $7,900 annually) than the average of thirty advanced countries (about $4,700), but the United States also has one of the lowest *participation* rates of preschoolers in the world.[4] Whereas in many industrialized countries nearly 100 percent of the children are enrolled in some form of early childhood education (public, private, or religious), in the United States it's roughly 50 percent—and this relatively small proportion is divided between schools of all levels of quality. With the exception of a few Head Start programs run with unusual vision and know-how, to get quality, you have to pay for it in America.

So, particularly for the youngest Americans, the onus of quality falls on involved parents. If you want kids to learn about the world, you better get started on your own. And you don't need to wait for the little ones to read or grasp global politics to educate them about diverse cultures and their oneness with the world.

Examples abound of how the youngest children have the easiest time learning a new language, adopting different cultural practices, and making new friends. As multiple respondents to my email survey pointed out, their young children didn't display the baggage (i.e., fear, hesitation, prejudgment) of older kids or adults in adapting to living in a new country. They had no preconceived notions or filter to get in their way of immersing themselves in their new environment and culture, so they really plunged in. This confirmed my own experience with my youngest daughter, who was only three and a half when we stayed in Africa for three months and adapted most comfortably to her environment. She had the most African friends, she gained a new sense of beauty—gravitating toward African images of beauty and away from European—and was the only one among us who came away speaking English with a Gambian accent.

Let children form their own opinions. When exposing your young child to stories, art, music, and new friends from cultures that are foreign to you, unless you have a particular expertise or experience with that culture (or maybe, even if you don't), *try to say as little as possible that introduces your opinion* about the culture and its different ways of doing things. If you let your little ones form their own, independent opinion and experience around that cultural phenomenon, you will probably learn a lot from them and the experience becomes theirs, something they "own." Parents have asked me how I prepared my children for what they were going to experience abroad. For the most part, I did very little briefing. I let them just be and form their own view. Then, after they had witnessed different aesthetics and ways of doing things, we talked about it and processed it together.

As mentioned in the previous chapter, toys and games with a global slant are most abundant for the preschool audience. Similarly, the selection of picture books for this age group representing different cultures is vast. Beginning when my girls could walk, going to our local library has been one of our favorite outings. Often we would participate in the storytime programs, which librarians had carefully organized around various themes. These might include a cultural celebration, a region of the world, or a folktale from the United States or abroad. Then, it was

"Meet" kids in other countries by following their typical day. Various websites introduce kids from other countries. For example, Kids Web Japan, at web-japan.org/kidsweb introduces life in Japan. You can learn about a typical day in various Japanese schools, what's cool in Japan today, high-tech gadgets used there, or take a video tour of different towns. The site is sponsored by the Japanese Ministry of Foreign Affairs and is intended for children ages ten to fourteen, but I think it's appropriate for younger children, too.

such a treat to fill our canvas bag with books of all kinds. It didn't take much research on my part to gather books that represented cultures and perspectives that were new to us, from stories taking place in New Orleans and Harlem, to the Caribbean, China, and Mexico. In order to collect quality books with international themes, I simply needed to be on the lookout for them, and so many of these have become my children's favorite picture books. For more assistance, consult your librarian, and see the book list at the end of each chapter and on www.growingupglobal.net.

PUBLIC SCHOOL IN AFRICA—MADE REAL

Among the highlights of my family's experience living in West Africa, volunteering in the nearby public elementary school stands out. The neighborhood we stayed in contained a wide range of homes, from a few luxurious villas behind high walls and comfortable middle-class homes, to "compounds" housing dozens of people between thatched or tin roofs and dirt floors. We soon learned so much about our local community and its customs, daily life, and people through the school serving that neighborhood. Anyone who could afford to pay even a few dollars per month in tuition would not send their children to the government's "Lower Basic School," but there were still plenty of people for whom that school, with its less-than-$1 per semester tuition and time taken away from the family's work, was a stretch.

The school's physical amenities reflected the minimal expectations for learning: a tin roof connected by poles made from knotty and unfinished wood. Barred, glassless windows faced the school's courtyard where the community's water pump was located. No indoor plumbing—students and teachers used a shed in back of the school and squatted over a hole. Electricity was found in only a few adminis-

Consider Sponsorship.

"Sponsor" a child's education to make a real difference in someone else's life, while your kids gain an appreciation of their own education and opportunities. Your financial support helps the sponsored kids remain in school and often provides the incentive for them to succeed.

A family I know sponsors a girl around their own daughter's age through beadsfor education.org for school and boarding fees (about $400 per year). They hope to travel to Africa eventually to visit "their family."

There are hundreds of organizations through which you can sponsor a child's schooling. See the appendix or Google the topic. In the case of BEADS, it's a small organization that's grown through word of mouth.

trative rooms, but was rarely functioning. School took place in two shifts to accommodate population growth, but at each sitting, classrooms still squeezed in about fifty children sitting together in rows on benches.

There was no "substitute teacher" while the teacher was absent nor were there any teachers' helpers. If they were lucky, a teacher might have a textbook, but never the children, and their library—which neighbors said the school "was fortunate to have"—contained shelves of long-outdated, donated cast-off books, mostly from well-meaning British schools. I got my first sense of the library's quality when the sixth graders I was teaching, ages eleven to fourteen, were taking turns looking at an activity book designed for six-year-olds that had been filled in (probably years ago) by its original owner somewhere far away, and other books I saw described scenes from Victorian-era English history. Initially, I seethed at the injustice of the materials made available to these children who were eager to learn, but in time, had to fight back feelings of complacency—that "that's just how it is." Many organizations conduct book drives for the needy around the world, and our neighborhood school in The Gambia demonstrated that there is still a desperate need for more. (Room to Read and Building with Books are two great organizations contributing books around the world.)

Then there was the matter of getting to school. Most kids walked a long distance (often several miles) in worn rubber flip-flops and had already worked for hours with their families by the time they arrived. This meant many children arrived at school exhausted, and for those who were late, their greeting came in the form of a beating with a stick on their backsides.

After a few weeks in the country, I realized that I recognized clusters of children walking to school as I returned from dropping off Sophia at her private preschool. The traffic circle I'd stop at was about two miles from the public school, and the children had already walked a distance to get there. As soon as I pulled over my borrowed, twenty-year-old car to offer a ride to a few kids I recognized, about a dozen children sprinted toward the car so they wouldn't miss the precious "lift" to school. In the United States, what I did would be unacceptable, but in one of the world's poorest countries, where gasoline costs more than double the price I pay in Pennsylvania and automobiles are an unreachable expense for most, I felt too greedy to drive by these kids in an empty car. And seat belts? They're relevant where it's assumed there's a seat in the car for all. Children would pile in, about three deep, so I carried, on average, twelve kids where there was seating for four. On random days when the air-conditioning sputtered on, the children in the front would excitedly whisper to their friends in the back about the wonderful luxury they were all about to experience—probably for the first time. The sheer joy they gained from getting a ride to school was enough to make my day.

Witnessing firsthand (but really, not *experiencing* it, as we always knew we were going back to our comfortable home and school—and car) what education is like for millions of African children—a heavy dose of deprivation mixed with enough delight and wonder so that learning can begin—will forever impact our lives. Every child who eagerly raised his (or her) hand in my class, who scooted over in the car so that more friends could get in, who finished housework early to attend our Saturday enrichment class, or who carried a full bucket of water to the classroom for hand-washing, demonstrates the desire for education, and this desire forms the heartbeat of every school everywhere.

Processing the information: Our experience reflects the fact that over one billion children, or *one out of three of the world's children,* experiences "severe deprivation" with regard to shelter, water, health, and education.[5] Parents can share these circumstances with their children without turning the stories into a guilt trip, but this is not an easy task. If your children attend a well-equipped school in the United States, how would they know that everyone else isn't in a similar environment if they're not shown? Show them in stages—don't overload them with too many facts and harsh realities at once.

For younger children, you could start by reading a story about children's lives and schools, like *Wake Up, World!: A Day in the Life of Children Around the World* by Beatrice Hollyer, *Back to School (It's a Kids' World)* by Maya Ajmera and John

Ivanko, and Ifeoma Onyefulu's vividly photographed titles like *A is for Africa* and *One Big Family: Sharing Life in an African Village.* Or, read from the compilation of children's lives around the world in UNICEF's *Children Just Like Me,* described in more detail in Chapter 1. A story from a child's perspective presents age-appropriate perceptions of the world (without statistics!). You can ask your child to point out differences and similarities in the pictures and stories from their own life, as they enjoy "getting to know" someone whose life is different from their own. Without the guilt trip this exercise also shows kids elsewhere can be happy with much less "stuff."

For kids around age ten and older, the younger child's storybooks will still illuminate, but you can graduate to chapter books depicting life and schools abroad, like *The Diary of Ma Yan: Struggles and Hopes of a Chinese Schoolgirl* by Ma Yan and Pierre Haski, *Facing the Lion: Growing Up Maasai on the African Savannah* by Joseph Lemasolai Lekuton, and *Monsoon Summer* by Mitali Perkins. Websites with a charitable or international mission that have been mentioned already in this book, ranging from un.org, to bbc.com and peacecorps.org, and more focused websites, like Educate Girls Globally (Educategirls.org) also offer new insights and ways to connect with children abroad. As described previously, there also are many ways to get involved directly in sponsoring a child's education. See the appendix to learn more about service-oriented organizations.

What did we learn from the Arabs?

Did you know that the best early universities and libraries in the world were located in Islamic capital cities like Cairo, Damascus, and Baghdad? And early Muslim scholars pioneered innovations in math, botany, and medicine? We even have English words that originated from Arabic, including:

Alcohol	Cane	Guitar	Lute	Sugar
Algebra	Coffee	Hazard	Orange	Tambourine
Almanac	Garble	Lemon	Racket	Tariff
Amber	Ghoul	Lilac	Safari	Zenith
Apricot	Giraffe	Lime	Sandal	Zero

For eighth graders on up, read *Come Back to Afghanistan: A California Teenager's Story* by Said Hydar Akbar and *Miriam's Song: A Memoir* by Miriam Mathabane, as told to Mark Mathabane of South Africa, or other titles from numerous school reading lists. Depending on the age, questions and discussion might naturally follow. But they might not, and that's okay. Let the new information and experience sink in and introduce new concepts slowly.

Allowing the concepts to take their own time sinking in is an example of why "growing up global" is a process, not a race to the finish—it becomes part of the reality kids grow up with and learn to recognize from an early age. Your children's reaction most likely will be very different from yours and that is your test as a parent. Their impressions are just that—*theirs,* which they own. My older daughters certainly didn't share my reaction to the concepts I introduced to them, neither in elementary school nor later, when we were in Africa. Sometimes I took their quiet to be indifference, but later, in small ways, I noticed that the information and observations would surface when I wasn't expecting it.

Even within one family, each child's reaction will be very different. Our oldest daughter seemed the least affected by the many stories and examples she heard and saw over the years, but by her freshman year of high school, she surprised us by writing profound insights about some of her experiences for school assignments. She owns those ideas for herself and will carry them authentically through her life. I tried hard not to express disappointment if she didn't share the passions for social causes I did, and she has proven to me that she has her own—complex and sound—ways of looking at the world, and that these emerge in time.

Girls' education will change the world. My daughters assume that they have every right to anything boys have, especially in education. Many women as well as men have worked hard to ensure this entitlement. But severe disparities still dominate the world. Learning about this, our children not only can better appreciate their own schooling, but also relate to those who are deprived of this basic right. This is not an issue that only parents of girls should care about—it also intimately affects boys.

Over the past decade or two, a powerful transformation of thought has occurred among policy makers and experts from virtually every ideological and political background—that *girls' education is one of the best investments a country can make.* The Nike Foundation has determined that investments in adolescent girls (what they call "The Girl Effect") will show the biggest impact for their dollars. In poor countries this improves a community's health, its chances for increasing incomes, and even can cause political extremism and violence at all levels to decline. Educating future mothers directly benefits future generations. In poor African countries like The Gambia and Burkina Faso, the presidents have made a clear commitment to girls' schooling, sending a strong signal to men and women, and we saw the repercussions beginning to affect everybody in positive ways.

When my daughters were in elementary school, we supported a small initiative for girls' education in Bolivia. They were proud to give teachers the pins made by the Bolivian girls, knowing they were making a difference in someone's life and sharing the impact in their own school. We periodically talk about these issues, each year adding a little bit more of the societal complexities to our conversation. Universal education forms an important piece of the global development puzzle, and our children can feel linked to the problem as well as the solution.

IDEAS YOUR SCHOOL CAN USE TO GO GLOBAL

We know by now that one International Day at school, with a carnival-like atmosphere, will not make our children globally minded. At its best, a day-long celebration will heighten curiosity, teach a lesson, and launch a process of exploration—usually among those already inclined to these ideas, and from families that encourage global knowledge. In the worst case, these events have reinforced an "otherness." Looking at how different the foods, games, and traditional clothing are, some children can feel doubly alienated and remote—especially if that is their one and only contact with those customs. If the exposure to international concepts is limited to the International Day, then it is natural that this topic would be seen as an isolated issue (if at all) by the child, not part of their own reality.

To avoid such disconnection, international understanding can be integrated into the overall curriculum and become a part of the school's own culture. This is a huge leap for some schools, but the acceptance that every school needs to train students who will be able to compete in the global economy is leading educators and communities to conclude that this step is inevitable. A successful integration of international topics in the school day increases empathy and connection with diverse people; it also helps to hone critical thinking skills and make the study of topics like science, math, and foreign language apply to very real issues confronting the world. If this integration does occur, then a program like an International Day will feel more like a culmination of the learning that has been taking place, not a stage show. It would also reinforce your efforts at home. Here are some of the specific steps a school can take to realize this vision:

1. *Teachers can take a fresh look at their curriculum and their physical classroom.*
   ○ In each lesson of English, science, social studies, or even math, is there a "global" perspective that can be brought in, or an impact on someone in another country that could be explored?

Sell a chocolate bar—
change the world—support your school.

Try an alternative to selling wrapping paper for a school fundraiser, and raise global consciousness while you're at it. Equal Exchange offers fair-trade coffees, teas, chocolates, and other treats, and Global Goods Partners sells handcrafted gifts made by artisans earning a fair wage. Through both of these organizations, the school keeps a sizable percentage of the sales revenue and makes a just difference for people living in some of the world's poorest countries.

- Do the art and music programs incorporate contributions made by world cultures?
- Do classrooms have a world map (as well as a U.S. map) hung on the wall in a convenient place?
- Do the items used to decorate the classroom take advantage of diverse cultural styles that are available, particularly among nationalities represented in class (e.g., on a tablecloth, a piece of art on the wall, an educational poster, a craft project, etc.)?

2. *Take advantage of the experiences and perspectives of parent volunteers, international families, and staff.* The tasks in the previous step might seem overwhelming to a teacher, but some of the parents of children in the class might have experienced living or traveling abroad, or can share their own cultural perspective. The more organized the teacher, the more the class can benefit from the parents' experience or willingness to help. For example, if the teacher finds certain topics would be enhanced by outside assistance, an advance note with specific requests can be sent home. Parents don't need to be experts on the topic, but be willing to make the effort to get the right information for the class.

Another often-overlooked source for authentic information is through service staff at school or with other employers in town. Don't fail to include the important experiences that the cafeteria worker from Guatemala or Sudan or the maintenance manager from Jordan might be able to contribute to the vitality of your school community. More important, don't treat these workers as invisible. This also applies to including the contributions of parents who may not speak English fluently. Special effort may be required to involve them, but their children's education is likely a priority—that may be a big reason they came to this country. See these citizens as a rich, untapped resource in your community.

3. *Use teleconferencing to "meet" children in different countries.* This technology has become relatively cheap and easy to use. One place to "Meet" or collaborate with students from other schools is through iEARN (International Education and Resource Network) at www.iearn.org or Global Nomads Group at www.gng.org.

   Caryn Stedman, the 2004 winner of the National Council for Social Studies Award for Global Understanding, set up a video teleconference between her students and students in Baghdad so they could share perspectives just sixteen days before the Iraq war started. She also set up a post-invasion teleconference so students could talk about life before, during, and after the war.[6]

4. *Find a partner school.* Just as there are sister cities, your school can initiate a partner school or twinning program. Partnerships might connect pen pals or go as far as advancing environmental and scientific knowledge, through NASA's GLOBE (Global Learning and Observations to Benefit the Environment) Program, which your school can join at www.globe.gov.

5. *Discuss the origins and trading routes of products you use on a daily basis.* In English schools, Oxfam UK prepares curricula to help elementary students on up to trace the journey of an item like a banana or a T-shirt sold in a local shop. Where did it come from? How did it get here? How many people were involved in getting it to your local store? Who earned what in the process? Global Exchange, from the United States, offers a curriculum showing kids where one of their favorite products, chocolate, comes from. Children from schools around the nation have taken action, like writing to the presidents of major candy bar companies to protest child labor and other conditions that go into their beloved candy. This is the type of project one or several parents can assist with.

6. *After-school programs for everyone, not just children from affluent families.* OneWorld Now! serves economically disadvantaged students in Seattle public high schools with after-school classes in Chinese or Arabic, leadership workshops, summer study-abroad scholarships, internships, and college preparation help. The International YMCA, a branch of the YMCA of Greater New York, offers resources to other YMCAs in providing after-school international enrichment programs and summer exchanges, training, and other opportunities. Both of these not-for-profit organizations, as well as local employers, might be called on to help a school with limited capital begin its own new program.

7. *Public school districts, of varying funding capacities, can launch their own international schools, in partnership with the community.* In Chicago, leaders recog-

nized the need to train the city's children to be globally competitive. They saw the large influx of immigrants as an asset, and strengthened ESL and foreign language programs. Predominantly Hispanic schools teach Mandarin Chinese along with ESL, so the children can be trilingual by the time they complete middle school. These children aren't a burden to the system; they're helping strengthen it. The government of China and corporations like Motorola have donated funds and teaching materials to help advance the goal of a substantially increased number of students learning Chinese. The Chicago Public Schools support the Confucius Institute (Confuciusinstitutechicago.org), house it at a public high school and provide learning resources for parents, teachers, and students in learning Chinese. Chicago now has the largest Chinese language program in the United States.

At the John Stanford International Elementary School in the Seattle school district, the University of Washington's Language Learning Center provides curriculum development and staff support for the mandatory Spanish or Japanese language immersion program. The business community provides mentors and funds to support foreign language requirements. Its students test better than district standards in reading and math, even though those courses are taught in Spanish or Japanese for half the day (the other half of the day classes are in English).[7]

8. *Build up your library's resources—and go an extra mile.* Get to know your children's school librarian and learn about the selection of books, so that you can make a difference with your donation and your time. When looking for new books for the library, try to find titles depicting life in diverse cultures as well as non-American classic stories—particularly from the cultures of families represented at the school. A gentle reminder to parents to give books can come in the

Learn from other schools.

The Office of Language and Cultural Education, www.olce.org, of the Chicago school district is a good place to see how bilingual and world language programs are run. The site also has resources for teacher training and support and a publications section that includes various curriculum guides prepared locally on Arab, Mexican, Chinese, Korean, Polish, and South Asian heritage and culture.

form of a dedication card sent home around the date of the child's birthday, or about a month before the holidays. The card goes on the book's first page, showing "This is a gift from . . . In honor of . . ." It could have a picture depicting the world or diversity to remind donors you are aiming for a range of perspectives in the new books.

You can go an extra mile in stocking your school library by adopting or partnering with another library in a needy community (in the United States or abroad) in which to donate new or used books and duplicates.

9. *Use outside expertise to help you.* The Asia Society's InternationalEd.org site supports schools' efforts to go global, with analyses of numerous issues and school experiences, as well as a state-by-state look at initiatives underway and the results to date. Use this information to inform and influence your school board and elected officials, particularly at the state level.

IMPROVE YOUR GEOGRAPHY KNOWLEDGE

Geography knowledge is a building block for learning about the world, but U.S. schools have paid relatively little attention to the subject. In the 2006 National Geographic/Roper poll, half the eighteen to twenty-four-year-olds surveyed could not find New York on the map and just thirty-seven percent of them could find Iraq, even though tens of thousands in their own peer group have been deployed in war there since 2003. Just before the war, in the 2002 survey, thirteen percent of those surveyed knew where to find Iraq—and more than twice as many knew the remote South Pacific location of that season's *Survivor* TV show.[8]

Our schools may feel too overloaded with material they must teach, so geography falls between the cracks. Spinning a globe and imagining where you'll visit next or live in twenty years, or competing with friends or family over who knows the most countries on a continent can be fun. My mother-in-law astounded us with knowledge she retained from her childhood about seventy years ago in Iran, learning each country on the map, with capital cities and key industries. Almost like a jump-rope song, she could still recite "Chile: Santiago, copper; Argentina: Buenos Aires, cattle" and so on through each continent, to my children's and my amazement.

Here are five ways to get started supplementing geography learning at home or in the classroom:

1. *Discover rich websites and blogs.* "GoogleEarth" anywhere: Find your home, then school, then move on to the deserts of the Sahara or wherever you'd like to go. For the stories behind the places and more, go to National Geographic. Their

kids' website at www.kids.nationalgeographic.com contains interactive games online, as well as crafts, maps, news, experiments, and recipes to try. Their My Wonderful World initiative, described previously, is a campaign to "give kids the power of global knowledge" and a must-visit for anyone reading this book. See sections for parents, educators, kids, and teens filled with activities, as well as ways to get your community on board the campaign for global knowledge. The Discovery Channel's education arm at school.discoveryeducation.com has good geography games and lesson plans. See the Peace Corps's teen page for geography and culture quizzes, recipes, music samples, and profiles of past and present volunteers—great and real role models for kids. This site also might get younger people excited about overseas service. In addition to the blogs associated with these sites, see StrangeMaps.wordpress.com and OgleEarth.com.

2. *Use teacher resources.* Education World is a free Internet resource for teachers. *Where in the World Is Mrs. Waffenschmidt* rivals Carmen San Diego: She goes out in the world hunting for specific places with historic and geographic clues that help bring the locale to life. The *Geography A to Z* series on Education World can be played as a family game with a map or globe, or even turned into conversation over the dinner table. See education-world.com.

3. *Beyond almanacs—read the world.* A nice resource to leave on a coffee table or take on a long car ride and use for quizzing on global knowledge is *The Geography Bee Complete Preparation Handbook: 1001 Questions to Help You Win Again and Again!* Our friend David Broida is trying to read one book by an author from every country in the world. You can do this yourself, as well as with children's books. Yahoo and Wikipedia, the online encyclopedia, among others, each have lists of countries for creating a checklist (type "country list" in the search box) and starting the process—or spin your globe. Lonely Planet's *The Travel Book: A Journey Through Every Country in the World* serves as a vivid, accessible resource for looking up countries, including a book to read from each nation. Hop from region to region for variety, cover an entire continent, or coordinate your geographic readings with themes taught at school, or upcoming holidays, or news stories, or places you'd like to visit. Make sure to include books set in various locales for kids' summer reading.

4. *Keep globes and maps handy handy handy.* World map placemats at the table, area rugs in the playroom, an atlas or other geo-book on the coffee table. Jackie Eghrari, a physician outside of Washington, D.C., told me, "My kids have had globes and world maps as decorations in their rooms since they were sleeping in cribs." She adds that where some people spend money on clothes, fine food, or wine, she and her family travel whenever possible, to as many different places as they can.

5. *Play geography-themed games,* like the *1,000 Places to See Before You Die Game, Where in the World Is Carmen San Diego,* Highlights's *Top Secret Adventures* game, the various *Borderline Games* (USA, World, Middle East and Europe, and Africa editions), *Take Off!* and *World Dash.* Younger kids might enjoy Learning Resources's *Pretend and Play World Traveler Kit* (or make your own world travel kit with an old suitcase or a hatbox). Look for skill-appropriate puzzles of world maps and places of interest, like Usborne's *The Great World Search,* a puzzle-search book that takes you around the world. Use Educational Insights' *The World Giant Discovery Atlas* as a kid-friendly atlas or open it up to play *I-Spy* and quiz games, like our friends Esther and Bernie do with their grandsons. The boys liked this Chanukah gift so much that Esther got an extra copy of the *Giant Discovery Atlas* from a local specialty map shop to keep at home so that the grandsons can call to stump her with a question when they phone from their home a few hours away from hers. Have fun with the *World Traveler Magnetic Dress-Up Doll* from Mudpuppy, which includes changeable backgrounds and outfits for imagination games to take place all over the world—or just decorate a file cabinet or fridge!

Note that companies are changing their inventory often, so some of these exact titles may not always be available. Get product updates at www.growing upglobal.net. The previous chapter, Play! contains more geography games for various ages, too.

———

Education plays a crucial role in helping our children gain a global perspective, and parents can work with their kids and schools to enrich the experience. Just as the learning process can be dynamic, so are the global rankings of how a nation's kids do from year to year. The media and so many popular business books seem to have moved focus from the economic battle with Japan and the rising European community to that of emerging markets like China and India. While children in the United States are among the bottom performers of wealthy nations on multi-country test ranks and the headlines would have a reader stirring in anxiety about the future, this nation still produces the greatest innovations, has the largest economy, and continues to break records every year for the number of new immigrants wanting to build their dreams here. So, while there is great cause for concern, re-form, and getting involved, it shouldn't be motivated by panic and crisis, and there is great strength to build from.

Model international-focused public schools in places like Seattle and Chicago, and the flexibility and creativity demonstrated by some districts and teachers show that acceptance of a broader worldview and readiness for change are thriving (in pockets) all over the country. The places that succeed most in providing an international education are not those that are motivated by test performance or by the race for global economic dominance, but are the ones that possess a longer term view. At a time when American schools are becoming more, not less, segregated by race and the courts uphold the ruling that desegregation of schools cannot be mandated,[9] the schools that are proactive about attracting diversity and academic talent also are innovators in international education. No one is forcing them, they just know it optimizes the learning environment. When Hispanic children in ESL classes simultaneously begin to master Mandarin Chinese, they demonstrate their vitality—trilingual residents from hardworking families will be a great asset, not a drag on their community. When a middle-school social studies class nurtures a relationship with children in Baghdad or the Palestinian territories, each pen pal and teleconference participant on both sides is a future peacemaker. When an art class helps children create masks in the style of rainforests in Java or Brazil or the Congo, a wider aesthetic appreciation is cultivated, and a window is opened on a previously baffling culture. Ultimately, when the school environment allows these initiatives to flourish, deeper and wider bonds of friendship are reinforced among all the members of its community as well as with the wider world community, creating true global citizens.

RESOURCE BOOKS CITED IN CHAPTER 4—THAT YOU MAY FIND HELPFUL, TOO

Material World: A Global Family Portrait, cited in Chapter 1.

Frida, Jonah Winter (author) and Ana Juan (illustrator) (New York: Scholastic, 2002).

Diego, Jeanette Winter (New York: Random House Children's, 1994).

Katie Meets the Impressionists, James Mayhew (New York: Scholastic, 2007).

Dinner at Magritte's, Michael Garland (New York: Penguin, 1995).

Wake Up, World!: A Day in the Life of Children Around the World, Beatrice Hollyer (New York: Henry Holt and Co., 1999).

Back to School (*It's a Kids' World*), Maya Ajmera and John Ivanko (Watertown, MA: Charlesbridge Publishing, 2001).

A is for Africa, Ifeoma Onyefulu (New York: Puffin Books, 1997).

One Big Family: Sharing Life in an African Village, Ifeoma Onyefulu (London: Frances Lincoln Ltd., 2006).

UNICEF's *Children Just Like Me,* cited in Chapter 1.

The Diary of Ma Yan: Struggles and Hopes of a Chinese Schoolgirl, Ma Yan and Pierre Haski (New York: HarperCollins, 2005).

Facing the Lion: Growing Up Maasai on the African Savannah, Joseph Lemasolai Lekuton (Washington, DC: National Geographic Children's Books, 2005).

Monsoon Summer, Mitali Perkins (New York: Laurel Leaf [Random House Children's], 2006).

Come Back to Afghanistan: A California Teenager's Story, Said Hydar Akbar (New York: Bloomsbury USA, 2005).

Miriam's Song: A Memoir, Miriam Mathabane as told to Mark Mathabane of South Africa (New York: Free Press, 2001).

The Geography Bee Complete Preparation Handbook: 1001 Questions to Help You Win Again and Again!, Matthew Todd Rosenberg and Jennifer Rosenberg (New York: Random House, 2002).

The Travel Book: A Journey Through Every County in the World, Roz Hopkins, publisher (Australia: Lonely Planet Publications, 2005).

ADDITIONAL RESOURCE BOOKS RELATED TO CHAPTER 4

Nurtured by Love: The Classic Approach to Talent Education, Shinichi Suzuki (Secaucus, NY: Suzuki, 1983).

1000 Places to See Before You Die, Patricia Schultz (New York: Workman Publishing, 2003).

Talking Walls, Margy Burns Knight (author) and Anne Sibley O'Brien (illustrator) (Gardiner, ME: Tilbury House Publishers, 1992).

Chapter 5

Break Bread

How can you govern a country that has 246 varieties of cheese?

CHARLES DE GAULLE

This quote from France's prominent twentieth-century leader gives a sense of how closely intertwined food is with national identity, culture, daily life, and even a nation's security and stability. It's the most basic physical requirement for human survival, but beyond this, a culture's foods tell so much about its people. Food probably offers the most accessible and natural way for a family to begin experiencing a different culture without traveling far away.

At around six P.M. in some neighborhoods, you might be able to take a walk and experience a global palate of smells: Korean cabbage, Southern BBQ, and stews from China, India, Greece, Mexico, and countless other places. I became aware of this fact one summer evening when Sophia was around three. I put her in her red wagon for a walk while our roast cooked in the oven. Perhaps our hunger sharpened our sense of smell: We started a new game, like a scavenger hunt, to figure out what the neighbors might be having for dinner as we were drawn from one continent to another, walking between the houses.

We fabricated funny, imagined stories about the strangers in their houses and their evening meals. We knew what they looked like, as we waved hello or goodbye on the driveway, but the rest was a mystery. By the end of the summer I made a conscious decision to start asking some of the neighbors with whom I had a little bit of contact about their cooking. This opened so many doors. Busy working mothers found time on a Sunday afternoon to show me how they premade some of the dinners for the week; I shared the bountiful bok choy from our cooperative farm harvest with those who appreciated it far more than my own children and they sent some back, having transformed it into something a few in my family liked and others found curious; and we miraculously found time to get to know one another—beyond the mandatory wave on the driveway. This validated once again that food is a portal to getting to know a culture or a friend. As busy as we are, we all find time to eat.

LOOK AT WHAT THE WORLD EATS

A great way to imagine what people are eating is by exploring the pages of *Hungry Planet* by Peter Menzel and Faith D'Aluisio. *Hungry Planet* is a book to be experienced—the family portraits, photos of different types of food, and the environments and preparation of the food remind us that eating is a collective experience as well as a commentary on the state of the human condition. You may be struck, as my girls and I were, by all the plastic bottles of Coca-Cola and generic colas displayed in family cupboards from Bhutan to the Australian Outback, Bosnia, and Mexico. The differences also tell so much about each family's health, prosperity, hopes, and values. At times I keep our copy of the book on the family-room coffee table. Sophia and I like to pick out one picture of the families and their week's groceries; we look for foods she can name, and then for those she doesn't recognize.

One day, when we started looking at the pictures, I reprimanded her for deliberately dropping her crumbs on the picture of the family from Mali, West Africa. I saw it as messy and careless, and disrespectful to the book and the images on it. She protested, "Mommy, I want to share my bagel with them." That's when I realized how much meaning the book contained for everyone in our home.

A lighter treatment of a similar topic, written about and for children is Oxfam's *Let's Eat! What Children Eat Around the World.* This book takes one representative child in five disparate countries (France, Mexico, Thailand, India, and South Africa) and shows what they eat and how it is prepared, providing a glimpse into a special day in each of their lives, along with the food on that celebratory day. This is a nice selection for kids from pre-K through elementary school.

For older children, *Hungry Planet*'s montages of photos, from fast food to bizarre, exotic street foods, paint a fascinating picture of current life on our planet. The book also includes essays, like "Food with a Face," by Michael Pollan, who later released the brilliant *The Omnivore's Dilemma* and *In Defense of Food: An Eater's Manifesto.* The essay gets us to think about our relationship with the animals we eat and is followed by two pages of photos of animals as food. As Pollan observes, "Meat comes from the grocery store, where it is cut and packaged to look as little like parts of animals as possible. The disappearance of animals from our lives has opened a space in which there's no reality check, on either the sentiment or the brutality."[1] In a two-dimensional book you can't smell or feel the fresh meat, but the vivid images will expose readers to a different side of where their meat comes from and how closely others in the world must get to the gorier sides of their food. Pollan doesn't argue that we should never eat meat, but that our society needs to go back to the ancient ways that "respect their animal-prey." Children don't need to be shielded from the knowledge of where their meat comes from and what it really looks like—it makes them aware of the food chain they are in the middle of, and can open their minds to many other connections that propel their daily lives. The signs of globalization, from omnipresent sushi to supermarkets, tell their own story in the book, as well as so many other commentaries about what and how the world eats. It's a great way to get the whole family thinking about their consumption and more, their world community.

WHAT'S FOR LUNCH?

Like the photos of a week's worth of groceries, different kinds of weekday lunches tell so much about their cultures. Imagine a Japanese lunchbox that carries meticulously rolled sushi, vegetables, and condiments, each in a different compartment; an American PB&J sandwich in a plastic bag; and various East and West African cultures that share lunch from a communal bowl.

Each of these "working lunches" gives a cultural message. The Japanese and Zen mentality of being "present" in all aspects of one's life, from the monumental decisions to the miniscule, might be seen in the Bento Box. The act of rolling a small portion of food into a thing of care and beauty is in harmony with the culture's worldview.

The American sandwich in a bag reflects the value our culture places on speed, convenience, and accomplishment (get the lunch over with so you can get back to work) as opposed to tradition. When we send our children off to school, there is a strong component of socialization that goes along with the sandwich in the bag. By middle school, who they sit with and are included among, for so many kids, determines a large share of their self-worth and day-to-day happiness. As early as elementary school, lunch can be a pretty jarring experience. In most schools, the children are rushed (given about twenty minutes to get their food, find a seat, gobble their lunch, and clean up their place) and shushed, then hurried to the playground for recess that can last anywhere from thirteen to forty-seven minutes, if they are lucky enough to have any recess at all.

In France, the children who stay for school lunch (many will go home for the long lunch period to eat with their families) are universally fed a multicourse meal every day—what many Americans would consider a "gourmet" meal—with homemade soup, salad, a meat or fish course, bread, and a light dessert, usually including some fruit and a cheese course. A BBC study[2] of a typical Parisian primary school found a menu of "adult" food in smaller portions: a starter of grapefruit, followed by grilled chicken with green beans, then a cheese course and rice pudding for dessert. The day's snack was a tangerine. One day a week, French fries ("pommes frites") were served, but with a salmon lasagne. Each meal is accompanied by plain water to drink. There is no choice, so children must either eat up or go home for lunch. At least two hours are set aside for lunchtime, which includes the leisurely meal as well as a healthy dose of playtime. The cost of the meal is subsidized, so it is equally available to all children—the government considers it their duty to provide the healthy midday meal. The growing number of French families that are skipping the traditional meal in favor of fast foods adds to the government's imperative to make sure the kids get the slow meal during school lunch.

Some American schools are moving toward healthier and "slow" foods and eating experiences. The "slow food" movement (Slowfood.com) attempts to source ingredients locally, heighten interest in the food we eat and its impact on the world, and counteract its opposite—fast foods. If you haven't heard about this being instituted in your community, you may want to contact the food supervisor in your school district. To help arm you with information on the benefits of slow food and the changing school lunches in communities around the country, Chef Ann Cooper, "Renegade Lunch Lady," has a blog and website, Lunchlessons.org, with links and ideas from all over the country.

Eating lunch from the communal bowl in Africa had a profound impact on me. Far from being something to pity, it seemed to have less to do with scarce resources and was more about the primacy of the group (clan, village, family) in all the actions of the individual. As the point was clearly made to us in West Africa, as long as you have a large family (including distant and extended family), you are not poor. The person who is alone is poor. When you are surrounded by people—assuming there is peace—then the food, medicine, shelter, and clothing can all be shared and there is a better chance that there will be enough to go around.

For the school celebrations at the Lower Basic School in our Gambian neighborhood, almost all the children brought large portions of tasty chicken or fish and rice dishes to share with their friends and teachers. At significant expense to the family, parents cooked full hot meals that children carried to school in pots wrapped in cloths and balanced on their heads, as opposed to the standard-issue cheese pizza usually served at my kids' parties. There was enough for each child to eat their own dish of food, but I didn't see any of them eating alone—this was a party after all! A highlight for the children seemed to be getting me, the foreign guest, to eat from everyone's pot. I first met the enthusiastic invitations to dig in

Getting little ones (and big ones) to try new foods

Learning about different foods goes only so far if you won't taste them. In homes where kids eat a wide range of foods, I have noticed three key elements put in practice:

1. Don't give them an "out"—prepare *one* meal that everyone will eat. Sometimes adults will need to compromise and have less "exotic" foods, or a "safety" dish that can accompany something new, but this shows that a family meal is just that.

2. Be an example—be willing to try new foods yourself. The example of their peers who will try different foods is an equally powerful aid.

3. Vary the types of food you serve at home and the types of restaurant you visit.

    Famed restaurateur and chef Alice Waters, in her children's book *Fanny at Chez Panisse*, shares delightful stories from the perspective of her then-seven-year-old daughter Fanny, on how she got over foods she thought she didn't like. When she refused the halibut on fig leaves, her mother didn't give up trying to get her to try the dish: *"Remember the time you said you didn't like ricotta cheese on your pasta, you only liked Parmesan?" "Yeah." "And then you tried just a little bit and ricotta became your favorite cheese?"* Recalling how she overcame other foods she thought she couldn't stand finally convinced her to try the new dish, and of course she loved it. For a stubborn adult at the restaurant, chefs disguised one type of meat as another, and of course, he loved it as a result. Though its honor is questionable, with my own children, "bait-and-switch" has been a useful tactic to get them to try things like tofu and turnips.

with my fingers with a combination of shock and dread, but knew that I couldn't refuse the kind offers. Once I let go of my horror, I realized the food tasted delicious, but I still must admit, it is not a practice I felt comfortable with or would continue. When the meal was finished, I was fascinated by the intricate and seemingly ancient and effective hand-washing from a bucket of water in the room that each child and adult conducted. We had eaten from the same pot, dug our fingers into the same bowls, and washed from the same bucket. Now we were friends!

These distinctions in how a meal is prepared and consumed can be grasped even by quite young children. They demonstrate how there are so many ways to accomplish the same goal (lunch) and that each one can be interesting and fulfilling.

Anyone who has played tea-party with little ones knows that the act of creating a beautiful presentation and some ceremony can make even a sip of water special. This sort of meticulousness might appeal to little girls more. But don't deprive the boys of a creative game of tea-party—help them find a way to make it interesting. You can show your boys and girls examples of tea ceremonies like the Japanese, Chinese, or Russian versions to better appreciate the experience of meticulous preparation, and note that great chefs (possibly most accessible by watching the Food Network) can be both women and men. A beautiful or careful presentation of food isn't just a girl-thing.

FOODS WE ALL SHARE

At the Chinese restaurant next to our pharmacy and dry cleaner, "kids' food" usually consists of a *lo mein* noodle dish, a bowl of sticky white rice, and dumplings. Nothing too spicy or rich or funny-textured. They are familiar and unique at the same time. These are the foods to ease into. They resemble the foods our young children eat most other days, like spaghetti and pancakes. So many children's authors have noticed the range of food similarities across cultures, devoting entire picture books to the common foods. In some school districts, curriculum includes learning about the foods we eat—where they come from and the common heritage various foods share, like noodles in Italy, China, and Egypt. Because few of the foods we consume every day actually come from North America, this is a great way to show how our daily consumption is linked together with faraway places around the planet.

Bread: There are several books for kids that drive home the message that bread comes in so many forms, from so many places, but it's a common, delicious comfort food spanning cultures. In *Bread, Bread, Bread* by Ann Morris, photos of

Start slowly.

A gentle transition to new forms of bread can begin with peanut butter and jelly on a tortilla or pita bread in the lunchbox. Work your way up to pumpernickel or seeded breads, flavored naans, and scooping up stews with various flatbreads—get used to different textures, looks, and tastes one step at a time.

They eat that?! Share stories of the most exotic food you've ever eaten or heard of.

If your child stays a very picky eater beyond age ten or so, it's not a bad idea to expose them to foods you consider to be *really* exotic—then what you're trying to get them to taste may not seem so strange. My most bizarre food experience probably was eating a whole guinea pig in Peru. It was lying on its back, with paws straight up, stiff in the air, smothered in a tasty tomato sauce. Among my daughters, this experience of eating the *cuyi* is one of their favorite stories. There's also:

• Live octopus—Japan

• Whole pigeon—China

• Fried crickets on chips and salsa—Mexico

• Lamb head, all of it: eyes, brain, tongue, etc.—all over the Middle East

• Haggis: sheep heart, lungs, liver mixed with oatmeal and stuffed in the sheep's stomach bag—Scotland

• Live cobra heart—Vietnam

The last one comes courtesy of Anthony Bourdain's *No Reservations* show on the Travel Channel. Along with Andrew Zimmern's *Bizarre Foods,* these programs take eating unusual foods to new, entertaining heights, and have become favorite TV shows in my home. Look for showtimes on www.travel.discovery.com. Don't let unusual foods be presented as only some sort of freak show—by slowly introducing new foods to your family, your family's eating can become more adventurous, naturally.

clearly diverse people enjoying various forms of bread, and simple accompanying text, will appeal to the youngest children. The index at the end includes a guide to the country of origin for each photo. In *Everybody Bakes Bread* by Norah Dooley, Carrie is sent around her idealized, diverse neighborhood on an unattainable er-

Food Books and Cookbooks

Learning about diverse foods and making them in your own home creates a sort of relationship with the food and the culture. Kids are more willing to taste something they made (or helped make) themselves. A few good places to start:

• For the littlest ones, the World Snacks series from Tricycle Press by Amy Wilson Sanger, with titles like *Hola! Jalapeno, First Book of Sushi,* and *Yum Yum Dim Sum* celebrate diverse foods through fun pictures and poems. Mollie Katzen of *Moosewood Cookbook* fame gets preschoolers excited about healthy and varied eating in *Pretend Soup and Other Real Recipes: A Cookbook for Preschoolers and Up* and *Salad People and More Real Recipes.* These include international foods, but they are not the sole focus. The smart, pictorial recipes keep the focus on younger children's involvement with food.

• When the kids want to get more involved in the kitchen, age-appropriate multicultural cookbooks present kid-friendly recipes, history, and background on foods and cultures. You can start with *The Kids' Multicultural Cookbook* by Deanna Cook or *Kids Around the World Cook!* by Arlette M. Braman. Also, there's *The Kids' Around the World Cookbook* by Deri Roberts.

• Older kids will enjoy Lerner Publications' *Easy Menu Ethnic Cookbooks,* a series for teens from various authors with specialized cuisines covering virtually every corner of the world, from Cuban and West African to Mediterranean and Korean, plus holiday, and dessert books.

• For a more sophisticated palate, travel the globe with Jeffrey Alford and Naomi Duguid through their acclaimed books, including *Flatbreads and Flavors: A Baker's Atlas; Seductions of Rice; HomeBaking: The Artful Mix of Flour and Tradition Around the World; Hot, Sour, Salty, Sweet,* and others. The fantastic adventures of this couple and their two children are brought alive through insightful essays, doable recipes, and enticing photos.

rand and discovers so many at home baking bread on that rainy day. By visiting them, she gets to enjoy Jewish *challah,* Barbadian coconut bread, Indian *chapatis,* Lebanese pitas, cornbread from South Carolina, *pupusas* from El Salvador, and finally, her great-grandmother's sweet Italian bread.

For older elementary kids, *Loaves of Fun: A History of Bread with Activities and*

Recipes from Around the World by Elizabeth Harbison starts with some of the shared ancient history of bread ranging back to the lumpy, uncooked mixture of grains and water of around 73,000 B.C. in Asia, where breadmaking began, to 4000 B.C. Mesopotamia (modern-day Iraq), where the grains were first cooked over a fire, and 1500 B.C. Egypt, where yeast was first used to make leavened bread. The fact that Egyptian tomb drawings include pictures of people making bread and that pharaohs were buried with their bread—they might need some in the afterlife—illustrates how essential bread has been for so long. Egyptians were even known by ancient Greeks as the "bread eaters." Mexican *tortillas* and Indian *chapatis* can be traced back to the pounded breads of Mesopotamia and Egypt.

Ancient Romans used bread ovens as temples and their bakers were among society's most respected members; the Jewish celebration of Passover is marked by consumption of unleavened bread, as was necessitated in the exodus from Egypt; and bread serves as the symbol of the body of Christ during Catholic mass.

In modern times, protesters have gone to the streets over the price of bread, slang in various languages uses the word *bread* to mean money or wealth, and folk songs depicting a wide range of emotions are sung about it. The practice of scooping up food with tortillas, pita, or spongy, sour Ethiopian *injera* can be traced back centuries before the use of utensils, and elaborate combinations of meat, vegetables, and dairy products on a pizza, in a dumpling, or on an empanada predate the use of plates—on every continent.

After sharing a bit about the traditions of bread, you can try to stretch the experience of your children by packing their school lunch with a different form of bread than the usual loaf you might reach for at the grocery store.

Rice: After wheat, rice is the second-most consumed grain on the planet. In my home growing up, basmati rice served as the base of an array of meals and we bought it in fifty-pound sacks from specialty stores. Today, you can get basmati rice at most grocery, health food, and warehouse stores like Costco and Sam's Club. Our rice dishes were completed by a meat or chicken and then mixed with dill and other herbs, or nuts, cinnamon, carrots, or tomatoes and green beans, or sour cherries or barberries, lentils and raisins, and topped with saffron.

People often clump together the style of cooking Persian rice with Indian or Lebanese or other pilafs from the Middle East and the Mediterranean, and many of the children's cookbooks or food books I have reviewed generalize all of the food styles as "Middle Eastern." But to anyone who has grown up with these foods, there are clear differences—not just from country to country, but between regions or even subgroups within a region. You can try following a few rice recipes from various countries for a family dinner to begin tasting the differences for yourself.

Notice and discuss the variations between rice dishes from Spain, Peru, Iran, Lebanon, India, China, Indonesia, or just about any other country. Are they sticky or fluffy? Savory or sweet? Spicy or herby? Moist, buttery, or dry? Drenched with a stew or cooked with the meat and veggies as part of a single pot?

To start slowly in transitioning to new forms of rice, simply replace the standard rice you might usually cook with basmati or jasmine rice. For the more health-conscious, brown basmati and jasmine rices also are available widely. Because few of us have seen how rice is grown and where it comes from, a book like *Rice Is Life* brings the rice fields of Bali to life and has been a joy to read with my youngest child. For elementary and middle schoolers, *The Sacred Harvest: Ojibway Wild Rice Gathering* depicts the importance of the crop to the Ojibway people living in Minnesota and touches on some aspects of daily life for modern Native Americans, to which few American kids are exposed. The geographic contrast between the story set in Bali and another in the lakes of Minnesota reflects the universality of rice.

Noodles: It is widely believed that Marco Polo brought noodles from China to Italy and this later turned into the nation's signature food—pasta. Many children familiar with the offerings in a large American grocery store have seen Italian-American pasta sold in an array of shapes: wide (lasagna), thin (linguine), thinner (spaghetti), thinnest (angel hair or capellini), curly, square, short tubes (ziti), long and wide tubes (manicotti), bow tie, and elbow. Instead of always reaching for the usual linguini or spaghetti, vary the form and shape of your standard white-wheat pasta. Then, go further by trying green and red and deep brown pastas from the supermarket. A step beyond this is to try varieties made of the many different in-

If the World Were a Village by David Smith is a must-have book for readers of *Growing Up Global*. To help kids (and their parents) get their heads around the distribution of resources among the world's 6.2 billion population, the author condenses that number to one hundred and uses clear pictures to make his points. The manageable numbers show how much more food, electricity, technology, and education we get in the United States compared to the rest of the world. This approach can help us think about how we might rebalance our individual consumption. When we feel a connection to others on the planet, the task becomes more relevant.

gredients available in specialty stores. Norah Dooley's *Everybody Brings Noodles* celebrates ethnic variations, like egg noodles prepared in the Chinese or Jewish (kugel) style, Greek orzo, Japanese soba (buckwheat) noodles with seaweed, rice vermicelli prepared in the Vietnamese style, Latin American macaroni salad, and linguine with Italian pesto.

A different kind of starchy staple: For many it's hard to imagine a meal without a good share of bread, pasta, potato or rice. In much of sub-Saharan Africa, another staple is served at virtually every meal. It's grounded maize and water paste, known as *nsima* or *nshima* in Malawi and Zambia, *ugali* in Kenya, Uganda, and Tanzania, *fou fou* in West Africa, and *mealie meal* in South Africa and Swaziland. This was brought by the Portuguese from the New World to Africa in the 1500s to feed slaving outposts. It curbs hunger, but depletes the soil of nutrients, is not drought-resistant, and deprives the body of essential vitamins and proteins.[3] Prepare this gluey paste for your family to get a sense of the big challenge for African food security, as well as to taste the essential staple on most of the continent. Just mix plain cornmeal with some water over the stove like a porridge, until the consistency is "gloppy." You can eat it plain, as most people do, with salt and butter, or with a stew or broth next to it. A fascinating site to explore with interested family members is the U.S. government's Famine Early Warning System Network at www.fews.net. Here you can find regularly updated, country-by-country data that tracks food security issues, including weather patterns where famine is a threat.

Host a world meal. A variation on serving *nsima* or mealie-meal is to host a "World Meal," which consists of a limited amount of rice and beans with water as the sole beverage. This is the average meal for the average person on the planet. You and your family can serve this for a group of friends and encourage them in turn to cook a World Meal for others. Several elite private schools across the United States give this meal periodically to their students (with the encouragement of the parents). The school collects the money saved from not preparing their usual meal and donates it to a particular charity. This sort of initiative forms part of a school's community outreach and environmental mission.

A variation on the World Meal (also known as a "hunger meal") is to sit "haves" and "have-nots" next to each other at the same meal. Some churches, civic groups, and even businesses have held dinners like this, not telling participants in advance of the setup. When one person sits down with a sumptuous meat-rice-bread-butter-salad dinner and the person next to him has only bread or a bit of rice and water, issues around justice become more tangible and great discussions about the world situation can follow. The dinner illustrates the fact that people don't go

Watch what kind of face you make.

Our friend Tom Teti has been acting, producing, and teaching professional theater for over three decades. He described to me his formative experiences with foods and how he uses this to teach acting:

Most Catholics dreaded Fridays in the fifties and sixties because it was a fish day and not a meat day, but my family loved it because we got all this "special" food that others didn't, and wouldn't, eat, like calamari, tuna steak, and lots of greens. My friends would come into our house, make a face, and say, "Ew, what's that?" with the ugliest expression you could imagine.

When I taught school, I brought in things that were different for kids to try, for the food value, but also to explain where they came from, which became a geography game with the map. When they didn't want to try it, and made that face, I would tell them to freeze, that we were going to have a funny face competition, then quickly take them to a mirror and show them what they looked like. "And this is because you don't want to taste an artichoke! How would you feel if I made that face when you offered me a cookie that your mother baked?" Manners enter into it, being more polite when refusing something. But for some reason, people seem to think they can unload their basest reactions on exotic foods, and don't understand the great social advances that can be made by accepting another's gift of something to eat.

hungry because the planet can't produce enough food to feed everyone, but usually because resources aren't fairly distributed. Kids aged eight and up can grasp at least part of this concept. If you'd like more information on organizing such a meal, Oxfam America's Hunger Banquet offers ideas, a network, and a place to donate funds for poverty and hunger alleviation.

Beyond the common carbs: Bread, rice, pasta, and maize meal aren't the only examples of shared eating experiences across cultures. Fruits and vegetables offer a healthy, tasty, and often surprising way to experience world cultures. As a sign of a shrinking world, fruits like mango and pomegranate that were recently considered exotic are stocked in mainstream supermarkets. In just a generation, suburbia's food choices reflect more "global" choices than ever before.

My mother recalls experiences in the United States in the 1960s and even into the 1980s, when "We were so excited to find an eggplant in the grocery store and once we took it to the cashier, we would be ready for the manager to be called over to help figure out what the thing was and how to check it out. I bought parsley in bunches to use in stews; no one else thought of it as more than a garnish, so they only needed a few sprigs. They imagined I was feeding hundreds of people! Also, for years the only way to get plain, unsweetened yogurt was to make it myself. It's only recently that plain yogurt is available in the supermarket."

Instead of going for the usual Red Delicious apple or Bosc pear, take your kids grocery shopping to feel, smell, and see fruits they might be unfamiliar with, like prickly pears, papayas, starfruits, Asian pears, blood oranges, and plantains. If you like canned fruits, try lychee. These fruits are often more expensive, but if you compare the cost to a sugary snack they might eat, you might feel justified in the expense. When shopping for potatoes, try a different color, shape, or size—like the residents in the Andes mountains of South America, who cultivate dozens of different types (my favorite are purple). Look for new salad ingredients; vary the types of lettuce, tomato, and cucumber, and try fragrant herbs and new types of vegetables, nuts, dried fruits, and dressings. Take this quest to your nearby farmers' market, where the local might expose you to the global.

For a really different experience, go produce shopping in an ethnic grocery store. What are your Dominican, Indian, Mexican, Syrian, Chinese, and Vietnamese neighbors buying for their salad and their pantry? Not only will you find some exotic varieties, but some of the prices might be more reasonable than the supermarket that isn't equipped for selling such specialty items.

Tea, *té, cha, chai*—all from the same word in Chinese—is universal. Gaining popularity in America, it's been the national drink in dozens of countries for centuries. Particularly in countries where alcohol consumption is less acceptable in public places, hot tea flows freely, and teahouses are the hangouts, much like the neighborhood pub. (Russia and Japan are exceptions here: In both, strong liquor is drunk publicly, and at the same time, traditions around tea drinking throughout the day remain vital.) Herb teas and lightly caffeinated green teas provide variety and new flavor alternatives to sugary drinks for my kids on special occasions or as part of an afternoon snack. Dried hibiscus flowers from China or Senegal (available in some health food stores or ethnic markets) infused in boiled water and then served hot or cold make for a healthy and "global" drink. Using mugs and cups in whimsical, artisan, or classic styles adds to the "experience" of the tea—or try the tea-party approach mentioned earlier in this chapter.

MCDONALD'S—THE GLOBAL-AMERICAN BRAND

While so many foods reflect local culture and others are ancient and universal, certain brands embody the global conglomeration of consumption, like Coca-Cola, McDonald's, and more recently, Starbucks, which plans to close hundreds of U.S. locations but open 3,500 foreign outlets by 2011.[4] All have come to symbolize the United States abroad, and the first two earn most of their revenue abroad. McDonald's has over 31,000 restaurants, over half of which are located outside the United States, in 118 countries.[5] Many of its products are going global with the brand—burgers, fries, and sodas remain the mainstay.

China's first drive-through McDonald's—a joint venture with a gas station chain—opened in 2007, reflecting the growing car culture there. In France, McDonald's still incites angry protests from farmers and other food purists, but it doesn't hold back over one million people who eat there *per day* in over one thousand locations. Many Americans traveling abroad break down and get a familiar McDonald's meal, and as *Hungry Planet* and other media sources show, McDonald's is the preferred meal of most children, even if it is a financial stretch for the family. (In most foreign locations, their patrons are the elite, not the working class.) At an overseas McDonald's, you may have to pay extra for packets of ketchup, whereas mayonnaise is standard on French fries. Everyone I asked about their experience with McDonald's abroad says something like: "I don't know why, but it tastes so much better than American McDonald's." In many places, the chain has wisely incorporated some of the time-honored national tastes into its menu. For example:

- India: The popular Maharaja Mac is made of lamb or chicken—no beef is served due to Hindu dietary restrictions. The McAloo Tikki is the veggie burger.
- Israel: Kosher McDonald's will not serve cheeseburgers, as dairy cannot be combined with beef in a kosher diet.
- Morocco, Egypt, Jordan, Saudi Arabia: McArabia is a regular, large burger, but with meat that is *halal* (prepared according to Islamic dietary rules). Because of the restriction on eating pork in Islamic countries, the use of the word *ham*-burger is avoided. There is also the McTurko in Turkey, a lamb or beef kabob sandwich.
- Malaysia, China, Hong Kong: The Prosperity Burger rolls out for Chinese New Year.
- New Zealand: The Kiwi Burger was reintroduced due to popular demand in 2007 and is made with a beef patty, egg, tomato, lettuce, cooked beetroot, onion, "special sauce," and mustard on a toasted bun.

- Norway: Grilled salmon and dill sauce make the McLaks sandwich.
- Finland: A bun made of rye instead of wheat is available.
- Hawaii: Several unique items, including the Spam sandwich—"spamwich."
- Costa Rica: For breakfast you can get *gallo pinto,* the traditional seasoned rice and black bean dish.
- Japan: Menu items include the Koroke Burger, a sandwich of mashed potato, cabbage, and katsu sauce; Ebi-Chiki (shrimp nuggets); and Ebi Filet-O (shrimp burgers). There's also the popular Green Tea milkshake.
- Philippines: McSpaghetti and McRice burger on a fried rice-cake patty are popular, as is corned beef with rice for breakfast.
- Canadian Maritimes and Maine, USA: McLobster roll in the summertime, as in the region's specialty at a lobster shack.

DO YOU HAVE A KIDS' MENU?

Beyond the Western fast-food or chain restaurants, it is not typical to find specially designated kids' menus in many parts of the world. Nonetheless, wherever you travel you won't be far from pizza or Chinese food, even if it tastes nothing like what you expect. When we have traveled abroad with our children, I have found that prepping them to eat the local food (e.g., "no complaining; taste whatever is set before you; if you don't like it, no shrieking or strange faces; just set it down on your plate or in your napkin") has made all the difference in our experience. They often have enjoyed a local specialty that they never would have tried at home, like roasted duck in Peru and peanut-tomato-chile stew in The Gambia, more than the local versions of pizza (with corn, jalapeño peppers, mystery meat or fish, and no cheese) or burgers (with a fried egg on top!), which often turn out like odd imitations of their most familiar foods.

Eating out around the world shows other cultures' lifestyles and values, seen in everything from the *halal* or kosher meat preparation to the design of the seating area. For example, in Saudi Arabia, where women are completely covered in public and lead such separate lives from men, a seating plan must be arranged so they won't be rubbing elbows with unfamiliar men at a nearby table, and certainly not at a bar. Anecdotes around eating out help bring to life the experiences of families abroad. I shared them with my children when we were sitting at a restaurant and we compared how some of the differences stacked up to their own experiences. It also made them more aware of the manners expected of them in eating different styles of food, from burgers and fries with their hands in a more boisterous setting, to a nicer restaurant with cloth napkins on their laps, multiple forks to choose from, and speaking in muted voices. Then there's the skill of eating a whole new type of food, whether it's a saucy, bursting sandwich bought at a food cart, an unknown local specialty at a neighborhood stand, or a fish in its shell in a sit-down environment.

Eating out in Russia: Modern, foreign restaurants in Moscow and St. Petersburg and those catering to foreigners are the only places to find a kids' menu, and these are in a style similar to American restaurants—but they are uncommon. As my friend Venus, who lives most of the year in Moscow, told me, "Traditional Russian establishments wouldn't have a kids' menu, and parents sitting with their children are often smoking." The favorite foods for Russians span all ages. Everyone likes dumplings, known as *vareneki,* which can be sweet (filled with sour cherry preserves) or savory, with cottage cheese, meats, or vegetables. Other favorites are *piroshkis,* a rising dough dumpling filled with things like cabbage, meat, or mushrooms; *blinis,* probably the most commonly found of all, like a crepe filled with butter, sour cream, smoked salmon, or ground meat; *salad olivié,* potato, egg, and chicken salad mixed with carrots, pickles, peas, and sometimes raw onions; and another salad with beets, garlic, walnuts, and mayonnaise. Traditional *borsht* soup remains popular, along with open-faced sandwiches topped with butter and salmon or sausage or salami. The main meal of the day is at midday, where schools provide a hot, sit-down meal for the children.

Eating out in Thailand: My aunt, Sammi Nagaratnam, has lived in Thailand for over twenty years. She told me:

> Thai children eat in restaurants all the time. This is an eating-out culture. It is easier and cheaper to eat at a restaurant or stall than to cook at home. Parents are all working and there is generally no time to cook—of course some do, and some families have maids.
>
> Children eat what everyone else eats. You can order either a plateful/bowlful of rice or noodle-based food, or order a number of items to go with rice. One person can order several dishes. So, for example, for breakfast a child may have noodles with fishballs (not fish balls!) or sliced red pork or chicken, or they may have rice with chicken or pork or some curry, or fried rice. Really there is no big division between the food for breakfast and other main meals during the day. Anything can be eaten at any time. Now it has become more of a trend for children and teenagers to have milk and bread with some very sweet spread that's all artificial. The bread is always white and not nutritious. Some only have a glass of milk, and then fill themselves up at breaks with sugary drinks and sweet and salty snacks or chips.

A lot of fat children are a result, also a rise in diabetes and other problems. But the majority still eat normal Thai food, available on every street corner and everywhere. (I can't begin to describe to you how much food is available.) Children will eat carbohydrates, protein, vegetables. They will also have cut fruit for snacks—like pineapple, rose apple, guava, apples, melons, and whatever else is available. With food they will drink water, or more likely some awful sweet iced drink (green or red!), sweet iced tea, Coke, Sprite, etc. Nothing with low sugar.

Saudi Arabia: A friend who grew up in Saudi Arabia told me:

The kids I have seen in Saudi seem to get excited about pretty much the same things that kids anywhere else do (i.e., fries, pizza, burgers, and various other fast foods). Of course, the "fast foods" in Arabia also include such things as Man-a'eesh (za'tar spice and bread) and various forms of cheese, meat, spinach, yoghurt pastries that are made in a very similar fashion to pizzas. Sandwiches such as falafels and shawarmas also are considered fast food. Having said that, I think it is safe to say that the majority of restaurants in Saudi do not have a specific kids' menu.

As for behavior in restaurants, parents there seem to be less concerned with what the kids are doing and would generally tend to leave them to roam around, especially if they are boys. However, you have to remember that in Saudi, the "family" section of the restaurant is physically separated from the "singles" side. Also, the more strict families tend to sit in cubicles that are totally enclosed so that the women are not seen by strangers. As such, if the kids do roam out of the cubicles, it is usually the men, the maids, or the older children that [who] to chase after them.

Mexico: Our neighbor Jorge, who grew up in Mexico, pointed out that the kids' dining-out experience is usually reserved for the elite. When his family's house-keeper was taken to a Kentucky Fried Chicken (established in Mexico in the late 1960s), she revered this as a "once in a lifetime experience." McDonald's, which has been in Mexico since 1985 but has surpassed KFC in popularity, is a convenient choice for "yuppies' kids," and after the passing of the North American Free Trade Agreement, there has been a noticeable spike in food and drinks imported from the United States. So, in many respects, they are eating what we are eating, but what we consider "Mexican food" varies significantly between our two countries. For example, the cheese and sour cream we see on Mexican food is not common there. Comfort food might be chicken soup, but theirs is made with what he considers "real chicken," including the feet and neck—nothing is wasted.

For the most part, work during the week is hard work and so the days of rest are taken seriously, too. As a reflection of this fact, weekend meals are distinct from weekday meals and might include an entire goat cooked in an in-ground oven, and *tamales,* packets of corn dough with a savory or sweet filling, typically wrapped in corn husks or banana leaves. Fast food for most Mexicans is equated with the homemade foods of the street cart vendors. In the case of all these traditional Mexican foods, there is no food particular to children. "Kids eat what adults eat, but in smaller portions." For those who can afford modern restaurants, it is not uncommon to find a special play area for children. They are usually accompanied by a nanny there, but parents also send off the children to play in an area even if the families can't see them, so the adults can enjoy a peaceful meal—their safety is not questioned.

DON'T AVOID THE CHOPSTICKS

Nothing says world citizen like kids who are comfortable eating with chopsticks. To get started, parents might wrap a rubber band around two sticks for their kids. The back-and-forth tension from the rubber band helps simulate the up-and-down action of sticks properly held and avoids beginners' frustration. Discourage "spearing" of food with chopsticks as this is considered rude in all Asian cultures. Here's how to hold chopsticks:

First, hold the upper chopstick like a pencil, about one-third of the way from its top.

Next, place the second chopstick against your ring finger (or middle finger—whichever is more comfortable), holding it with the base of the thumb. It should be pointing the same way as the first chopstick.

Move the upper chopstick with your thumb, index, and middle fingers. Don't move the lower chopstick. Grab food between the lower and upper chopsticks. Get the hang of it by moving the top chopstick up and down several times while keeping the lower one still—before you pick up the food. You can start by holding the middle sections of the chopsticks for easier handling, and eventually move up your hands to about one-third from the top, for maximum leverage.

For preschoolers, a story of using chopsticks (and another set of instructions on how-to) is found in *Cleversticks* by Bernard Ashley. Along with practicing your chopstick use while waiting for your food at a Chinese restaurant, can you and your kids find out which animal corresponds to the years you were born? This is often as easy to learn as looking down at the red disposable placemat at your place setting in the neighborhood Chinese restaurant, many of which list Chinese zodiac signs and corresponding years. Among many Asian cultures, knowing if you are a horse or a rat or a rooster is as basic as many Americans remembering if they are a Libra or a Pisces or a Capricorn. You don't have to attribute your personality traits to your zodiac, but it can serve as a fun icebreaker.

SPICE UP THANKSGIVING WITH A MULTICULTURAL MENU

Thanksgiving is one of the great unifiers of Americans—from those whose ancestors arrived on the *Mayflower,* to modern, first- and second-generation immigrants. Whatever their beliefs, few Americans shun the practice of starting a four-day weekend (if they don't work in retail) to join family and friends around the table for a big meal and invoke their gratitude. When I was growing up, part of Thanksgiving's appeal was in the fact that it was one of the few meals prepared by my mother that incorporated totally American recipes, from green bean casserole with French-fried onions to pumpkin pie, and no Persian rice, thus helping us feel truly American. For many others, the meal's appeal is in the merging of home culture with a new American tradition.

My friend Rohini Pande grew up in New Delhi, and her husband Michael Gordy is a Jewish New Yorker. Their Thanksgiving meal is infused with Indian spices and cooking methods that they apply to the traditional fare. From the slow-cooked curried turkey to the basmati with cranberry and dried red chili peppers, turmeric- and five-spice-tinted sweet potato soup, and stir-fried green beans with mustard seeds and coconut, their now-traditional menu has Rohini's family coming all the way from India to join the fun, and their friends all over the country getting ideas for adapting their Thanksgiving meals with these recipes.

Kathleen and Chakib Bouhdary, an English and Moroccan couple who are raising their three boys in Pennsylvania, spent a Thanksgiving on holiday visiting family in Morocco. The in-laws knew this meal was important to the children, so they went to great lengths to prepare an "American Thanksgiving" dinner. As Kathleen told me: "They were kind enough to prepare turkey for us on Thursday, but it was rather different for the boys eating it off a centrally served single plate and ripping the meat off with their hands!"

You don't have to go to such lengths to put a new spin on Thanksgiving, but you could look to your cultural heritage, or that of a visiting friend's, or a favorite ethnic food style. Start slowly by incorporating a new spice or herb, or add a different side dish. And don't forget variations on leftovers. Turkey enchiladas, green bean and rice pilaf, dumplings, and piroshkis make the next day's meal almost as exciting as traditional Thanksgiving. A few of these recipes can be found at www.growingupglobal.net.

Another way to add meaning to your Thanksgiving is to invite a few foreign students from a local college or exchange students to your celebration. My family had two Chinese students over last Thanksgiving, spurring our children to think more about the traditions we had when explaining them, and learning about the home customs of our trendy Chinese guests. Our friends Dick and Carolyn Veith started inviting students living at International House of Philadelphia to their home for Thanksgiving over thirty years ago, and remain friends with most of their guests. When planning foreign vacations—from Norway to Chile—the Veiths have made a point of visiting the students they had formerly hosted; they might even stay at their homes. The Veiths's own children, now adults, grew up with international students as part of their family experience. Their spouses are from other countries and they raise their children biculturally.

DEDICATE YOUR WEEKEND TO "TRAVEL" TO A NEW CONTINENT OR COUNTRY

If travel to a foreign country is beyond the means of your family's budget, try the next best thing: Map out a weekend in New York or Minneapolis or Miami or Seattle or Toronto or any number of North American cities within your geographic and financial reach—and give it a global spin, as if you were traveling to a new continent. It definitely takes discipline and creativity to make it work, but with these, you can focus on a singular cultural experience in a great North American city—and no vaccinations are necessary.

A great way to begin is to find an event or exhibit or limited-run movie that will "anchor" your weekend. For example, go to a website like Afropop.org, Eyefortalent.com, or Globalrhythm.net; you will find numerous world music concerts taking place in various cities. Pin down a date and a concert your family would like to attend, then the weekend can revolve around that culture or, more generally, that region of the world. If you know you would only like to go to a particular city, you can look up its arts events calendar, the online city guide, or simply Google something like "world music Chicago" (or whatever city you are interested in). Before you get too excited about a concert, make sure the venue will allow children. International ensembles often have to play at bars or clubs (due to the limited size of their audiences) that won't let in anyone under eighteen or twenty-one. If it looks like the group you want to see is playing at one of these venues, look up the band's own website to see if there might be alternate dates or locations that welcome families. Sometimes they might also be at the local art museum, botanical garden, or an ethnic restaurant on one of the afternoons of the same weekend as the concert. If you see they have only one performance for the weekend at an adults-only locale, and it's still over a month before the date, you could try emailing the band or their agent to ask if they'd consider performing in a particular family-friendly place like a café or community center. What have you got to lose?!

Eating is a highlight of many families' travels, so this is the next anchor in your "continent in a weekend." It doesn't have to be expensive or formal to be good. For example, if you are going to a concert given by a Senegalese or Malian Kora player, then find a West African restaurant for your lunch or dinner that day. Crisscross the continent with another memorable meal, possibly from North Africa (e.g., Moroccan or Tunisian food) or Ethiopia. Both of these cuisine styles have become firmly established in many American cities. In addition to a musical event, you could visit the natural history museum to delve into some of the ancient civilizations and the environment from that part of the world. You also could find out what sort of relevant collection the art museum in that city offers.

And don't forget shopping. If there is a sizable ethnic community, take some time to walk in the neighborhoods (usually also the same place where the restaurants are located). Step into their shops—for food supplies, household items, gifts, traditional clothing, baked treats, a long-distance phone card, anything. This might prove more interesting than museums to some, and you can come away from the weekend with reasonably priced souvenirs and goodies. Other weekends could revolve around Andean and Mayan cultures, the Middle East or Southeast Asia—check the city's yellow pages. You could devise themes, depending on the ages and interests of your family—anything from your heritage to locations in literature that you love or the origin of some of your favorite foods. Themes can be quirky, too, like Bollywood (Indian) movies, former Communist countries, or the countries where your outfits were made (read the labels to decide your "route"). This might be a good time to look up old friends. Chances are, wherever you went to school you have friends from a different ethnic background than you. Reconnecting old friends and their "new" families with yours can help you see their city from their cultural perspective.

If you would like to undertake a trip like this with younger children, look for venues that host international children's performers, or better, international children's festivals. For example, the annual Philadelphia International Children's Festival at the University of Pennsylvania brings together some of the best children's performers in the world, all in one weekend. A walk on Penn's campus to the Museum of Archeology and Anthropology, followed by a meal at a nearby restaurant (choose from Vietnamese, West African, Ethiopian, Pakistani, Turkish, Japanese, Persian, Central American, Russian, Thai, Irish, Afghani, Brazilian, and many more) will keep you busy. Numerous cities, ranging from Seattle to Hampton, Virginia, and just about every major town in Canada also organize quality international children's festivals.

Don't overlook the ethnic offerings in your own backyard. Google "ethnic restaurants in . . . (your city or state)." I tried this for countless locations, large and small, with great results. It confirmed that not only is Chinese food ubiquitous, but it seems that depending on your region, so is Thai and Vietnamese, and in some cases, Lebanese and Mexican. (And I'm not even counting Italian, which is almost considered "American" food these days.)

For example, the website Indyethnicfood.com highlights the cultural diversity in and around Indianapolis through its restaurant offerings. While the index includes big all-American chains like Olive Garden (filed under "Italian") and Longhorse Steak House ("Texan"), it excludes Taco Bell and does have listings under Afghan, Vietnamese, and many Middle Eastern cuisines. There's also a Recipe tab on the site under Global Kitchen with recipes from cultures ranging from Amish to Zimbabwean.

If you're ready to explore New York, Joseph Berger, the *New York Times* columnist, has written *The World in a City: Traveling the Globe Through the Neighborhoods of the New New York*. In this part travelogue, part story of immigration to what is arguably America's (and possibly the world's) greatest city, Berger discovers that the world can be found in New York City, and "for the price of a subway ride, you can visit Ghana, the Philippines, Ecuador, Uzbekistan, and Bangladesh." The New York shown by Berger has been transformed by the sheer numbers and diversity of its ethnic population, who help spice up the life of a vibrant city and its boroughs. If Arab culture fascinates or baffles you, he guides you through the Queens neighborhood of Astoria where you can snack on baklava, drink dark Turkish/Arabic coffees, and watch some Al Jazeera TV in a local bakery. And just a few blocks away, you can take in Brazilian mango juice or meaty barbecues and even go bikini shopping. The longer established Greek community can be found nearby, with a visit to an orthodox church, a yogurt shop, or a theater.

On this type of trip you can contrast the way various cultures commingle. In some parts of the city they live side-by-side, with little blending, and in others, a true melting pot prevails. Both are experiences worth seeing for yourself. Berger reinforces the point made from 2005 U.S. Census data: The immigration trends experienced in New York are being repeated in record numbers in other major cities, and, significantly, in America's heartland—from South Dakota to southern Georgia, Indiana, and Iowa. So, you can take a virtual trip to the Far East by going to New York City, but also to St. Paul, Minnesota, and Fremont, California.

CHICKEN SOUP—AND MORE—FOR THE SOUL AND THE BODY: FOODS THAT HEAL

Chicken soup, the now classic healing food from Eastern European Jewish heritage, has become a ubiquitous and universal remedy using food. Science still hasn't found a better cure for the common cold. Friends have reported to me how important the broth has been to everything from recovery after childbirth to feeding cancer patients in the midst of chemotherapy. With so much wisdom passed among generations around the world, I wanted to know what other remedies stemmed from the kitchen, from wise grandmothers all over the globe. Here are a few sent to me (see p. 117).

Another form of "kitchen wisdom" I thought was exclusively from my own Persian heritage is the categorization of foods into hot-cold classification. It turns out this system is found in the cultural wisdom in various parts of Central and South America, India, China, and Arab cultures. The idea is that each food has certain characteristics (e.g., pineapple is "hot" and cucumber is "cold"). A balanced blend of hot and cold needs to be present in the diet for the body and mind to achieve health and harmony. My trusted Persian cookbook, Najmieh Batmanglij's *New Food of Life* describes this system[6] as do many anthropological studies. If you search "hot cold food classification" online you'll find thousands of references to diverse cultures. As our Western thinking becomes more influenced by the wis-

PROBLEM	FOOD SOLUTION	COUNTRY OF ORIGIN
Bruises	Shell a boiled egg, put inside a thin cloth, break it into chunks, rub while it's in the cloth, onto the bruise.	China
Bruises	Similar to the hard-boiled egg above, but with pieces of red meat.	Korea
Bruises	Rub enough turmeric powder on the bruise to cover it completely.	India
Colds, flu	Boil plenty of ginger and green onion roots in water, drink as a hot tea.	China
Colds, flu, asthma, anything else respiratory	Cut garlic cloves into a mug of whole milk, let it sit in the fridge overnight, strain, drink the liquid in the morning.	Bolivia
Coughing, asthma	Boil a stick of cinnamon, thyme, lime, three heads of garlic, and half a purple onion in water, sweeten with honey after it boils for about half an hour.	Mexico
Dandruff	Mix two parts olive oil with one part fresh lime juice, rub on the scalp, cover head with an old scarf overnight, wash off in the morning.	United Arab Emirates
Diarrhea	Boil water and rice until water is just white, strain out the rice and drink the white water hot every half hour until the diarrhea subsides.	Mongolia
Diarrhea	Rice soup—boil together water and rice, with lemon juice.	Cyprus
Diarrhea and vomiting	BRAT diet: bananas, rice, applesauce, toast	North America
Sore throat or strep throat	Hot milk with butter, baking soda, and honey	Russia
Underarm odor and perspiration	Rub fresh lime and its juice in armpits.	Paraguay
Underarm odor and perspiration	Make a paste of baking soda and a little water to rub under armpits.	Italy
Upset stomach	Stir dried dill into soft-cooked rice and serve with plain yogurt on the side.	Iran

dom of Eastern or traditional cultures, we can feel more confident applying some ancient wisdom to our modern methods, for a merging of the best the world has to offer, and ultimately, for attaining optimal well-being.

————

If you are what you eat, then you also can eat your way to becoming a "global" person. Food can serve as a unifier on so many fronts: Invite a friend to join your family for a meal, taste a culture's variations on your favorite foods, or even learn from your friends' experiences at McDonald's in multiple countries. Kids everywhere might adore Happy Meals, but they are also capable of trying and enjoying a range of foods—and their parents' attitude toward unusual dishes plays an important part in their acceptance of new foods. As a family, the new foods you try together form an adventure right at home. There are so many picture books, chapter books, and coffee-table books that introduce the way people eat; these open a window to diverse ways of life. These can encourage more adventurous eating while also showing the common bonds humanity shares.

Are there certain types of foods or cultures or presentations of the food that most appeal to you? How do the members of your household vary in their views of what attracts them? To kick-start your world travels on a budget, you can plan creative day or weekend trips around the theme of a culture of interest, with food—at new types of restaurants as well as from ethnic grocery stores—as a highlight. Closer to home, look for ethnic shops in your community; vary the types of restaurants you eat at; ask for chopsticks at the Chinese, Japanese, Vietnamese, Thai, Malaysian—whatever Asian—restaurant and introduce a new dish each time, to ease your family into this lifelong adventure. In short, look around at all the possibilities food offers for opening doors to the big, small world.

RESOURCE BOOKS CITED IN CHAPTER 5—THAT YOU MAY FIND HELPFUL, TOO

Hungry Planet, Peter Menzel and Faith D'Aluisio (Berkeley, CA: Ten Speed Press, 2005) and *Material World: A Global Family Portrait.* (San Francisco: Sierra Club Books, 1994).

Let's Eat! What Children Eat Around the World, Beatrice Holliyer (New York: Henry Holt and Company, in association with Oxfam, 2004).

The Omnivore's Dilemma: A Natural History of Four Foods and *In Defense of Food: An Eater's Manifesto,* Michael Pollan (New York: Penguin, 2006 and 2008).

Fanny At Chez Panisse: A Child's Restaurant Adventures with 46 Recipes, Alice Waters with Bob Carrau and Patricia Curtain (New York: Harper Collins, 1992).

Bread, Bread Bread, Ann Morris, photographs by Ken Heyman (New York: Lothrop, Lee & Shepard Books, 1989).

Everybody Bakes Bread, Norah Dooley, illustrated by Peter J. Thornton (Minneapolis, Carolrhoda Books, Inc., 1996).

Loaves of Fun: A History of Bread with Activities and Recipes from Around the World, Elizabeth M. Harbison, illustrated by John Harbison (Chicago: Chicago Review Press, Inc., 1997).

Rice Is Life, Rita Golden Gelman, paintings by Yangsook Choi (New York: Henry Holt and Company, 2000).

The Sacred Harvest: Ojibway Wild Rice Gathering, Gordon Regguinti, illustrated and photographed by Dale Kakkak (Minnesota: Lerner Publishing Group, 1992).

First Book of Sushi, Hola! Jalapeno, and *Yum Yum Dim Sum,* Amy Wilson Sanger (Berkeley CA: Tricycle Press 2001, 2002, and 2003).

Pretend Soup and Other Real Recipes: A Cookbook for Pre-Schoolers and Up and *Salad People and More Real Recipes: A New Cookbook for Pre-Schoolers and Up,* Mollie Katzen (Berkeley CA: Tricycle Press, 1994 and 2005).

The Kids' Multicultural Cookbook, Deanna Cook (Vermont: Williamson Publishing Company, 1995).

Kids Around the World Cook! Arlette M. Braman (New York: John Wiley & Sons, 2000).

The Kids Around the World Cookbook, Deri Roberts (New York: Larousse, 1994).

Easy Menu Ethnic Cookbooks series, various authors (Minneapolis: Lerner Publications, 1991–2004).

Flatbreads and Flavors: A Baker's Atlas; Seductions of Rice; HomeBaking: The Artful Mix of Flour and Tradition Around the World; Hot, Sour, Salty, Sweet, Jeffrey Alford and Naomi Duguid (New York: William Morrow & Co., various years, beginning 1995).

If the World Were a Village, David Smith (Toronto: Kids Can Press, 2002).

Cleversticks, Bernard Ashley (author), Derek Brazell (illustrator) (New York: Dragonfly Books, 1991).

The World in a City: Traveling the Globe Through the Neighborhoods of the New New York, Joseph Berger (New York: Ballantine Books, 2007).

New Food of Life: Ancient Persian and Modern Iranian Cooking and Ceremonies, Najmieh Batmanglij (Washington, DC: Mage Publishers, 1996).

ADDITIONAL RESOURCE BOOKS RELATED TO CHAPTER 5

Mama Panya's Pancakes, Julia Cairns (Cambridge, MA: Barefoot Books, 2006).

Also, see Barefoot Books' "Travel the World" selections for kids through age ten.

Chapter 6

What Do They Believe?

I love you when you bow in your mosque, kneel in your temple,
pray in your church. For you and I are sons
of one religion, and it's the spirit.

KAHLIL GIBRAN

Learning about the world's religions through the baggage-free lens of our children and from diverse people in our home communities offers a natural way to explore gently the positive aspects of world religions. To raise children who truly feel at home in the world calls for literacy in the world's spiritual teachings. Gaining such literacy might start as an intellectual exercise about tolerance, but ultimately can be motivated by something more basic and profound—appreciation and love.

I was lucky to grow up in a home where traditions and beliefs from Judaism, Islam, Christianity, and other faiths were naturally woven into the fabric of our lives, and rich friendships with people from each of these backgrounds, as well as Hindus, Buddhists, Baha'is, and agnostics comprised our social interactions. As a child I didn't think it was unusual. I didn't know otherwise.

One generation in our family decided to break from past, divisive patterns. They were not highly educated or well-traveled, but they made a conscious effort to live their ideals, thus benefitting subsequent generations. Looking back, I consider all this a great gift from my grandparents and parents, and more, a liberation—to be free from the idea that I was superior based on the God I worshipped, and to be comfortable asking questions about what was important to various people.

Gaining a broad worldview can be serious business, and if people are willing to strap bombs on themselves over their beliefs, or look someone in the eye and tell them they are "going to Hell," then the topic of religion cannot be avoided. America's Founding Fathers enshrined a vision that still seems progressive today: *E Pluribus Unum*—"out of many, one"—and a unique model for the world, a nation free from the tyranny of any single religion. Their great patriotism is at the same time a global vision of inclusive ideals.

RELIGION—THE LAST HOLDOUT

The twentieth century set the stage for social and scientific forces that hold the promise of bringing together the human race. Biological and genetic discoveries confirm our oneness, communications and commerce defy national boundaries, and social breakthroughs ranging from the implosion of apartheid and legalized racism along with the inclusion of women into so many spheres of influence—each testify to an irreversible process transforming human relationships. Organized religion remains the last holdout. Ironically, its very reason for being is the cause of brotherhood and peace.

Despite the long record of suffering and divisiveness caused in the name of religion, forward-thinking people still might find hope in it. Religion, or better said, faith, reaches to the roots of motivation, awakening "the capacities to love, to forgive, to create, to dare greatly, to overcome prejudice, to sacrifice for the common good, and to discipline the impulses of animal instinct."[1] Furthermore, when societies have tried to organize in a spiritual vacuum, the results have been disastrous.

Armed with this seemingly contradictory scenario, what's a globally minded parent to do? The simplest route may be to embrace humanism, renouncing whatever provokes such divisiveness, and many wonderful, worldly people have done this. The harder approach—but, I believe, the ultimately satisfying, edifying, and uniting approach—is to reach out to find the essence of what has inspired the human race for millennia and share this with our children. When you set aside the agenda-driven opinions of powerful political and religious leaders, note that the vast majority of believers do not subscribe to the fanaticism of the few. The underlying message of the original inspiration—in the Quran, the Bhagavad-Gita, the Torah, the Bible, and other holy books, as well as the positive contributions each one has made to society—evokes a different, more hopeful story. The essence of these great texts is like a light that has been obscured by centuries of personal interpretations and power struggles.

Metaphors that help teach how to deal with the differences: Metaphors or analogies from familiar concepts help to simplify the understanding of why there are so many religions and how anyone can make sense of them. Many of these were first elucidated by the prophets, great sages, or religious scholars who devoted their lives to studying or practicing the teachings of the world's great faiths.

The aim is not to boil them down to a meaningless broth or to simplify complexities into black-and-white, but to put differences into a context, acknowledge the distinctions, and be able to live with variations in thought and interpretation. Metaphors using nature and familiar concepts are as useful for helping children as they are for lifelong seekers of truth.

A little naïveté goes a long way.

Adults often pine for their days as children, when they saw the world in simpler terms. When looking at the teachings of new/other religions, you might need to tap into that old innocence. If you go to too many discussion boards, blogs, and anger-filled websites, you will find plenty of cynicism, from critiques on doctrinal and administrative matters to propaganda from extremists—and some of this could be valid. The alternate approach here is to look at the faiths for the spiritual essence they convey. If your aim is to impart some knowledge and benefit to your children, leave the arguments and negativity aside. This might go against your rational mind. It doesn't have to. Find the goodness, emphasize that, and recognize that you don't have to swallow the entire package including rituals, dogma, and divisions. Think of your search like the Eastern legend of the lotus flower. The lotus flower rises from deep, muddy water, until finally, a thing of beauty emerges, aspiring to the light.

The fingers of one hand: Bede Griffiths, a Christian who spent much of his life in India, explained that the various religious traditions are like the fingers of one hand. Each one is distinct, but they trace their source to the same palm.[2] Looking at them superficially, each finger looks different, but they come together at a deeper place. The hand functions well when the fingers work alongside one another toward a unified goal, but remain distinct.

Lamps with different lampshades: I grew up as a young Baha'i child learning that the various faiths can be thought of as lamps that have guided or enlightened humanity. Each lamp might have a different shade, but its core—the light inside—confers its power and usefulness. Young children (and older, artistic ones) can appreciate this concept by decorating a basic lampshade. Adornments can range from simple to messy to elaborate, but the light that goes inside will be the same for each. Universally, metaphors of light and fire and flame (like an eternal flame) permeate sacred scriptures.

A stained-glass window—like a beautiful mosaic: In his book *The Illustrated World's Religions,* scholar Huston Smith "likens religions to stained-glass windows that refract sunlight in different shapes and colors." This analogy allows for significant differences between religions without pronouncing on their relative worth.[3] Each of the faiths makes up a piece of a beautiful mosaic, each contributing some aspect of a bigger picture that sheds light on its recipient or on the world. Each piece is beautiful, and when taken together, they complete a full image.

A handwoven rug or tapestry: Huston Smith also employs the analogy that "It is as if life were a great tapestry which we face from its wrong side. This gives it the appearance of a maze of knots and threads that look chaotic." The wisdom traditions, or faiths, help "infer from the hindside of life's tapestry its frontal design. As the beauty and harmony of the design derives from the way its parts intervene, the design confers on those parts a significance they are denied in isolation."[4] To judge the quality and the workmanship of a handwoven rug, it must be looked at from the back side. Take your children to a rug store or a place selling tapestries to get a sense of the "backside" of the weave. Compare the quality of different reverse sides, feel the knots, compare the back to the side that is to be displayed, notice the view when only looking closely at the side with knots versus taking a step back to see the rows in their entirety—the bigger picture. If all we knew of life was the side with the knots and threads, we would miss out on some of the awe and wonder and beauty the world has to offer.

The sun's light, which shines on all: Analogies to the light of the sun are used throughout the world's religions. In one example, God is like the sun, which gives heat and light and life, and which no human being can ever fully comprehend or approach. You can explain to your child that each day the sun rises in a slightly different spot and its qualities and rays are slightly different from the day before. In spite of changing seasons and the movement of the sun on the horizon, we know there is one sun, and this sun gives us physical life. Similarly, there is One Perfect Source, God, even though different reflections of God's qualities have come to earth to educate us regarding His teachings and qualities. These various Rays of God's love have come to us at different times and with different names, like Buddha or Jesus, but each of them reflects an aspect of the Love of God and His qualities. Their "light" teaches us about a greater power, and about the spiritual qualities we need to reflect that power. The different manifestations of light do not conflict or contradict one another, and the recipient of the benefits of the light does not need to choose between which day's light is better.

A symphony or jazz orchestra that makes music together: When talking about unity in diversity in any form—between people from different ethnic, racial, political, economic, or faith backgrounds—the metaphor of making music as a symphony can be grasped by children of all ages. One instrument played on its own is beautiful, but when many are joined together, working in harmony while not all hitting the same notes, a new and beautiful sound is created. Beyond the symphonic melodies, the metaphor of jazz, where musicians must keep their ear attuned to the sounds created by the other players, might be even more apt.[5] Jazz musicians are engaged in an interactive process of creating, listening to one another, and playing their music simultaneously; one piece is never played exactly the same way twice; and the resulting sound might take a little getting used to when one is first exposed to the genre. Play a symphony or jazz CD while discussing this topic with your children, and as you're listening, point out complexities of the music and some of the places that may sound harmonious, discordant, daring, sensitive, conflicting, or triumphant—this is like the process of diverse people allowing one another to share their true beliefs.

You also can bring this metaphor to light by exploring various genres of faith-inspired music together, from gospel and Christian rock (perhaps in Spanish!), to the Jewish–reggae–hip hop of Matisyahu, and many more. Search for Muslim- or Buddhist- or "whatever-inspired music" online.

THE BUILDING BLOCKS ARE THE SAME

When children are raised in an atmosphere that consciously encourages knowledge and friendship across diverse perspectives, they will benefit thoroughly—at school, work, and in personal relationships—while strengthening the development of their own identity. I have seen one response to the question of "Who am I and why am I here?" is to have some appreciation of "Who are they and why do they think they are here?" Realizing that the search for answers to these questions is universal, one might feel less alone and out of place, and perhaps gain wisdom and insight from fresh sources.

The idea that children should be exposed to the teachings of diverse faiths is a new phenomenon, begun only in the past century, when modern communications and multicultural communities created an imperative to understand one another's beliefs. In recent years Australian officials recognized this issue can't be ignored to build a harmonious multicultural society: Public schools offer a world religions curriculum taught by representatives of diverse faiths as part of the day's lessons. To help your children make sense of the world's religions, start by talking about these common principles:

• *A common social ethic:* Religions share a moral code or laws for their faithful, and this has been synthesized by author Huston Smith as: "avoid murder, thievery,

What kind of Christian?

Catholic, Baptist, Presbyterian, Mormon, Seventh-Day Adventist, Orthodox, Methodist, Quaker, Coptic, Lutheran, Anglican, Christian Scientist, Pentecostal, Evangelical, or another denomination? Members of one of the faiths on this list may not accept another as a true Christian, whereas those followers may feel sincerely devout. The *World Christian Encyclopedia* cites over thirty thousand Christian groupings active in the world.

For children, these divisions could be particularly confusing. You can explain that as Christianity has grown into the world's largest religion, followed by Islam, followers have had different ideas about how to interpret the Bible. This results in different rules and rituals, but the basic core is the same. Compare some of the practical differences among three churches near your home. You can also contrast these with Christian worship in Greece or Central America or East Africa. (Find out about them online, ask a friend from that country, or ask a local church that might have a foreign church partner.)

Most major religions, from Judaism to Buddhism to Islam, contain multiple branches, arising from various interpretations of holy texts.

lying and adultery." These may seem obvious, but the fact that there is agreement here points the way to a world ethic of what is right and wrong. And while the portrayal of a forgiving Lord is prevalent, the cause of justice—manifested in various forms—is universally revered.

- *Universal virtues and being a "good" person:* The world's religions agree on the general outline of what makes a "good" person, based on universal virtues. Smith summarizes these into three categories: "humility, charity and veracity."[6] Along with virtues like honesty, respect, gratitude, patience, self-control, and kindness, the most basic virtues are embodied in the Golden Rule, summarized in Chapter 1. If the family of man embodied this one principle, imagine the world that could result. Children as young as three or four appreciate the Golden Rule, like a shorthand reminder of proper behavior that all share.

- *The search for answers to mystical questions is a universal human experience.* The great founders of the world's religions, including Jesus and Buddha, experienced intense anguish in their quest for truth, identity, and acceptance. Read their life stories with your children to reveal the spiritual struggle that all have had to endure and overcome. In an age when so much is handed to privileged children, these lessons demonstrate that obvious answers are rare, and life is really about overcoming multiple struggles, not ease and comfort.

- *A Great Spirit moves all creation and is the source of love.* While this Spirit is unknowable and infinite, sages might spend their entire lives in search or devotion to it. It (He/She) is called by various names, including Yahweh, Ahura Mazda, God, Allah, T'ien, Tao, Nam, Brahmin, or Nirvana, and It breathes life into us and is behind the mysteries of the universe that inspire awe, humility, gratitude, beauty, and truth. For the Abrahamic religions—Judaism, Christianity, Islam, and the Baha'i Faith, as well as Zoroastrianism and Sikhism—this force is One God. In Hinduism, Buddhism, Jainism, some Native American, earth-based and other belief systems, this is the spirit of a Divine Unity, and specific attributes are embodied through various gods. Each of those gods reflects one element of the Perfections that monotheists see embodied in One Creator, and for others, may be more similar to the individual saints. All teach that humanity was created in the image of the Lord, which is perfect, so mankind is uniquely ennobled and empowered by this potential for getting closer and closer to Perfection.

- *Humans strive to commune with the Divine through prayer and meditation.* The form of the prayer varies, from group prayer in a specified location to the privacy of one's own room, from chanting mantras to silence to recitation of a prescribed text or verse or series of names or words or an experience with nature, but the goal is the same.

- *There is a world beyond this world.* The world of the spirit is eternal, and in spite of its mysteries, humans strive to gain perfection in order to prepare themselves for it. The material world perishes; materialism feeds the ego and competes with spiritual growth.

- *An expectation of the fulfillment of the Spirit or a messianic age, preceded by a period of calamities and followed by a form of "heaven on earth" and great peace.* Mus-

What is Zoroastrianism?

It's a monotheistic religion founded in Persia around 6000 B.C. It teaches there is One Creator, which is Eternal, Pure, and True, symbolized by fire. At the time of Christ's birth, the Zoroastrian faith had wide influence, and particularly is thought to have strongly impacted the beliefs and practice of the Abrahamic religions. The Magi, or the three Wise Men, who visited the baby Jesus were Zoroastrians. When Islam conquered the region, Zoroastrian numbers dwindled dramatically and many migrated east, to India. Today, there are fewer than 200,000 in the world, the biggest concentration in India. These are the Parsi, distinguished for their achievements in education and business.

lims look forward to the coming of the Qa'im or Mihdi; Christians await the Second Coming of Christ; Jews, the Lord of Hosts; Hindus, the tenth Avatar, known as Kalki or Vishnu Yasha; Buddhists, the Buddha Maitreya; and Native Americans from Alaska to the tip of South America have various names for a similar spiritual renewal or expectation.

- Despite all the wars that have been waged over religion, ultimately *each seeks to create lasting brotherhood and peace.* Share with your children what the actual scriptures say:

  ◦ *Judaism:* "Strengthen the bonds of friendship and fellowship among the inhabitants of all the lands. Plant virtue in every soul and may the love of Thy name hallow every heart." (Jewish tradition, *The Union Prayerbook*)

  ◦ *Hinduism:* "Whoever sees all beings in himself and himself in all beings does not, by virtue of such realization, hate anyone. . . . When, to that wise sage, all beings are realized as existing in his own self, then what illusion, what sorrow, can afflict him, perceiving as he does the Unity?" (*Isa Upanishads*)

  ◦ *Zoroastrianism:* "The best way to worship God is to ease the distress of the times and to improve the condition of humanity. This is true religion; to cleanse oneself with pure thoughts, pure words, and pure deeds. (Zoroaster, *The Zend-Avesta*)

  ◦ *Buddhism:* When the mind becomes tranquilized and concentrated into perfect unity, then all things will be seen, not in their separateness, but in their unity wherein there is no place for evil passions to enter, and which is in full conformity with the mysterious and indescribable purity of Nirvana. (From *The Surangama Sutra*-Sanskrit Sources)

  ◦ *Christianity:* "Blessed are the peacemakers; for they shall be called the children of God." (Matthew 5:9)

  ◦ *Native American:* "The sacred hoop of any nation is but one of many that together make the great circle of creation. In the center grows a mighty flowering tree of life sheltering all the children of one mother and one father. All life is holy." (From the wisdom of Black Elk, Chief Seattle)

  ◦ *Taoism:* "Affirm everyone and everything. Freely extend your goodwill and virtue in every direction, regardless of circumstances. Embrace all things as part of the Harmonious Oneness, and then you will begin to perceive it." (Lao Tzu)

  ◦ *Islam:* "All of God's creatures are His family. He is most beloved of God who does real good to the members of God's family." (Muhammad, *The Holy Quran*)

  ◦ *Baha'i Faith:* "Ye are the fruits of one tree, and the leaves of one branch. Deal ye one with another with the utmost love and harmony, with friendliness and fellowship. . . . So powerful is the light of unity that it can illuminate the whole earth." (Baha'u'llah, *Gleanings from the Writings of Baha'u'llah*)

> ## Muhammad, in the Quran, Sura 11:130, affirms the divinity of the Jewish prophets and Jesus.
>
> "We believe in One God, and that which hath been sent down to us, and that which hath been sent down to Abraham and Ishmael and Isaac and Jacob and the tribes; and that which hath been given to Moses and to Jesus, and that which was given to the prophets from their Lord. No difference do we make between any of them."

These quotations help to expose young people to various belief systems based on their own merits and not on someone else's interpretation. There's much talk about the religious teachings, why not go to the source?

WHERE TO TURN WHEN YOU WANT TO LEARN MORE

With contact between members of various faiths increasing daily, learn what they teach through compilations of basic religious teachings, for children and for adults. Originally, I was going to include a brief summary—the elevator speech—of what each of the major faiths taught. But the more I tried to compress, the more profound ideas seemed to ooze out of the neat package I was trying to stuff each faith into. As parents, we don't have to explain everything to our children in a tidy summary, either. The answer to some questions can be "I don't know," and to others, "What do you think about that?" or "I see it differently." Take your responsibility to provide spiritual education to your children seriously. They will appreciate the road map you've given, but will need to take their own journey. Some good starting points for learning about and experiencing various faiths include *The Kids Book of World Religions* by Jennifer Glossop and *A Faith Like Mine: A Celebration of the World's Religions Through the Eyes of Children* by Laura Buller.

If you want to look up world religions with middle or high schoolers, see the Voice of Youth Advocates (VOYA) website (voya.com); under Booklists see "World Religions Resource List for Teens." These recommendations made by librarians from around the United States address interests of teens and adults.

If you're looking for more background targeted for yourself first, before you set out to enlighten the kids, try Huston Smith's *The Illustrated World's Religions: A Guide to Our Wisdom Traditions,* Stephen Prothero's *Religious Literacy: What Every American Needs to Know—And Doesn't,* and *Sourcebook of the World's Religions: An Interfaith Guide to Religion and Spirituality,* edited by Joel Beversluis. The approach in each of these books is quite different; so you have to see which one speaks to your information-gathering style: a scholar's wise summary of sweeping themes (Huston), essential need-to-know "facts" (Prothero), or excerpts from the actual writings, history, and various avenues of interfaith action (Beversluis) from multiple perspectives.

Two websites I find to be helpful are Beliefnet.com and the BBC's Religion and Ethics site, www.bbc.co.uk/religion. Beliefnet offers discussion forums, active worship opportunities, and regular updates; you just have to wade through some of the clutter of heavy advertising. The BBC's site offers news and information on faiths and issues in a clear format. Refdesk World Religion Resources provides a long list of links to just about every faith, philosophy, religious text, and movement on the Internet; it's at www.refdesk.com/factrel.html. For a quick reference to basic religious terms from a variety of traditions, go to religionstylebook.org, a guide for journalists.

Face-to-face is still best. There is no shortage of information sources for learning about world religions; but if you're seeking to find out about a new faith (or many faiths), try to speak with an active member or devout follower, as the first, best way to learn the teachings. When your children see that you are interested in learning about your friends' beliefs (not to convert them or judge them or to convert yourself), then you are sending a signal that this type of discussion, respectfully conducted, is entirely appropriate and possible.

My eldest daughter had numerous Muslim friends (from multiple countries) in middle school in Africa, where they fasted, prayed, and wore a head scarf to school. When I asked about where and how her classmates would perform their prayers she didn't know the answer. But the next day she was able to ask and learn directly from the girls. I began a respectful and open conversation with legitimate questions to my daughter, and she in turn drew on that experience for an honest exchange with her friends. A book or website could answer many questions, but the human dimension creates a different type of memory.

LEARNING FROM THE STORIES

In many countries, Bible stories are accepted as a basic building block of many educated people's knowledge. For the most part, these stories reflect the shared heritage of Christians, Jews, and Muslims, as the stories of Bible prophets are confirmed in all three religions' holy books. One Muslim-American mother told me, "My kids love the stories and movies about Moses and Joseph—they are their superheroes!" These stories are widely available from numerous publishers and in multiple forms; and don't miss an opportunity to hear them from a storyteller (this could be a rabbi, an imam, a nun, a grandmother, or on a CD).

A business strategy, a political position, and an SAT test might each include cases referring to the patience of Job, or the struggle between David and Goliath, or a Judas among us. But what if they might also include reference to the peace under the Bodhi tree or Khadija's entrepreneurship or the courage of the Letters of the Living or Ganesh's luck? Would these mean anything to you, or to your children? And more, could knowing them assist your life?

The lessons of these great stories, like learning about other beliefs, offer numerous life tools—well beyond the advantage of winning in the game show *Jeopardy!* Knowledge of the intense tests borne by Mary or Abraham or Ali or Siddhartha Gautama helps to make us stronger in the face of our own suffering. Children who learn of Jesus' or Abdul-Baha's acts of charity gain consciousness of an ethic of compassion and a vision for involvement with those less fortunate than themselves, from even the youngest age. Stories and examples from all the world's faiths work simultaneously to enlighten and connect believers from different traditions to universal life lessons. In my life if I felt I was dealt an injustice, remembering that a similar situation is found in ancient texts like the Bible or the Upanishads or even in Greek mythology helped me feel better—at least I wasn't alone.

The process of learning Bible stories and their equivalents from other faiths can be simple. Each tradition contains some basic myths and stories, and thanks to the surge worldwide in communications and publication, they are widely available. Here are a few good titles to begin with:

- *Sacred Myths: Stories of the World's Religions* by Marilyn McFarlane. This compilation for ages ten and up presents stories from Christianity, Judaism, Islam, Hinduism, Buddhism, Native American, and "Sacred Earth" traditions. This book specifically covers the larger religions, and there are numerous other titles juxtaposing mythologies of the world, including Greek, Roman, Egyptian, Mayan, and many others.

- Demi, the prolific author-illustrator, has produced reverent and beautiful picture books, appropriate for ages five and up: *Muhammad, Jesus, Mary, Buddha, The Legend of Lao Tzu and the Tao te Ching,* as well as *The Dalai Lama, Mother Theresa, Gandhi,* a story of Purim, and numerous other titles sharing folktales from various cultures.

- *Stories from Judaism:* DK Eyewitness Books' *Judaism,* like its books on other major religions and mythologies, is a good start. Well-known Bible stories—Adam and Eve, Noah, Abraham, Joseph, and so many others—are stories from the Hebrew Bible, known as the Old Testament to Christians. Also see *The Jewish Child's First Book of Why* (for preschoolers) and *Classic Bible Stories for Jewish Children,* both by Alfred Kolatch. Middle schoolers might enjoy *While Standing on One Foot: Puzzle Stories and Wisdom Tales from the Jewish Tradition* by Nina Jaffe and Steve Zeitlin or *God's Mailbox* and *Does God Have a Big Toe?* (with Oscar de Mejos) by Marc Gellman. Collections of Jewish folktales, especially *Stories for Children,* by the prolific Isaac Bashevis Singer, offer a sense of the rich Eastern European, Yiddish culture that has been passed down through generations. Also see *Next Year in Jerusalem: 2,000 Years of Jewish Stories,* retold by Howard Schwartz.

  As painful as it may be, reading stories from children's experiences in the Holocaust can be introduced to kids from around the ages of ten and up—getting a sense of this horrible chapter in world history adds an important dimension to a child's worldview and is not to be avoided, particularly since genocide continues in the world today. *The Devil's Arithmetic* by Jane Yolen is a good title on the Holocaust for ages twelve and up.

- *Stories from Christianity:* A Bible storybook can be found in millions of American homes and the market has responded with a dizzying array of specialized titles. There are so many compilations of Bible stories, you need to see for yourself which kind you prefer—from the classic Golden Books version, the early readers' best-selling *The Beginner's Bible: Timeless Children's Stories* from Zonderkidz, to manga-illustrated Bible stories, Princess editions, and teen stories. Whatever you do, don't let yourself get too overwhelmed to skip learning key Bible stories with your children, regardless of your system of beliefs.

- *Stories from Islam:* In addition to Demi's *Muhammad,* try Traditional Religious Tales' *Islamic Stories* and *Muslim Child: Understanding Islam through Stories and Poems, My Name Is Bilal,* and, for middle schoolers and up, delve into *Ayat Jamilah: Beautiful Signs: A Treasury of Islamic Wisdom for Children and Parents* by Sarah Conover. Despite the size and growth of Islam, there are relatively fewer child-friendly books on the subject; stories are often passed down orally.

Sects education: Sunni or Shiite?

If you follow the news, you've heard of "clashes between Sunni and Shiite," particularly in Iraq, but who are they, and what's the difference?

Most of the world's 1.5 billion Muslims will simply say they're Muslim, not distinguishing between Sunni and Shiite (or Shia), the two main branches of Islam. The basics of both center around the Holy Book, the Quran (also known as the "Koran") and the Five Pillars of Islam—the profession of faith, prayer, fasting, pilgrimage to Mecca, and charity.

The key differences arose over interpretation of who Muhammad's successor should be after his death in 632 A.D. The group that came to be known as Sunni believed the next leader, the Caliph, should be selected in consultation from among the prophet's most capable advisors and friends. The other group, the Shia, believed Muhammad specifically appointed an "imam" (Ali, his cousin and son-in-law was the first), from within his own family, which determined their line of succession. These hereditary imams are regarded by the Shia as saints and infallible. The original Sunni-Shia split set off violence: Ali was killed in Najaf about thirty years after Muhammad's death; Ali's son Husayn was killed about twenty years after that, in Karbila—towns suffering new waves of "sectarian violence" in today's Iraq.

The Sunnis eventually emerged as the dominant group, ruling over much of Eastern Europe through Central Asia until the fall of the Ottoman Empire after World War I. Of all the world's Muslims, 85 to 90 percent are Sunni, including most Muslims from Africa, Southern Asia, and the Arab countries. Notable Sunnis range from Osama bin Laden to Muhammad Yunus, the Bangladeshi Nobel Peace Prize—winner who pioneered microcredit for the world's poorest. Iran is the primary Shia (or Shiite) country in the world, with about 90 percent of its population subscribing to this branch of Islam, and Iraq has a smaller Shia majority (about 60 percent of its population; but historically, and under Saddam Hussein, the Sunni ruled). Famous Shias include the (imam) Ayatollah Khomeini and Nobel Peace Prize—winner and women's and human rights activist, Shirin Ebadi.

- *Stories from Hinduism:* Traditional Religious Tales' *Hindu Stories* picture book, *Hanuman* by Erik Jendresen, *Rama and the Demon King: An Ancient Tale from India* by Jessica Souhami, *Little Krishna* and *How Ganesh Got His Elephant Head* by Harish Johari, *The Story of Divaali* retold by Jatinder Verma, and many others depict the stories behind the Hindu deities and values. A fun book for teens and up (but even fascinating to my four-year-old, in its watered-down version) is *The Little Book of Hindu Deities: From the Goddess of Wealth to the Sacred Cow* by Sanjay Patel, a movie studio animator. Review the storybooks to see how they suit your child's sensibilities, as they can involve ten-headed beasts, battles, revenge, and other gruesome themes. If you're looking for the spiritual lesson behind some of the Hindu stories, see *Our Most Dear Friend: An Illustrated Bhagavad-Gita for Children*. Again, review the contents first, then decide how you'll treat the book with your children of various ages (e.g., will you explain the theme of reincarnation if you don't subscribe to it? How do you feel about the dramatic photos and illustrations?). With *Our Most Dear Friend,* for example, you can highlight how the mythology teaches the universal themes (like good versus evil) and lays the foundation for the Hindu spiritual perspective, if you're not ready to discuss theological differences.

- *Stories from Buddhism: Prince Siddhartha: The Story of Buddha* by Jonathan Landaw pleasantly tells the story of Buddha's life, as well as *Buddhist Stories for Children: Wisdom of the Crows and Other Buddhist Tales* by Sherab Chodzin and Alexandra Kohn. For older elementary kids and up, Anne Rockwell's *The Prince Who Ran Away* also discusses the life of the Buddha. Look for picture books by eminent Buddhist poet philosopher Thich Nhat Hanh, where Buddhist concepts like living in the present moment and "interbeing" are illustrated, complemented by various titles by Demi, mentioned previously.

- *Stories from other traditions:* Many of the compilation books introducing various faiths give a background of the stories central to other world religions. For more details on stories for kids from lesser known faiths, go to their dedicated websites. For example, creation stories and other tales from the Zoroastrian tradition are more accessible through zoroastriankids.com. For stories and legends from Sikhism (the fifth largest religion in the world), try sikhnet.com, go to the Sikh Youth tab, and click on the Sikh Stories Coloring Book link. *Confucius: The Golden Rule* by Russell Freedman is a good book for ages nine and up. The now-classic *Tao of Pooh* by Benjamin Hoff presents a brief, approachable way to understand Eastern religion, probably for teens and up. For the Baha'i Faith, you can download or purchase the Storybook Series on the Faith's Central Figures at www.core-curriculum.org or read *Ali's Dream* by John Hatcher. *Brilliant Star* magazine offers additional short stories and perspective for kids from a Baha'i view.

READY FOR A CLOSE-UP? VISITING OTHER RELIGIOUS PRACTICES

By now you might be eager to visit local congregations of various faiths, to see what actually goes on. With your child, look up "churches" in a local online directory, or the old-fashioned way, in the telephone book. Make a list of the different

Play Snakes and Ladders.

Experience firsthand the Hindu morality game (known as the "Ladder to Salvation") that was later adopted by Victorian England and modified for play today—without the moral element. Original versions of the Hindu game are described online. You can adapt today's more generic board game with your own labels: Identify which virtues lead you to ascend the ladder and which vices or "snakes" make you drop.

religious groups represented in your community, and note that not everyone under "church" is actually considered a "church." Are there some groups you have never heard of? Use source materials mentioned earlier in the chapter to find out about a few of them. You can plot the origins of each group on a map of the world. Do you have any friends who attend one of these whom you could ask to join for a worship or celebration service? The seventh-grade Sunday School curriculum at most Unitarian-Universalist churches consists of learning about and visiting various faith groups in the community. You can see their program of activities to get ideas and contacts for your own family's visits.

When visiting other houses of worship, call ahead, so you and your children can be more at ease during the service, knowing what behavior is appropriate. Nonetheless, here are a few etiquette rules to keep in mind:

- Among Muslim, Orthodox and some Conservative Jewish, and some Pentecostal and Eastern Orthodox Christian congregations, women and even men are expected to have a covering for their heads and, at a minimum, to dress modestly with arms and legs covered. To be safe, girls also should come in long sleeves or at least take a shawl over short sleeves if it is a hot day.
- In some of these same congregations, expect women and men to be seated separately. Boy children can sit with their mothers.
- During your visit, some congregations will expect each participant to offer a small amount of money as an offering, while other faiths won't allow contributions from visitors, only from members.
- In general, be alert to the customs others are engaged in. Notice if shoes are taken off, how singing and reading are conducted, who is expected to partici-

pate, if it is appropriate to ask questions or stay silent and wait until the program is over, if women and men shake hands with each other or not, if cameras or notebooks are acceptable to bring inside, and so on. The act of paying attention to these courtesies forms an important part of the visiting experience and will be appreciated by your hosts.

A good resource with more details is *How to Be a Perfect Stranger: The Essential Religious Etiquette Handbook,* Fourth Edition, edited by Stuart Matlins and Arthur Magida.

WHAT THE ARTS CAN HELP KIDS LEARN

Mosaics. Miniatures. Murals. Stained-glass. Bookbindings. Ceramics. Masks. Bronze figures. Illuminated manuscripts. Wood sculpture. Landscape architecture. Oil paintings. Architecture. Calligraphy. Mandalas. Tapestries. No matter what one feels about religion and God, there is no question that great movements in the arts owe some of their flourishing to the world's faiths. There seems to be a direct link between the lasting effects of a religion and the artistic creations inspired by it.

The renowned Uffizi Gallery in Florence is just one of the notable museums throughout Europe serving as homage to Jesus Christ and His Church, and one would be hard-pressed to walk through a major art museum in the United States and not find significant collections inspired by Judeo-Christian themes. At our hometown Philadelphia Museum of Art, whose steps Rocky Balboa immortalized in pop culture, we can walk through rooms of gilded religious art from fourteenth- and fifteenth-century Christian Europe, then find ourselves at the blue mosaic archway that re-creates the entrance to an ornate sixteenth-century mosque, follow it to see relics inspired by Islamic civilization, then walk down the hall to a Japanese Zen Buddhist temple amid other quiet representations of Buddhist life in the Far East.

With so many conflicting media images, particularly around Islam, a visit to one of many museums or university collections throughout the United States can create a unique appreciation of the religion's impact over the past millennium-plus. Your family might not be ready to visit a mosque or Muslim prayer service, but a visit to a museum with the intention of learning about the earthly impact of the religion can help begin tearing down barriers. The Freer and Sackler Galleries in Washington, D.C.'s Smithsonian complex house probably the most comprehensive selection in America; also see the Detroit Institute of Arts, New York's Metropolitan Museum, the Brooklyn Museum, the Museum of Fine Arts, Boston, the Cleveland Museum of Art, the Los Angeles County Museum of Art, and others with extensive collections of Islamic-inspired art. The L.A. County Museum has an informative site about the history and different periods of Islamic art, including photos of pieces in the gallery, at www.lacma.org/islamic_art.

Can you guess where the first and only Islamic history museum in America is located? Jackson, Mississippi. Part of the Mississippi Arts Center, the International Museum of Muslim Cultures opened just six months before the 9/11 attacks. A group of Muslims living in Jackson identified the need "to educate the public about Islamic history and civilization and to help provide educational tools for teaching global consciousness, historical literacy, and multicultural appreciation." This is the same place where my husband had gone to visit a cousin working for the U.S. Army Corps of Engineers in 1980 and was told by a store clerk who discovered he was from Iran: "You dead, boy," and where larger civil rights battles were staged, from the arrest of the Freedom Riders to the thirty-year delayed trial of civil rights leader Medgar Evers's assailants. The Muslim museum in Jackson has struggled to retain visitors partly because of local residents' fears after 9/11, but it remains a sign of the spectacular diversity and cultural surprises that can be found in every corner of a continuously changing America.

Visit a university campus. Universities large and small, private and public, across the country provide ideal environments for meeting international students, practicing (or learning) a foreign language, engaging in an interfaith dialogue, and taking a family outing. Many contain rich collections of art inspired from Islam, Buddhism, and other heritages. The University of North Carolina–Chapel Hill's Ackland Art Museum's extensive collection from their Five Faiths Project (original art from Hinduism, Buddhism, Judaism, Christianity, and Islam), the University of Chicago's Smart Museum of Art, Harvard's Sackler Gallery, and the University of Michigan Museum of Art are among a few examples of Islamic collections in American universities. The University of Georgia houses a mega website called Islamic Art, Music, and Architecture Around the World. (Google those words to get the link right away.) The universities with extensive South and East Asian religious art are too many to name here. Check the resources at universities near you for collections of manuscripts, modern and ancient art, lectures, programs for children, interfaith Thanksgiving services, and more. Ask to get your name on mailing and email lists, take walks on campus, and look for notices, demonstrations, or other signs of faith and art.

Food for the soul

Just as the body needs nourishment, so does the soul. You can explore with your child how prayer—offered in whatever way agrees with you—is like "spiritual food." As with physical food, prepare it and "consume" it deliberately and organically—set aside some time and don't force or manufacture the experience. Conversations at the dinner table or on the drive to school can explore this metaphor (e.g., Are you paying attention to what you feed your soul; How often; Do you like to take in the same thing each time or vary it; etc.). Children of all ages can explore a tangible metaphor like this one.

CREATING SPACE FOR THE SACRED IN YOUR HOME

Representations of the Divine as depicted in the arts can come home with you, to adorn walls, play on your stereo, and inform the arrangement of furniture (i.e., feng shui from Taoist belief). You can take this a step further by designating a room or a special spot in your home or plant a garden where family members can take time out for prayer, reflection, and meditation. Cultures and faith groups all over the world have highly developed notions of this practice and there is much we can learn from them. The ritual of going to a special, peaceful, beautiful spot in your home or garden and carving out a few minutes each day, maybe just before bedtime or right after school or in the morning before breakfast, serves both a practical and spiritual purpose—it helps with focus and introduces the sacred into our daily lives. The older children get, the harder this might be to bring into the home and daily routine. Instead of one place for the whole family, adolescents might be more comfortable with a special spot in the privacy of their own rooms—this is okay, too, and shows your respect for their need for a personal reflection space.

When entering the sacred space at home, start by coming in with clean hands and face. Many of the world's religious traditions call for ablutions before entering into prayer or a holy place. Even if it seems you don't need to wash up before entering the sacred space, the conscious effort to cleanse one's hands and face can serve as an important precursor to a state of prayer, like a daily baptism from the usual routine.

The universal practice of reverence—largely disappeared from Western culture—also is manifest in the act of taking shoes off before entering the space, another lesson from virtually every Eastern tradition. In Islamic, early Christian, and other traditions, the floor is covered with a "prayer rug." You might choose a rug woven by women in Tibet, Afghanistan, Guatemala, or another location where your purchase would make a difference in their lives. Drawing upon the Hindu, Buddhist, and certain Christian traditions, something like an altar can be created. Consider adorning it with fresh flowers, light a candle or some incense, display a family photo in a beautiful frame, and possibly another picture reminding you of happiness or people from a different culture; you can include a special gift given by someone you love as well as an object symbolizing your faith—whatever carries meaning for you and is conducive to you or your family's spiritual thoughts.

Keep some inspirational reading on hand. I find that having the original holy writings of various faiths—whatever you most relate to, or would like to learn from—allows you to experience the actual words that have inspired millions, instead of relying on interpretations. I gained exposure to these original works as a child and it has been a cornerstone of my own spiritual literacy. At first their style may seem very difficult to understand—especially for young children—but taken in small, bite-sized portions (perhaps a sentence at a time) a level of comfort can be achieved by even the youngest among us, who might find it most natural if they have become accustomed to the style of the Bible or Baha'u'llah's mystical *Hidden Words* from a young age. A small CD player with some inspirational music nearby can add to the environment, all so separate from the rest of the home's busyness. This tidy, sacred room or corner engages the senses to convey a universal experience of reverence and communion with the Divine, drawing in the members of the family, and often serving as a uniting force when there is so much to pull families apart.

Open the sacred space to friends. Expanding on the idea of a sacred space, your home also can serve as a place where people from diverse faith backgrounds can come together to experience the Divine in its diverse forms. You can make it clear that your aim is to create a safe, nonthreatening environment not aimed at conversion, but a spiritual conversation and discovery of shared beliefs. By sharing inspirational and sacred writings and expanding the circle of friends with whom you would broach the topic, you are creating a haven of peace in your home and helping to unite the community in which you live. The "devotional gathering" is a place for inspiration and understanding, ideally among people from different backgrounds. To get one started requires a shift in attitude—how you're willing to spend your social time, the spaces in which you can experience the sacred—not just in an institutionalized setting, and your willingness to go out on a limb to share these ideas with friends and coworkers who might misinterpret your intentions at first.

Around the turn of the twentieth century, artists and intellectuals attended "salons" in fashionable cities. The devotional gathering is akin to a salon, with the purpose of creating a sacred experience and a feeling of unity among the participants, but it's not just for elite adults. In ninth grade, my eldest daughter began inviting her school friends from many faith backgrounds for a "youth devotional." She and possibly one or two others find readings and prayers on a set topic, like "Overcoming Obstacles" or "Our Environment" or "The Meaning of Love" or "Peace." They read several short passages as a group, listen to some music on the theme (including music by international artists), or perform on an instrument and sing for one another, and this can be followed by dinner and maybe a movie, sometimes related to the theme and other times completely irrelevant to the topic. Parents have told me they are thrilled that their children are having a profound experience in a safe environment and the kids are learning about the world and one another.

For much younger children, families have organized "bedtime prayers" among a few family friends. In this case, the young children are excited to go to what feels like a pajama party just before bedtime. They might meet around seven P.M. (or whatever works for the families participating). Before arriving the children need to be briefed that this is not a playdate or a long visit. Rather than letting them rip right into the playroom, a peaceful place in the house is prepared for the group to sit down and share a very short program of prayers from different faiths (even five minutes can make a lasting impression). It is amazing to see the ability of children to display reverence and respect when they see the example of their peers and their parents. A special treat after the "bedtime prayers" program might be milk and cookies together. Because the devotional program for the children is brief, but it is such a special gathering, they inevitably ask when they can come back for bedtime prayers. If it is possible for the families, organizing this on a regular basis (like once per month) is well worth the effort.

CHECKING YOUR PREJUDICES—AND FEARS—AT THE DOOR

Among the repercussions after 9/11 was the profiling and harrassment of so many people who were innocent, upstanding citizens. And if someone like our local cardiologist or nearby nursery school teacher carried a Muslim name or place of birth (like a scarlet letter on their American passports), they knew to arrive at the airport almost an hour earlier than the other passengers on their flight, prepared for "random" security checks.

One notable news story of that time showed members of the Sikh religion being singled out, confused for Muslims by law enforcement and then by their neighbors and classmates. Such treatment was not fair to Muslims or to anyone else. But many don't seem to realize that Sikhs are not Muslim. They do wear turbans and long beards. Their beliefs are distinct from Islam, forbidding the cutting of hair. This took many Americans by surprise on multiple fronts. What's a Sikh? There are people who can't cut their hair? Actually, the Old Testament bans trimming of the beard, so how odd does that make the Sikh custom? Mistakes by law enforcement or angry neighbors who may not know the reasoning behind the Sikhs' practices led to false arrests, property damage, and psychological isolation. They also spurred many kitchen-table conversations.

A friend shared that her thirteen-year-old son was studying the world's religions—consisting only of Christianity, Islam, and Judaism—in his liberal northeastern U.S. private school. He brought home a question that arose during class and asked his mother: "How freaked out would you be if a Muslim fell to the ground and started praying next to you in the back of the airplane?" Her response: "I wouldn't be freaked out; I'd see it as part of the person's deep faith." Inside, though, she thought, "Of course I'd be freaked out," and then she quickly changed the subject because it was too uncomfortable to discuss with him. I posed these scenarios to followers of multiple faiths and took some key lessons from their responses.

1. *Recognize your child's concern and isolate the sources of anxiety.* The scenario my friend's son described is close to the 9/11 hijacking, so alarm is understandable. But would you feel differently if the prayer took place in public at the train station or at school? Determine which specific part(s) of the scene bothers your child—and you—the most.

2. *Acknowledge your own biases.* Sherri Hauser, a minister at Bryn Mawr Presbyterian Church in Bryn Mawr, Pennsylvana, suggested, "Rather than try to appear like 'I have no prejudices whatsoever,' acknowledge that you, too, grapple with these issues." If done in a spirit of learning and trust, this type of conversation with more mature children creates an open channel for discussing difficult issues.

3. *Explain what is going on. If you don't know, look it up or ask someone else.* If you hear a Muslim ask which direction is East, or Mecca, it's because that is the direction to which they pray—toward their holiest place. If they go to the washroom and then set out a little rug to stand on, that's because they perform ablutions (a ritual of washing up) before prayer and pray while standing on a clean spot. A Muslim mom told me, "The [five-times daily prayer] is a way to

stop, take a break, take account of our lives, thank our Creator, and ask His protection. Particularly during travel, many might pray for their safety, and for the safety of all on board the plane. He believes the angels are surrounding him during his prayer. . . . The Muslim believes he is praying to the same God of the Christian and Jew."

4. *Familiarize yourself with some core beliefs and find out the meaning of the prayer that involves standing, kneeling, and bowing prostrate.* Beyond the discussion of *why* they are doing the prayer, learn *what* they are saying and believe. Read the English translation of the Muslim prayer. The quotations about peace from the Quran and other holy books earlier in this chapter also are meant to be shared with your children to give them a direct sense of those sacred texts. For more depth, you can go to a clearinghouse like Beliefnet.com or websites of various faiths.

5. *Recognize common threads.* Rabbi Ethan Franzel of Main Line Reform Temple in Wynnewood, Pennsylvania, pointed out to me: "If you fly El-Al [Israel's airline] it's almost guaranteed there will be certain times where at least ten [Orthodox Jewish] men are praying together." I was struck by the fact that of all the people I spoke to about the airplane question my friend's son asked, the rabbi from a liberal congregation could relate most to the scenario.

   In addition to the beard and hair-cutting teachings found among the Sikhs and in the Bible, the New Testament (John 13:14-15) counsels: "If I then, your Lord and Teacher, have washed your feet, you also ought to wash one another's feet, . . ," As a result, some Christians wash feet before worship, like the principle of Muslim ablutions. Then there are shared rules about women covering their heads to pray, as well as fasting and disciplining children with the "rod." When you take a closer look at the context, aspiring to be a Christian "soldier" or engaging in *jihad,* which can mean both an individual's striving for self-perfection and spiritual struggle as well as "Holy War," then they may not be different, either.

6. *Look around; do you personally know anyone who practices this faith?* If you have a friend from that faith you probably won't feel quite so "freaked out." If you share a meal or a soccer game with someone in a turban (or a head scarf, hijab, sari, yarmulke, bonnet, etc.) you may appreciate their real concerns, interests, and motivations, instead of associating them first with their head covering.

7. *Learn from history.* History is full of examples of bias and hatred turning into full-scale persecution. As the remaining Holocaust survivors from WWII age, the opportunity to hear one of their firsthand accounts is precious. Try to attend a talk by someone like Marion Blumenthal Lazan (fourperfectpebbles.com) or speakers from the Kindertransport Association (the Jewish children from all

over Europe who were sent to England after Kristallnacht while their parents stayed behind) or other organizations with a speakers' bureau of courageous Holocaust survivors. Find out if your children's school (particularly for ages ten and up) schedules such guest presenters. If not, try to initiate a program with speakers from different perspectives. Contact the nearest synagogue for names of speakers. If you can't bring a speaker, you can watch video testimonies of survivors' stories online at the USC Shoah Foundation Institute for Visual History and Education site at college.usc.edu/vhi. Numerous films and documentaries, from *Paper Clips,* about a middle-school project in a Southern Christian community grappling to understand the Holocaust, to *Life Is Beautiful, The Boy in the Striped Pajamas,* and *Into the Arms of Strangers: Stories of the Kindertransport,* can also help bring this period to life or underscore its significance, for the appropriate ages.

Unfortunately, genocide has continued well past the end of the Holocaust. Today, others who can address the issue and teach lessons on religious tolerance can include refugees from Darfur and southern Sudan (e.g., the experience of the Lost Boys of Sudan), Bosnia, Kosovo, Cambodia, Rwanda, Iran, and Iraq. If it seems hard to believe that such atrocities continue today, find out what has spurred them, even if you start with an article from Wikipedia. Organizations like the Anti-Defamation League carry information and action ideas as well as reading lists for various ages and curriculum guides to be used by schools. Amnesty International's website exposes thousands of current cases of human rights violations with action steps to protest these injustices.

A "FAITH CLUB" FOR ALL AGES

The interfaith movement was introduced in America back in 1893, at a conference taking place concurrently with the Chicago World's Fair. Since then, a combination of clergy and laypeople with a sincere interest in peace-building has helped interfaith dialogues flourish all over the country. The popular 2006 book *The Faith Club* demonstrates how three adult women from three faiths confronted their differences and their own beliefs. The book offers guidelines for adults to begin their own "Faith Club."

You don't have to be all grown up to engage in profound learning and sharing. Some of the most creative and dynamic interfaith efforts involve youth and children. If children are engaged in a playgroup or a fun class learning about one anothers' beliefs, wouldn't comfort with diversity come more naturally as an adult? If you'd like to get engaged in a multifaith experience for your family, see if the interfaith organizations in your area offer multiage activities. Here are a few more ways to get started.

- *Playgroups for the littlest ones:* Start a "playgroup with a purpose," or see if your existing playgroup would like to explore ways of teaching universal principles, like the Golden Rule and virtues like kindness and generosity,[7] or celebrate different holidays together, through creative activities for the children. Parents with very young children have a distinct advantage, in that their children are more likely to be willing to try anything and they may not already be bombarded with extracurricular activities. Then, as the kids grow up together, more profound lessons can be explored. One version of this was featured on a March 7, 2008, National Public Radio story titled "Class Teaches Virtues to Children of Many Faiths." In the small group in northern Virginia, families came from Muslim, Greek Orthodox, Jewish, Baha'i, Protestant, and Unitarian Universalist backgrounds. They were united by the desire to learn from one another, help their children's spiritual development (beyond academics), and equip them with the confidence to be curious about belief systems that may not be their own. If you don't have a ready group of diverse friends to invite, try to start something at your local YMCA, or through the Newcomers Club, local MOMS group, Internet message boards for local activities, or also look for an existing interfaith organization and reach out to members of participating congregations.

- *Elementary and middle-school clubs:* A growing number of elementary and middle schools around the country celebrate holidays like Chinese New Year and Diwali. Would your children's schools be interested in starting an after-school club to prepare for various holidays from religions and cultures around the world? The clubs could prepare fun activities for a celebration, but more, they would set aside the time to learn about the significance or spiritual lesson behind the celebration. If this activity appears questionably "religious" for a public school environment, perhaps it could begin on the neighborhood level, at a local community center or after-school facility. Try to start with a core group from different faith perspectives so diverse learning and outreach begins on solid footing.

- *High-school activities and service clubs:* By high-school age, there is a bit more interest in peoples' actual beliefs. Many schools' curricula in world cultures includes a brief study of belief systems. A club that ties in dialogue engaging diverse students' views is a natural fit in such an environment. Christian prayer groups openly practice as clubs in public schools, so an interfaith or world faiths club should not pose a challenge to church-state separation concerns and an increasing number of teens are ready for such an experience. The Anti-Defamation League runs high-school clubs, and the Interfaith Youth Core (ifyc.org) offers a growing movement and resources for young people nationwide that could be tapped.

- *Youth groups outside of school:* Some interfaith organizations sponsor active programs for youth. My eldest daughter participates in the Interfaith Center of Greater Philadelphia's "Walking the Walk" program where youth and adult mentors from different faiths engage in dialogue, service, reflection, and building friendships over the course of a school year. She got involved reluctantly, but after just the first meeting she came away learning so much about other teens and their faiths, and this has impacted the formulation of her own beliefs.

———

The buildings, rituals, rules, stories, and mysticism representing various faiths reflect human experiences interacting with the Divine—without people, any religion would be considered "dead." Likewise, a deeper understanding of the people around us entails appreciation of different belief systems, especially as our communities become more diverse and our interactions involve people from across the planet. This is not a topic to be reserved for wise elders. Experience after experience shows that as children interact with various faiths and their adherents, their appreciation of diverse beliefs becomes almost second nature. Such a comfort level—with oneself and with others—will prove invaluable when confronting the challenges of adulthood. In many cases it has actually resulted in a more profound sense of faith because it cultivates a sense of oneness with all of God's children. Further, we have transitioned from an age in which one's faith was inherited and assumed, based on what village we came from. As population surveys show, a profound change is underway. People are growing up to "choose" their own beliefs. Exposure from a young age can help avoid a crisis of choice and help to create a feeling of comfort with spirituality and diverse beliefs.

Families of different faiths don't have to agree theologically with each other to recognize the value of each others' beliefs and cultivate lasting friendships. Similarly, one can appreciate the numerous art forms that have flourished as a result of inspiration from a particular faith without converting. Depending on how you, the parent, were raised, this openness to learning about other faiths with your children may be extremely difficult. It might force a profound questioning or require a new lens by which to view the world. But that may be a good thing. From the New Testament we learn that "In My Father's house there are many mansions." Feeling "at home in the world" stretches us to feel at home in any of these "mansions."

RESOURCE BOOKS CITED IN CHAPTER 6—THAT YOU MAY FIND HELPFUL, TOO

The Torah and Talmud
The Holy Bible
The Holy Quran
The Bhagavad-Gita
Various works of Baha'u'llah
Various works of Lao Tzu

The Illustrated World's Great Religions: A Guide to Our Wisdom Traditions, Huston Smith (New York: HarperOne, 1991 and 1995).

World Christian Encyclopedia, David Barrett, George Thomas Kurian, Todd Johnson, editors (Oxford University Press, 1982; 2d ed., 2001).

The Kids Book of World Religions, Jennifer Glossop and John Mantha (Toronto: Kids Can Press, 2003).

A Faith Like Mine: A Celebration of the World's Religions Through the Eyes of Children, Laura Buller (New York: Dorling Kindersley (DK) Ltd., 2005).

Religious Literacy: What Every American Needs to Know—And Doesn't, Stephen Prothero (New York: HarperOne, 2007).

Sourcebook of the World's Religions: An Interfaith Guide to Religion and Spirituality, edited by Joel Beversluis (Novato, CA: New World Library, 2000).

Sacred Myths: Stories of the World's Religions, Marilyn McFarlane (Portland, OR: Sibyl Publications, 1996).

Multiple books by the author-illustrator, Demi, including: *Muhammad, Jesus, Mary, Buddha, The Legend of Lao Tzu, The Legend of St. Nicholas, Tao te Ching,* and more (New York: Simon & Schuster, various years).

Judaism, (Eyewitness Guides), Douglas Charing (New York: DK Publishers Ltd., 2003).

The Jewish Child's First Book of Why and *Classic Bible Stories for Jewish Children,* Alfred Kolatch (Middle Village, NY: Jonathan David Publishers, 1992 and 1993).

While Standing on One Foot: Puzzle Stories and Wisdom Tales from the Jewish Tradition, Nina Jaffe and Steve Zeitlin (New York: Henry Holt and Company, 1996).

Does God Have a Big Toe? Stories About Stories in the Bible and *God's Mailbox,* Marc Gellman. (New York: Harper Trophy, 1993 and 1998).

Stories for Children, Isaac Bashevis Singer (New York: Farrar, Straus and Giroux, 1985).

Next Year in Jerusalem: 3000 Years of Jewish Stories, retold by Howard Schwartz (New York: Puffin, 1998).

The Devil's Arithmetic, Jane Yolen (New York: Puffin, 2004).

The Golden Children's Bible, Golden Books version (New York: Golden Inspirational, 2006).

The Beginner's Bible: Timeless Children's Stories, Kelly Pulley (Grand Rapids, MI: Zonderkidz, 2005).

God's Little Princess Devotional Bible, Sheila Walsh (Nashville, TN: Thomas Nelson, 2006).

The Manga Bible, Tyndale (Wheaton, IL: Tyndale House Publishers, 2007).

Traditional Religious Tales' Islamic Stories, Anita Ganeri (author) and Rebecca Wallis (illustrator) (Mankato, MN: Picture Window Books, 2006).

Muslim Child: Understanding Islam through Stories and Poems, Rukhsana Khan (author) and Patty Gallinger (illustrator) (Morton Grove, IL: Albert Whitman and Company, 2002).

My Name is Bilal, Asma Mobin-Uddin (author) and Barbara Kiwak (illustrator) (Honesdale, PA: Boyds Mill Press, 2005).

Ayat Jamilah: Beautiful Signs: A Treasury of Islamic Wisdom for Children and Parents, Sarah Conover and Freda Crane (authors) and Valerie Wahl (illustrator) (Spokane, WA: Eastern Wasington University Press, 2004).

Traditional Religious Tales' Hindu Stories, Anita Ganeri (author) and Carole Gray (illustrator) (Mankato, MN: Picture Window Books, 2006).

Hanuman, Erik Jendresen and Joshua Greene (authors) and Li Ming (illustrator) (Berkeley, CA: Tricycle Press, 2004).

Rama and the Demon King: An Ancient Tale from India, Jessica Souhami (London: Frances Lincoln Children's, 2005).

Little Krishna and *How Ganesh Got His Elephant Head,* Harish Johari (author) and Pieter Weltevrede (illustrator) (Rochester, VT: Bear Cub Books, 2002, 2003).

The Story of Divaali retold by Jatinder Verma, Nilesh Mistry (illustrator) (Cambridge, MA: Barefoot Books, 2002).

The Little Book of Hindu Deities: From the Goddess of Wealth to the Sacred Cow, Sanjay Patel (New York: Plume, 2006).

Our Most Dear Friend: An Illustrated Bhagavad-Gita for Children, Jean Vishaka Griesser (North Carolina: Torchlight Publishing, 1996).

Prince Siddhartha: The Story of Buddha, Jonathan Landaw (Somerville, MA: Wisdom Publications, 2003).

Buddhist Stories for Children: Wisdom of the Crows and Other Buddhist Tales, Sherab Chodzin and Alexandra Kohn (author) and Marie Cameron (illustrator) (Berkeley, CA: Tricycle Press, 1998).

The Prince Who Ran Away, Anne Rockwell (author) and Fahimeh Amiri (illustrator) (New York: Alfred A. Knopf, 2001).

Confucius: The Golden Rule, Russell Freedman (author) and Frederic Clement (illustrator) (New York: Arthur A. Levine, 1997).

Tao of Pooh, Benjamin Hoff (New York: Dutton, 1982).

Ali's Dream, John Hatcher (Wilmette, IL: Baha'i Publishing Trust, 1998).

The Central Figures: Baha'u'llah, Volumes 1, 2, 3, National Spiritual Assembly of the Baha'is of the United States (Wilmette, IL: Baha'i Publishing Trust, 2001).

The Family Virtues Guide: Simple Ways to Bring Out the Best in Our Children and Ourselves, Linda Kavelin Popov, Dan Popov, John Kavelin (New York: Plume, 1997).

How to Be a Perfect Stranger: The Essential Religious Etiquette Handbook, Fourth Edition, Stuart Matlins and Arthur Magida, editors (Woodstock, VT: SkyLight Paths Publishing, 2006).

The Faith Club: A Muslim, A Christian, A Jew—Three Women Search for Understanding, Ranya Idliby, Suzanne Oliver, Priscilla Warner (New York: Free Press, 2006).

ADDITIONAL RESOURCE BOOKS RELATED TO CHAPTER 6

Multi-Cultural Manners: Essential Rules of Etiquette for the 21st Century, Norine Dresser (Hoboken, NJ: John Wiley & Sons, 2005).

Acts of Faith: The Story of an American Muslim, the Struggle for the Soul of a Generation, Eboo Patel (Boston, MA: Beacon, 2007).

A Pebble for Your Pocket and *The Hermit and the Well,* Thich Nhat Hanh (author) and Vo-Dinh Mai (illustrator) (Berkeley, CA: Plum Blossom Books, 2002 and 2003).

World Religions 101: An Overview For Teens, Margaret O. Hyde and Emily G. Hyde (Minneapolis, MN: Twenty-First Century Books, 2009).

Chapter 7

Celebrate with the World

All the world is a birthday cake, so take a piece, but not too much.
GEORGE HARRISON

When I was thirteen and still living in Indiana, we had only a couple of Jewish kids in our grade in public school. One of them was my good friend Beth, and her Bat Mitzvah might have been the single most magical event of my life up till then. For starters, she sent out the nicest invitation (written in calligraphy on heavy paper) that I had ever seen. Then I needed to shop for not just one, but two fancy dresses. And then there was sitting in front during a ceremony that seemed so mystical to me—my first time in a synagogue—and listening intently as my friend seemed to speak in tongues. And when I thought it couldn't get better, we girlfriends were transported to the Marriott! for a buffet luncheon! meeting her sophisticated cousins from Chicago and Michigan! and dancing with our shoes off! It almost still makes my heart flutter. Somehow, my daughters don't get as excited about their Bat Mitzvah invitations as I did (and still do). Perhaps in 1970s Indiana, without a lot of entertainment available or diversity among my friends, Beth's Bat Mitzvah threw me an early lifeline for the global-seeking person I would grow up to be.

Looking back to this sparkling memory of thirty years ago, I now recognize that part of the magic for me came as a result of sharing in a wholehearted celebration. I knew almost nothing about what to expect; it wasn't "my" celebration. But possibly because of its newness and my family's anticipation of participating in my friend's milestone celebration, I was completely open to it—and I now recognize that it was a milestone in my own development, too. This impact can come from joining in on so many types of celebrations, not just a once-in-a-lifetime event.

Everybody celebrates something. If I call to invite you to a meeting or a service to learn about my religion, would you eagerly attend? Maybe not. But what if my family mailed a colorfully decorated invitation to yours to participate in an afternoon-into-evening celebration of Diwali, Eid, Passover, Purim, King's Day, Norooz, or Ayyam-i-Ha? You might not have ever heard of one or more of these holidays. It doesn't matter so much, though, because celebrations are universal. Whatever the financial, cultural, or religious conditions, human beings love to have a reason to throw a party, observe a happy occasion, or mark a historic event—and share that with their friends.

Participating in a religious or cultural holiday is about sharing a festivity; it's not a step toward conversion. It shouldn't feel threatening. When you feel comfortable participating in a celebration that is foreign to you—including familiar occasions, like birthdays, celebrated in a new way, which will be discussed in the second half of this chapter—then you are ready to experience it at its fullest. For younger children this could involve trying the foods associated with the holiday, getting dressed up for the occasion, and absorbing the wonder that is being offered. Many diverse cultural holidays include particular aspects oriented toward children, whether it is gift giving, playing games, telling stories, or sharing treats. They also might require some time sitting still and listening, a practice honed by kids all over the world. Your openness to these new experiences will show your child that it is safe, exciting, and fun to participate—even when it is completely new and possibly baffling to you.

While it might be universally rude to invite yourself to someone's home for dinner or a party, I have found that asking politely if our family can join in their celebration of a cultural or religious holiday is usually welcomed with a quizzical look implying *You're actually interested in our holiday?* And followed by *We'd love to have you!*

WHAT DO THEY CELEBRATE? HOW?

You can't invite yourself and your children to a new celebration if you don't know what your friend celebrates. When processing a new celebration you have had minimal or no contact with, you'll need to orient yourself, both before and during the event. There are a number of excellent resource books that will help you do this. Some that I like include:

- The vibrantly photographed *Children Just Like Me: Celebrations!* from DK Publishing. Like its predecessor volume *Children Just Like Me,* the *Celebrations* book brings the various holidays to life through stories of real children that the authors have visited around the world. Along with the eye-catching photos and easy-to-scan two-page spreads, I like the organization of holidays by seasons. When we get the big picture of global celebrations that take place in each of the four seasons, universal elements punctuated by the calendar come to light, at the same time that differences are acknowledged. For example, springtime festivals share the theme of new life and are celebrated colorfully and with flowers. Think of Easter, but also, Purim, Japanese Doll Day (Hina Matsuri), and the Hindi fes-

Celebration Literacy 101

Teach your children about some major holidays from around the world.

• *Chinese New Year* is celebrated on different dates around February each year, by about 20 percent of the world's population, with fireworks, parades, money gifts, special treats, and fifteen days' holiday. Join in a celebration with friends or at your nearby Chinese restaurant or Chinatown.

• *Diwali* is the two-day Hindu festival where streets, houses . . . anywhere is adorned with lights to welcome the goddess of prosperity, Lakshmi. Indian bakeries in the United States and worldwide do most of their business around this holiday, as sweets are exchanged by all.

• *Carnival,* celebrated throughout South America and most famously in Brazil, is the flamboyant street party three days before Ash Wednesday and the Catholic days of self-denial (through fasting or giving up a favorite thing) during forty days of Lent. In North America and many parts of Europe, this is celebrated as *Mardi Gras,* literally "Fat Tuesday."

• *Eid ul-Fitr* is a three-day holiday marking the sighting of the new moon and the end of the holy month of fasting in Islam. From Saudi Arabia to Malaysia it is the major holiday celebrated, particularly by Sunni Muslims. Visits and gifts to friends and family, new clothes, and hospitality to the poor and loved ones mark the occasion. In strictly Muslim countries like Saudi Arabia, birthday celebrations are discouraged, so this type of holiday gets all the attention.

• *National Days* or Independence Days are different everywhere, but celebrated in every country.

tival of Holi, where families play for hours, covering one another in dry, then wet powdered paints—like no other celebration I've ever seen—and Norooz, the ancient Persian New Year that actually takes place on the first day of spring; winter celebrations are marked with light and warmth (as in Christmas and Chanukah, as well as Diwali). Be aware that not everything is included in this lovely book—it's not meant to be an encyclopedia of celebrations—but it's a great start.

- Barron's Educational Festival Time! series, with titles like *Lighting a Lamp: A Diwali Story; Apples and Honey: A Rosh Hashanah Story; It's Party Time! A Purim Story; Lanterns and Firecrackers: A Chinese New Year Story; Hope and New Life! An Easter Story;* and *Fasting and Dates: A Ramadan and Eid Story.*
- National Geographic's *Holidays Around the World* series.
- The Rookie Read-About Holidays series.
- *Celebrating Ramadan* and *Celebrating Chinese New Year* by Diane Hoyt-Goldsmith.
- If Islamic holidays remain elusive to you, try *The Islamic Year: Surahs, Stories and Celebrations* by Noorah Al-Gailani or *Muslim Child,* cited previously.
- Finally, *How to Be a Perfect Stranger: The Essential Religious Etiquette Handbook,* Third Edition. I mentioned this book in the last chapter, but it's worth repeating, as a reference for etiquette, clothing to wear or not wear, gifts, food, and drink for visiting virtually any congregation in America. Each brief chapter also includes a summary of the religion's history and beliefs, dogma and ideology, and special vocabulary used by the congregation—useful information when invited for a special event.

To get oriented *during* the event, don't be afraid to ask questions. Generally, your hosts will expect questions from someone who is new to their traditions—otherwise you probably wouldn't be invited. But just to be sure, check ahead if it's okay to ask questions and find out if there are times when you should not speak, or if there are people around whom you should remain quiet or wait to be spoken to. Also, ask in advance if there are expectations for the children: How long are they expected to sit still? Will they be eating a meal there? Are there many sugary desserts fed to the children? What should they wear? If you try to restrict your children's sugar intake or are concerned for how long they are expected to sit still, try to clarify these questions in advance, but don't sweat the details.

(HOW) DO YOU CELEBRATE CHRISTMAS?

There are dozens of exotic-sounding celebrations around the world, but Christmas remains the most celebrated holiday in the world. In some places, Christmas is not associated with Jesus Christ, but has become thought of as a universal day of gift-giving. One friend related being asked by a trendy Japanese teenager in Tokyo: "Do you celebrate Christmas in America?" She only knew it as a Japanese holiday. Likewise, many secular Middle Easterners of Muslim heritage living in the United States have adopted it as their own family holiday, complete with the tree, outdoor lights, and elaborate seasonal parties.

Not every American celebrates Christmas. Despite the pervasiveness of Christmas, it's important that any globally minded person not assume that everyone celebrates it—even in America. I respect the desire to "put the Christ back in Christmas," but also recognize that it's not everyone's holiday. One book (and video) on recognizing that different families celebrate different holidays is *There's No Such Thing as a Chanukah Bush, Sandy Goldstein* by Susan Sussman.

The well-meaning stranger who asks the children in line at the grocery checkout, "Have you been a good boy for Santa? Is your Christmas list all ready?" is making a value judgment that everyone celebrates as she does. For a sizable (and growing, based on immigration trends) number of Americans who don't celebrate Christmas or pass along the Santa myth, this becomes an awkward exchange, and more, the whole season becomes something to dread—particularly for the kids.

Christmas is not my family's main holiday. At the same time, I prefer to say "Merry Christmas" rather than "Happy Holidays" if I know someone celebrates Christmas. As I explain hundreds of times each year over the holidays, we appreciate the sanctity of Christmas, we're not "baah-humbuggers"—we participate in the festivities and caroling and giving gifts to friends—and Santa does make a stop at our home when the kids are young; nonetheless, the cultural assumptions can be exhausting.

Jewish families have been dealing with this issue for generations in America. "Are you Christmas?" the kids in first grade all seemed to be asking my friend's son, Jeremy, as if we *are* our holidays. "I don't think so, but I'll ask my mom," he responded the first day back from Thanksgiving break. Jeremy's mom related this kind of experience to me as one of the biggest challenges to the idyllic country life they had chosen for their family, where they were one of the few non-Christian families for miles. All over the United States, young kids have to deal with this question that points to the heart of their differentness—their celebration is not the same as most of their classmates'. Many schools have begun including some treatment of multiple holidays, but without reinforcement of such diversity from home (which could start simply by discussing what they've learned about at school), such efforts probably won't stick.

Attend Chanukah and Kwanzaa festivities with your children. If you're not invited to a private home celebration, look for a special program in a museum, library, theater, or other civic venue. Give your child a richer perspective of why so many say "Happy Holidays" in December, sometimes interchangeably with "Merry Christmas," but remember that Chanukah is not "Jewish Christmas." It marks the miracle of the oil that lasted for eight days to light the lamp or menorah marking the liberation or rededication of the Temple in Jerusalem. Even if your family personally experiences these celebrations only every few years, by encountering the merriment that accompanies menorah lighting or kinara lighting (Kwanzaa) together with their parents, the memory will stand out far more than a lesson that's demonstrated only in class or heard about on talk radio in the context of an annual political correctness debate around the holidays.

Different cultures, different Christmases. Even among those who celebrate Christmas, there may be significant cultural differences—in decorations, foods, stories, gift giving, and even the date on which Christmas is celebrated. If your family celebrates Christmas, are there some new traditions from other cultures you could incorporate into your festivities to add meaning and connection with others in the world? Neighbors of ours have no Swedish ancestry, but the family has adopted the culture, ever since their grandmother spent one year in Sweden while she was in high school. Two generations later, Christmas has become synonymous with the Swedish customs—baking Santa Lucia Buns (*Lussekater*) and other Swedish-style holiday cookies, wearing the crown, telling the stories, kids preparing a ceremonious breakfast in bed for Mom and Dad, and participating in the nearby American Swedish Historical Museum's Christmas celebration. Similarly, another friend, whose British mother grew up in colonial India, fondly recalls Boxing Day (December 26) suppers always composed of various curries and naans (Indian flatbreads) in their very British home.

Talk to friends and neighbors about traditions they have incorporated for their holiday. Some possibilities for your celebration could include:

New decorations for the tree: When it's time to decorate, look for ornaments from different cultures. Decorations from Latin American, Russian, Asian, and many other cultures are readily available at specialty Christmas stores, fair-trade shops, Pier 1, Whole Foods Market, and even Target and TJ Maxx—if you look for them. Kids might enjoy selecting an ornament from a favorite country, being drawn to a particular style and then finding out about where it came from and what it represents, or reflecting their ethnic heritage in decorations. You may be able to turn a souvenir into an ornament with a bit of string and imagination.

Spice up the menu. In the past few years, boxed "panettone" bread loaves, quintessential Christmas food in Latin America and Italy, have been sold widely everywhere from department stores to supermarkets in the United States, replacing the traditional, ubiquitous fruitcakes. Some examples of Christmas food from other countries (look for recipes and serving suggestions online or in books) include:

- French Canada—desserts like doughnuts and sugar pie
- France—black-and-white pudding made of sausage containing blood
- Germany—gingerbread biscuits and liqueur chocolates
- Nicaragua—chicken with a stuffing made from a range of fruits and vegetables including tomato, onion, and papaya
- Russia—a feast of twelve different dishes, representing Christ's disciples
- Italy, Spain, Latin America—Feast of seven fishes on Christmas Eve
- Czech Republic—Carp for Christmas dinner. At the end of the meal, everyone gets a scale from the carp and keeps it in their wallet for the entire year to symbolize prosperity—it's a sign that the wallet will never be empty during the year
- Denmark—Rice almond pudding with lots of slivered, and just one whole, almond. Whoever finds the whole almond wins the coveted prize of a marzipan (almond paste) pig

Charity catalogue "shopping"

Save the Children's holiday gift catalogue helps donors—particularly the youngest ones—honor a friend with a charitable gift, while envisioning what they are giving and where it's going, with a clear price tag. For example, you can choose "Send a girl to school for one year, $56" or "Help a farmer grow apple trees in Ethiopia, $75" or "Help provide micronutrients and medicine to 25 children, $25." Your friend will receive a card and gift, acknowledging the donation you have made in their name. Save the Children also has a limited gift shop on their website with products you can purchase to support the organization. This was one of the early "cause" marketers selling projects to support their charity. Now the Internet is loaded with websites marketing appealing products that make a difference in the world; cross-search a cause you care about with cause-marketing gift catalogues and see what products come up!

Put on a play and learn new stories. Find other cultures' variations on familiar stories, or Christmas stories you've never heard of. A variation of the Nativity scene is played out in Mexico and northern Brazil, called *Los Pastores* or "The Shepherds," where shepherdesses, not shepherds, come to the manger and defend against the attempt to kidnap the Christ child. In warm climates like these, Christmas might be a special day to go to the beach or give flowers as gifts. Different scenarios impacted by climate, musical styles, and traditional or popular culture affect how Christmas is dramatized around the world.

Start on December 16 or 6. In many Latin countries, a procession begins on December 16 to mark the nine days Joseph and Mary walked looking for lodging from Nazareth to Bethlehem. Old and new friends are welcomed into the home for a meal, to make up for the hospitality Joseph and Mary were denied. Throughout parts of Europe, the season begins on December 6, with the arrival of St. Nicholas (often accompanied by the devil—to take in your year's bad deeds or to spank bad children—all in fun) and ends on January 6, Three Kings Day or Epiphany, the day the Magi from Persia visited the baby Jesus. These customs can bring parts of the Christmas story to life in a whole new way, bookending the season differently from how shopping days do.

Make it a time to bring people together. Perry Yeatman is a senior executive with Kraft Foods outside Chicago, and the co-author of *Get Ahead by Going Abroad.* Her husband came to the states from Denmark, and their Christmas celebration incorporates Danish traditions, like cooking an elaborate Christmas Eve dinner that includes roasting a pig with the rind still on it—which must be ordered months in advance—and lighting hundreds of specialized Danish candles on their live tree. They share the feast with about one hundred guests each year. These friends come from all aspects of their life—colleagues from work, day-care providers, sailing buddies, neighbors, and family members. "It's wonderful bringing everyone who is important to us together. When you see them enjoying interaction with new and different people and hear them say, 'I hope to see you at next year's party,' the effort feels worth it," Perry told me. She went on to say, "Becoming a global citizen shouldn't feel like a project for your family." Sharing the holiday traditions with friends from so many countries and walks of life feels like a natural outgrowth of what is important to the family. Without having to force a lesson on their children, they simply live it.

Skip the hype. More and more American families are consciously opting out of the consumer frenzy that's come to characterize Christmas. This often includes dedicating the funds to a special cause instead of spending them on gift indulgences for family members who have everything; traveling away from home and the mall during the height of the season to avoid the pressure to buy, and being able to focus on quality time with the family; or matching the amount spent on family gifts (or setting aside a certain percentage of funds) with gifts for others more needy. Children can be taught that this move can be fun and meaningful, not just a deprivation to them. You can prep their schoolteacher and others around you about your family's decision in order for them to reinforce this initiative and make it seem "cool" among their peers. The website redefineChristmas.org can help you think further about this.

HAPPY NEW YEAR?

The whole world seemed to celebrate together on December 31, 1999, ushering in the new millennium, with TV images of partyers all over the planet counting down the start of the Year 2000. If one were to go by the images on the screen, the dawn of Y2K seemed universal, with only time zones between us. This date corresponded to the Gregorian calendar, the world's standard setter, and most used calendar. But it isn't so simple. Different calendars correspond to various faiths, each with their own New Year and timeline, and within one faith, there might be various calendars (e.g., the Greek Orthodox Christian calendar differs from the Gregorian and within Hindu societies there are various calendars). The math isn't so easy, either. One year in a lunar calendar differs in length from a year in the solar calendar, explaining why Ramadan, Easter, or Passover always fall on a different day on our western, solar calendars. Various calendars have different New Year's, but they also have different months, days of the week, and years. To make things more confusing, even within one country there might be multiple calendars observed, particularly when business is conducted around the Gregorian calendar, religion around another calendar, and an older cultural calendar system is observed. For example, the year 2009 in the Gregorian calendar corresponds to:

- *Jewish:* Year 5769–70; New Year is marked at Rosh Hashanah, during the seventh month of the Jewish (lunar) calendar, which falls around September on different days in different years in the Gregorian calendar.
- *Buddhist:* Year 4707–08, commonly celebrated as "Chinese" New Year, also celebrated by Vietnamese, Thais, Koreans, Tibetans, and other Asian cultures.
- *Hindu:* The Hindu calendar began in Gregorian Year 3102 B.C. In 1957, the Indian government instituted a new system to unite dozens of variations in the

Marking the Jewish High Holidays

Following the first day of the Jewish year on Rosh Hashanah, ten days of repentance or reflection take place, culminating in Yom Kippur, the "Day of Atonement" and the holiest day on the Jewish calendar. Yom Kippur is observed with twenty-five hours of fasting and prayer. Leading up to that day, individuals might contact friends and acquaintances that day to ask their forgiveness for any offenses they may have committed during the year, or reconcile these privately.

Hindu calendar, setting the date at 1879 (because of a complicated system of epochs); so in 2009 the recognized year in India is 1934; New Year is celebrated with springtime festivals in March and April.

- *Islamic:* Year 1430–31, based on a lunar year, which is eleven days shorter than a solar year. New Year takes place on the anniversary of Muhammad's flight from Medina to Mecca, which in 2009 will be on December 18, and in 2010, on December 7.
- *Baha'i:* Year 165–66; the New Year begins with the first day of spring on the solar calendar, so it always starts on March 21.

Runaway Rice Cakes for Chinese New Year!

Ying Chang Compestine's story *The Runaway Rice Cake* offers a fun tale for Chinese New Year, a doable recipe for making good luck rice cakes, and it imparts a deeper message: of generosity, selflessness, and compassion. There's a universal side, too. The runaway rice cake resembles the gingerbread man, which is also a global story, as seen by *Musubi Man: Hawaii's Gingerbread Man, The Runaway Latkes, The Runaway Tortilla, The Cajun Gingerbread Boy,* and others. If your child isn't already familiar with the Gingerbread Man story that's traditionally told in North America, expose her to some of the international versions and see which one she prefers. You'll likely see it with new eyes, too.

Choosing an auspicious day

In many cultures, particularly those inspired by the Eastern religions of Hinduism and Buddhism, major events—from a first haircut to a wedding—must take place on an "auspicious day." This day is chosen usually by a priest, family elder, or other respected member of the community based on the "karma" of the lunar calendar or particular measures of astrology. It's also associated with the Eastern art of arranging objects, *feng shui*. Millions of people in the world subscribe to this methodology for bringing success, health, and happiness.

STARTING YOUR OWN TRADITIONS

You may not have grown up with many traditions, but there are little rituals and celebrations you can incorporate into the milestones of your family. Experiences of other cultures point to fun customs at so many turns. For example, in the book *Throw Your Tooth on the Roof: Tooth Traditions from Around the World* by Selby Beeler, we learn about customs that go way beyond putting a tooth under one's pillow for the tooth fairy to exchange for money. And there are other events in a child's life you can make special by learning from other traditions. For example:

- In Iran, to mark the beginning of spring—symbolic of renewal—families celebrate by wearing all new clothes. For some, it might be the one day in the year they wear something new, but it puts all in step with the fresh beginnings surrounding them in nature.
- In Mongolia, among nomadic families, a child doesn't receive his/her first haircut until after surviving the dangers of infancy, or as old as age five (for boys) and six (for girls). This becomes an occasion for close family and friends to gather. A specially chosen elder (like a godparent) makes the first symbolic snip, somewhere close to the face, and all guests take a turn to make a small trim. An expert will later finish the job and the hair is saved as a keepsake for the child. This is followed by hospitality, complete with food and gifts of money, toys, sweets, and sometimes even a baby animal, like a goat, for the child's own herd—though you could modify this and give a housepet!

- In Germany, on the first day of school, children are sent with a special bundle of candies to wish them "sweet" success in the year ahead.
- Like the Mormons, start a weekly Family Home Evening. This was established to reflect the importance of family life, and has been promoted by toy makers as a "family game night." Yours can include a special dinner, story-reading or telling, game-playing, and other activities to engage and unite the family.
- Once the weather turns warm and the evenings are pleasant, do like most people in the world and head outside. If conditions allow, a summertime evening ritual can consist of reading bedtime stories on a blanket on the grass, or having a picnic one evening per week. Like families in parts of the Middle East who sleep on the roof in the summer—as well as camping enthusiasts all over the world—sleep outside as a special treat (if mosquitoes allow).

LIFE CYCLE CELEBRATIONS

Birth. Coming-of-age. Marriage. Death. This circle of life has formed a cornerstone of social organization for thousands of years in virtually every culture. In our hurried, informal, modern lives a baby might be born with the neighbors' only knowledge of its arrival from the Mylar balloon announcing "It's a Boy" outside the door. A wedding is officiated at city hall, followed by lunch with a handful of close friends or family, or the couple goes to an island far from home for their nuptials. A teen gets Happy Birthday wishes sent to her via Facebook. A funeral often becomes too time consuming or depressing for anyone but close family to attend. As a result, many of our children have never participated in or considered the larger meaning of these life-cycle milestones.

Practices in other cultures offer examples for how to inject meaning and community into our various celebrations and family milestones. We find one culture's example of celebrating life's milestones in three of Nigerian author Ifeoma Onyefulu's picture books intended for younger children: *Welcome Dede!*, *Here Comes Our Bride! An African Wedding Story*, and *Saying Farewell*. These help open youngsters' (and possibly their parents') eyes to key rites of passage in West African society. Mexican-American artist Carmen Lomas Garza gives a rich taste of her memories of Hispanic life in Texas near the Mexican border in the bilingual books *Family Pictures/Cuadros de Familia* and *In My Family/En Mi Familia*.

Birth days: Like the Nigerian custom, in many other cultures the baby's birth or infancy is greeted with days of celebration, prayers for protection and prosperity for the baby, and generous hospitality shared with a wide circle of people.

Where we live, the most common rituals for the birth of a baby are found dur-

Did You Know?

A wide range of cultures—from Chinese to West African to Russian to Latino and Middle Eastern—will not throw a baby shower before the baby is born, won't coo over their baby as cute, adorable, yummy, and so on, and certainly won't choose a name in advance of the birth (especially before a naming or blessing ceremony takes place). The thought in so many places is that evil will find the child who's being paid such attentions, and loved ones will try to hide the child from the "evil eye" or simply from bad that often finds its way to a newborn.

In the wedding photos from many countries, you'll notice the bride doesn't smile. This doesn't mean she isn't happy (though she may not be thrilled). It could be that she's been told *not* to smile: A smiling bride looks like a bride who was desperate to finally get hitched!

---

ing baptisms and christenings. Jewish families conduct a *brit milah* (Hebrew for "covenant of circumcision") or Bris ceremony for infant boys on their eighth day of life; for girls it might be an announcement of the baby's name at the synagogue.

Transcending religious beliefs, the universal practice for a baby's birth takes place when friends or neighbors band together to cook for the family of the newborn. This relief to the postpartum mother of feeding her household is not so different from ancient practices—like the Chinese, Arab, African, or Indian traditions of newborns and mothers staying indoors for periods of up to thirty or forty days after birth, receiving food from others, and refraining from the heavy household chores that normally fill their days.

Some traditional cultures require a haircut or head shaving for infants or toddlers (Islam and Hindui). Others prohibit an early haircut (Mongolian and Navajo). Some require circumcision of boys; others oppose it until puberty or altogether. Some call for a sweet food placed in the child's mouth to prepare the tongue to utter sweet words or to have a sweet future; others shun anything but breast milk. In several cultures the baby's first outing is to a temple or holy place. My kids' first outing was to the pediatrician—possibly a ritual in its own right. In various faiths and cultures, as soon as a baby is born, a special prayer is whispered in the baby's ear. This ensures that the first sounds it hears in this world are holy ones. Muslims whisper the "call to prayer" in the right ear, which is the same as what is chanted over the loudspeakers of mosques worldwide, calling believers to prayer:

God is Great. I bear witness that there is no God but God. I bear witness that Muhammad is the Prophet of God. Come to prayer. Come to success. God is great. There is no God but God.

One does not need to be a Muslim to appreciate this practice that welcomes a new life into this world. I have not found a specific Christian prayer for this occasion, though many faithful have composed prayers for their newborn babies. You could prepare a verse from your own Holy Book, or even a favorite poem or other prayer to recite into your newborn baby's ear at birth. This practice is traditionally performed by the father and can offer an immediate bond between Dad and newborn.

When my children were born, our extended family hosted a "Welcoming" party for our babies, and we have hosted them for various friends. After the baby is about a month old, we invite friends and family to share in an inspirational program as a blessing for the baby, followed by a meal together. The showering of love during the sleep-deprived early weeks of parenthood proves particularly meaningful to the new mother and father. The act of sharing inspiration, food, and fellowship around the start of a new life honors a practice that is both ancient and universal.

One special way to time your "welcoming" can be inspired by the Native American Navajo laughing ceremony. According to Navajo tradition, babies have a relationship with the Holy People in a world of the spirit before their birth into this world. The baby's first laugh—usually when they're between one and three months old—is the occasion to celebrate, because it marks the moment when the child is preparing to speak, and thus to fully enter this human world. The Navajo believe that the qualities of the person who witnessed the first laugh will be inherited by the baby, so they try to keep away anyone who is stingy, dishonest, and so on, in the early days. The person who coaxed the first laugh also is supposed to host the party. During the "Baby Laughed" ceremony, the baby "serves" salt crystals to guests, which is meant to rejuvenate good character in all and represent a lifetime of generosity practiced by the child.

One doesn't need to have Navajo roots to enjoy a custom like this. It brings the family's loved ones together, and more, it celebrates the joy generated by the new baby. The celebration symbolizes virtues like generosity and gratitude as well as joy, hospitality, friendship, care, kindness, and patience. Take this idea a step further using the universal symbol of the 'Tree of Life.' If you create a welcoming program for your baby and you have older children, you can make a Tree of Life and have them help you adorn it with "leaves" representing the virtues the family and guests hope to see in the young baby. Older siblings' attitudes will be refined and uplifted by thinking in terms of positive attributes and by helping with the

SMILE—a proactive spiritual practice

This simple yet profound lesson is taught by various Hindu and Buddhist religious teachers. A saying attributed to Vietnamese Buddhist poet Thich Nhat Hanh: "If we are not able to smile, then the world will not have peace. It is not by going out for a demonstration against nuclear missiles that we can bring about peace. It is with our capacity of smiling, breathing, and being peace that we can make peace."

For moody children (and their parents), challenge them to smile from the core of their heart or belly or whatever is the deepest place they connect with. Then, have that smile radiate on out through their chest, up their throat, to their face and their thoughts—a purely natural antidepressant. It also aids in starting meditation. Mahatma Gandhi's famous quote, "Be the change you wish to see," reinforces this idea. "Becoming" that smile makes for a change that is genuine and pleasant.

Tree, and they get personally involved in a substantive element of the baby's welcoming party. They can cut out colorful paper leaves; guests can write their wishes for the baby's life on the leaves, and this becomes a family keepsake that everyone contributed to. The Tree of Life can be made by your children and incorporate a cultural style that reflects your family's heritage or beliefs, as it has so many incarnations, from Celtic to Armenian, Hebrew to Hindu.

Coming-of-age celebrations: Like my own experience growing up, and for many non-Jewish American families, the first authentic experience of a religion outside of one's own is at a classmate's Bar or Bat Mitzvah ("one to whom the commandments apply") at age thirteen. Where we live, it's customary for parents to drop the kids off outside the synagogue and leave. If you can spare the time, stay awhile for the ceremony (no invitation is required for this portion) and talk about it with your child once the party is over; or prep your child in advance to bring home a lesson that struck them from the program.

With greater diversity in some neighborhoods, there are more cultural expressions for "coming-of-age." Replacing the old debutante ball, Sweet Sixteen parties in some areas have taken on a grand scale, partly influenced by over-the-top parties on MTV's *My Super-Sweet Sixteen*. There's also the Hispanic Quinceañera

("KEEN-say-an-yer-a") celebration for girls at age fifteen, blending a large party with roots in Spanish and Aztec tradition, when daughters are introduced into society, and preceded by a Catholic mass. With the growth in the Latino population in the United States, non-Hispanic youth are increasingly participating in the Quinceañera, as guests and as members of the "court" of best friends. This type of participation might influence more young people to want celebrations at milestone years in their teens.

In the Baha'i Faith, there is no set ritual for coming-of-age, but fifteen is considered the "age of maturity," when faith is practiced consciously, not simply inherited. This implies responsibilities to develop one's own spiritual life, and consider how to be of service to humanity—a lifelong quest. The combination of Confirmation, Bat Mitzvah, and Quinceñara inspired my family to host a "turning 15" party for our eldest daughter—with a meaningful sharing of her beliefs, a funny slide show of her life by her dad, dinner, and dancing.

The "Upanayana," or Hindu thread ceremony, is observed among Indians of upper castes. Like the milestone marker for so many other belief systems, this initiation ceremony for preadolescent males marks the transition to awareness and adult religious responsibilities. As my friend Vijaya explained to me, "It is when the ethical component of life, when contemplation about principles of right and wrong kicks in, and the person transitions from being ruled by instinct to becoming a more subtle, analytical, conscious being." When a boy is entitled to wear the sacred thread conferred by a family priest, he is considered twice born, or born-again. A growing number of Hindu parents are incorporating this ritual with life in North America instead of discarding it as a practice of the old country, as perhaps was done two or three generations ago, when immigrants were more focused on blending in. For young women, the rite is marked upon menses, which used to signal eligibility for marriage, but today might simply involve a gift of jewelry or a first sari passed privately from mother to daughter.

These life-marking rituals in traditional Hinduism are called the *Samskaras*, or sacraments. Like a Christian or Catholic sacrament, they are a physical reflection of Divine grace marking particular stages in one's life and spiritual development. The Catholic church's confirmation is not alone in recognizing that emergence into adulthood bestows sacred and more complex responsibilities. If the infant baptism was the parents' decision, the confirmation symbolizes the young person's own signature on the decision of faith, often represented by the choosing of a saint or confirmation name, or verbally recommitting to the name(s) given the individual at birth.

In Native American Navajo culture, the ancient Kinaaldá ceremony marks a girl's passage from child to adult, also following her first menstrual cycle. The book

Kinaaldá: A Navajo Girl Grows Up, part of the We Are Still Here: Native Americans Today series, gives a nice depiction of the symbolic acts of this ritual. The Vision Quest practiced in multiple Native American cultures puts the focus on finding one's spiritual core through a multiday endurance test for young men in the wilderness. Today, this rite of passage has become widely used in substance-abuse rehabilitation and for adults seeking a fresh start in their lives—for whatever reason.

Like many of the Native American rites, coming-of-age practices for most people in the world involve endurance and, possibly, pain. A more obscure practice is the Balinese tooth filing ceremony upon puberty. Pointed teeth are thought to represent animal instincts, so they are evened out to ward off evil in the person.

Another painful but more common rite is circumcision for adolescent boys and girls. In the case of girls, this practice is more accurately known as female genital cutting or mutilation (FGM); it's such a serious danger to a girl's health that it is illegal in many countries. Despite this, women in parts of southern Arabia and Africa widely continue the practice, believed to enhance girls' marriageability. This issue clearly is unpleasant to talk about; but with young teens and up, they can become informed about what their peers worldwide continue to endure, particularly if they happened to be born a girl. Learn more about this issue starting with information from the World Health Organization (who.org) (enter "FGM" in the Search box), or from a grassroots organization like Tostan (Tostan.org), working on the front lines of positive community transformation to abandon FGM. *Tostan* means "breakthrough" in Wolof, a predominant language of Senegal and The Gambia. To support advocacy and care for women escaping this practice, learn about the Tahirih Justice Center in Washington, D.C, (tahirih.org).

Increasingly, worldwide, the ambition for girls is to obtain education and accomplish life-goals through their careers. This makes graduation a more important coming-of-age rite than ever before. However, this is a new reality, even in modern, Western countries. Until just a generation or two ago, all a girl could aspire to was a good match in marriage that would provide the basics for her and her children's survival. Thus, diverse cultures' rites upon menstruation carried heavy weight for young girls—as a sign that marriage was imminent. The time of menstruation itself also signaled various forms of isolation of women from the rest of their kin, for being "unclean." This still prevails today among traditional Hindus, observant Muslims, and Orthodox Jews. Among Eastern Orthodox Christians, taking communion is prohibited for women at this time. My daughter experienced a version of this practice firsthand on a field trip to a mosque. After the girls were ushered away from the ornate door decorated in gold-leaf calligraphy (the men's entrance) to a small, dark, side door (the women's entrance) by the middle-aged imam (clergy in charge of the congregation), he asked the adolescent girls if any were menstruating, because if they were, they could not enter the mosque. As she described, "It was so embarrassing. We all looked down, and of course, we mumbled 'no.' " This was my daughter's first taste of the type of isolation or separate treatment experienced by women since early history and continuing globally today.

Movies can serve as another source for learning different cultural perspectives on marking an individual's coming-of-age. In the next chapter I have included a set of movies classified under Coming-of-Age. These don't give overt examples of how to mark the adolescent milestone; instead they offer a lens into the ways people in different cultures have experienced the transition from child to emerging adult. Our kids have assumed that most transitions from childhood to adult entail getting lavished with gifts, but in reality, many of these customs involve hardships. I won't be dropping off my girls in a forest to fend for themselves, but I can talk about why (and among whom) this might be the case. How do these practices reflect the importance of the milestone? How will they impact an individual's identity and cultural values in comparison with typical rites of passage in our culture, such as obtaining a driver's license, going to a prom, or graduating from high school? You can honor and celebrate your children's coming-of-age with customs you might derive from world cultures and faiths. A special acknowledgment—coupled with a process of service and learning—can bestow meaning at a turbulent time in a young person's life, when they might need it most.

Weddings: Like other rituals, wedding practices from various cultures can teach modern people a great deal about the meaning of marriage, as a milestone marking the joining of two lives and the union of two families. I have been particularly struck by the impact a long marriage celebration (like those practiced in South Asia, West Africa, and elsewhere) can have on the couple and beyond them. After days of ceremony, the bride and groom's bond is almost literally cemented together. The families have made deep commitments to each other, guests have spent many hours interacting together, children become friends with the in-laws' kids, and the couple is wedded to more than just each other. They are part of a fabric that holds the community together. In many traditional cultures, the wedding might be the first day husband and wife have ever laid eyes on each other. As *L.A. Times* writer Swati Pandey reflected after attending her cousin's very traditional Indian wedding, this "rite of passage . . . combines a wedding, prom and first date, moving out of your parents' house and in with a man."[1]

The fascination with weddings has spurred books for all ages depicting the celebration. *Now We Can Have a Wedding!* by Judy Cox takes a "melting pot" approach to preparing a wedding feast for a couple from a multiethnic apartment building. Ann Morris's photographic global survey, *Weddings,* for four- to eight-year-olds, gives a glimpse of different traditions. This age group also might enjoy *Uncle Peter's Amazing Chinese Wedding, Beni's First Wedding* (Jewish), *Navajo Wedding Day: A Diné Marriage Ceremony, La Boda: A Mexican Wedding Celebration,* and *The Road to Mumbai* (Indian).

The book *Joining Hands and Hearts: Interfaith, Intercultural Wedding Celebrations* by Susanna Stefanachi Macomb isn't a kids' book, but may be helpful if your family has been invited as guests to a wedding of a different faith or culture, or significantly, if a family member of yours is marrying someone from a different background. Sensitivity of each family to the needs and values of the new in-laws will help unite the two cultures, and may particularly benefit your children: Their memories of when they became relatives with people who seemed very different on the surface will be fond ones, and hopefully, the families will become closer as the years progress. Of course, this fosters a nurturing extended family for the future children born from this marriage, too.

Learning from global experiences when coping with death: It's usually out of need and not a wish that we talk with children about death and funerals. If your family is grieving the death of a loved one it might be instructive to learn how other cultures cope with such loss. I found that in parts of East and West Africa, the scenario of death is not a taboo subject with most children. From the death of an animal on the road or a loved pet, to the significant loss of a young mother or sibling, children learn this is a reality early in life. Their coping mingles whatever organized religion they belong to, with their traditional practices from their ancient cultures. So, the funeral may be carried out in the Islamic or Christian method, but the grieving and mourning period—sometimes marked by singing and wailing loudly (a cathartic release that can seem a bit scary to unaccustomed bystanders), being fed by their friends and family, and not going back to work for a certain length of time—is based on particular ethnic traditions.

In West Africa, we found that work in many environments, from government office clerks to housekeepers and teachers, ground to a stop when a funeral was taking place, and that large, extended networks of acquaintances would participate in the funeral and then be obligated to go back to pay respects to the mourning family after the ceremony was long over. So, the death of a distant acquaintance created a significant ripple effect on a wide circle of people and it seemed people were often attending funerals.

In Mexico, the annual "celebration" of their dead is marked by a national holiday, the *Dia de los Muertos,* or the Day of the Dead (annually on November 1 and 2) and is enjoying renewed popularity in part to counter the commercialism of

Halloween exported from the United States. This combines indigenous Aztec customs with Catholic prayers of All Souls Day, so the souls of loved ones who have passed on join the living for a night. Festivities are marked by sugar cubes or chocolates shaped like skulls and coffins, pottery and toys like skeletons, the placement of altars, candles, and wreaths of traditional gold flowers or paper that adorn headstones, and offerings of encouragement and nourishment to the souls that have passed on, featuring the favorite foods of the deceased. This rite embodies the Mexican idea of remembering death, mocking it, joking about it, and ultimately, facing it head-on. The parties around gravesites acknowledge the acceptance of death as a natural phase in the unpredictable cycle of life—in contrast with its somber or taboo treatment elsewhere.

When diverse cultures have a close relationship with the earth and nature, they seem to more readily recognize death as a natural component of the process of organic life. Since our trip to West Africa, I no longer shield my children from the sight of a dead bird or a field mouse in the backyard or the blood of meat at the butcher's. I previously thought that contact with anything dead could upset and therefore "scar" them; now I see their young acceptance of these realities as a healthy communion with life and the world around them. (At the same time, we don't own video games that involve killing and we carefully monitor the violence in movies and TV that our daughters might be exposed to.) Similarly, if we see a bird's eggs or a nest, we might try to protect it or consciously leave it alone. Learning from the wisdom of indigenous cultures, I want them to be aware of the beginning and the ending of so many life-forms around us. We humans are one of many life-forms in this vast ecosystem, though our consciousness (some might say, our soul) distinguishes us.

Try some origami.

Sadako and a Thousand Paper Cranes is the true story of a young girl born two years before the end of WWII in Japan. After she is diagnosed with leukemia she learns that folding one thousand paper cranes will bring her good luck. Since then, Sadako has become a hero in Japan and the tradition of folding cranes for peace and hope has spread worldwide. You can read the story (note that it is considered a sad story by many children) or share a summary. Try the art of origami paper-folding and cranemaking as a quiet coping mechanism, like the Japanese do.

To get a better sense of this "circle of life," the picture book *Lifetimes: The Beautiful Way to Explain Death to Children* offers the example of nature—all beings have a beginning and an ending, with living in between. Dr. Leo Buscaglia's *The Fall of Freddy the Leaf: A Story of Life for All Ages* also offers a gentle meditation of life's purpose and ending. These examples from nature don't emphasize a religious view. You can introduce your specific faith's perspective on death and life beyond this world to supplement the view from nature.

HAPPY BIRTHDAY!

The origin of the birthday party as we know it goes back to legends of medieval Europe, when it was feared that people were vulnerable to evil spirits on their birthdays. The more friends and family members attending bearing gifts, the better could one ward off the spirits. Originally, these celebrations were possible only for kings and nobility, and this might explain the custom of wearing a birthday crown. The smoke from blowing out candles sent one's wishes up to the gods, and noisemakers scared the evil spirits away. I am amazed by how firmly these medieval European traditions remain today.

Other customs shape our celebrations, too. The Mexican birthday tradition featuring piñatas filled with candy and small toys has become totally integrated into U.S. birthday parties. Few would associate their Little Mermaid or Buzz Lightyear piñata with a Mexican tradition, but that's exactly what it is. Big parties for babies turning one are becoming the norm, following the worldwide practice in places where infant mortality was traditionally high, so families had much to celebrate when their little one made it through their first year. Today, particularly in ethnic communities in the United States—Korean, Vietnamese, Chinese, Arab, and African—this tradition continues and, in some cases, is compared to the grandeur of a wedding party, hosted in large banquet halls, with relatives flying in from around the world to celebrate.

CELEBRATING BIRTHDAYS AROUND THE WORLD

A cake, candles, song, presents, and friends seem to represent the universal components of birthday celebrations. The differences that remain are in the details, or are particularly found among stronger traditional (and often, geographically remote) cultures. In certain cultures, such as the Latin American, birthdays are usually celebrated similarly to North American, but with what seems to be a grander scale of everything: more food, more friends, more decorations, more presents, more dressed-up than an economically similar family here.

When I asked friends and contacts from various countries if they ever practiced the traditional customs I had read about for birthdays in their country, many responded that they had never even heard of these customs (e.g., rubbing butter on one's nose for birthdays in Canada). Some traditions do remain, though. Here are a few to consider, ranging from meaningful to silly:

Scandinavia: Our friend Michael Alexandersen, from Denmark, describes how traditional Scandinavian customs were celebrated in his home, and for the most part, continue today: "When I was a child, my family would wake me on my birthday by opening the door to my room singing a birthday song. Presents would be placed on the dining table, and are opened before breakfast. We hung flags from the ceiling and outside a window to show that someone who lives in our house was having a birthday. Children bring a cake made of cream puff covered with chocolate to share with their classmates."

Brazil, Argentina, and Paraguay: In traditional families instead of getting the best, first slice of cake, the birthday boy or girl gives the first slice of cake to their most special friend or relative, usually one of the parents. Instead of a "pinch to grow an inch" or spanks for the number of years, the birthday child receives a pull on the earlobe for each year they have been alive.

Ecuador: My friend Solange is working as a volunteer in Ecuador and told me: "After singing happy birthday to the *cumpleañero,* he or she is supposed to bite the birthday cake. As they bite, someone or various people push their face into the cake and get frosting all over them. The *cumpleañero* knows this is coming so tries to bite quickly and get away before getting pushed in. At my birthday three of us had a joint party, so we shared one cake and each had to take a bite from it!"

Russia and Germany: Birthdays are celebrated on or after the birthday, not before. Wishing someone happy birthday prior to the actual date is considered bad luck. When my friend was visiting her hometown of Bremen, Germany, she called to wish an old classmate "Happy Birthday" before leaving to go back to the states. My friend told me, "This otherwise modern woman gasped and said, 'Oh, let's pretend you didn't say that!' "

Israel and Egypt: Arabs and Israelis might not see eye-to-eye on religion or politics, but due to thousands of years of shared history and geography, they enjoy similar foods and certain birthday customs. For example, birthday parties are traditionally decorated with fresh flowers, fruits, and greens—symbols of life and growth to both.

Some don't celebrate birthdays.

People as diverse as devout Jehovah's Witnesses and traditional Saudi Arabians and most rural Africans don't usually observe individual birthdays. Religious convictions might shun it, or some cultures simply do not know the actual birth date. A friend who grew up in Tanzania related a perspective that's found the world over: "What's the point of celebrating a birthday when daily life is a struggle? Half my relatives don't know when their birthday even is." This reflects what a luxury it is to spend the money and time on a birthday that comes every year, focuses only on the individual, and doesn't have significant meaning or yield a tangible result. This also shows the difference between a culture that values individualism versus one that values, and depends on, community.

China: In one generation, conditions around birthday celebrations have changed drastically. Parents around my age say that when they were children, the idea of making kids the center of attention was shunned, as the country was largely closed to Western influence, firmly Communist, and poor. Today, however, with new wealth available to so many, fascination with modernity and consumerism, and the fact that most families have only one child, birthday parties in the cities have become lavish affairs where one family often tries to outdo the next. One tradition that prevails is the bowl of noodles for the birthday boy or girl: Extra-long noodles are fed to the celebrant to represent longevity in life.

Philippines: Like so many aspects of its culture, Philippine birthday celebrations combine Eastern and Western influences, like Asian noodles and various rice cakes for a long and good life, with balloon decorations and piñatas (reflecting the lasting influence after nearly four hundred years as a Spanish colony), and among the majority Catholic population, attendance of morning mass to start the day. Particularly for adults, the person who's celebrating the birthday will treat friends to a meal—as the host—and not the other way around as we do in the United States. Every birthday for every person, young or old, needs to be celebrated, even if very simply. Among less prosperous families, invitations to birthday parties are not sent out, but all the neighborhood is welcomed to the festivity.

Vietnam: As my friends from Vietnam have told me, only those who were born in the 1980s and later have grown up celebrating their birthdays, with the exception of certain elites who were raised around French colonizers at the turn of the twentieth century, and thus engaged in French-style celebrations. The country was poor, families had numerous children (nine to twelve kids was the norm for most people I spoke with), and with the long wars, a birthday celebration wasn't even considered (other than the traditional one- and three-year-old celebrations, but these were more to celebrate the child's survival amid high infant mortality rates). While weddings are typically elaborate affairs involving hundreds of people, the birthdays of young people today are more about holding a family get-together than indulging the birthday child. Demonstrating what a foreign practice a birthday party is, Vietnamese also sing "Happy Birthday" in English, like we do in America. Money is the typical gift, offered in a simple envelope. The special red envelope is reserved for Tet, or New Year (same as the Chinese New Year).

BRING THE WORLD TO YOUR BIRTHDAY PARTY

Creative parents have found all kinds of ways to incorporate global themes into a fun birthday party; here are a few ideas you can try.

Gigi's "Around the World" party: Gigi Shamsy Raye and Mike Raye, from a Dallas suburb, created an unforgettable theme for their twins' sixth birthday. "We 'took' our twins and friends around the world to visit countries of friends' families." She created invitations by reproducing an actual airline boarding pass and filled in party details like "Estimated departure (and return) time" and "Please call ahead to confirm seating" instead of the standard RSVP line. Activities included passport making, storytelling, and games from various countries. Friends from China, Russia, and elsewhere helped out with activities. They showed an "in-flight movie," had snacks from various countries, and instead of goody bags, kids got airplane sick bags filled with cool globe-themed tchotchkes like those found in the Oriental Trading Company catalogue (oriental.com).

Mina's sushi party: Thanks in part to supermarket and mall food courts, kids all over are starting to choose sushi over pizza or burgers. For her daughter Juliet's seventh birthday, my sister threw a sushi-themed party. On the invitation, she had a picture of Juliet dressed in a geisha-type costume (kimono-style robe, hair up in chopsticks, white powder and dots of red lipstick on lower and upper lip) eating a sushi roll. The picture made it clear: This was going to be a fun party! She mounted the photo on red card stock with the party info on the back. The main

Go to Ottawa to see the world.

Ottawa is the capital of Canada—it's Washington, D.C.—and is about a seven-hour drive from New York and a nine-hour car ride from Detroit. Among its attractions is the stunning Canadian Museum of Civilization. Within this impressive building (designed by the same architect of Native American ancestry as the Smithsonian Museum of the American Indian) is the Canadian Children's Museum. The children's museum's permanent exhibit is *The Great Adventure*, which takes kids on a virtual trip around the world. They start with getting a passport—similar to that at the Around the World birthday party—and get it stamped at various "destinations," like Nigeria, Indonesia, Mexico, Japan, and Egypt's Nile. Unload a ship's cargo, play global games, experience fabrics and clothing worn worldwide, visit diverse market settings, and more. If your family enjoys the virtual travel component of the birthday party, then schedule this family trip.

party "craft" would be to make sushi rolls. Her local Whole Foods Market made the inexpensive sticky rice in advance, then she prepared veggies for the kids to use as filling, along with sesame seeds to sprinkle on top. The kids designed their own flags to designate the rolls they made and shared their sushi with all at the party.

For dessert, her daughter wanted a "regular birthday cake," but the children could also try crepes with various fillings to keep with the "rolling" theme. Red goody bags were filled with chopsticks, the inexpensive but attractive rectangular sushi plates used by each child, and Hello Kitty stickers and pencils. Along with Hello Kitty, other Japanese-style characters include Pokemon, Power Puff Girls, Sailor Moon, and Avatar the Last Airbender (actually an American character made to look like it came from Asia) that could go with the theme. It's been awhile since this party took place, but my niece Juliet will still excitedly describe her most memorable party for anyone who asks.

OTHER BIRTHDAY PARTY THEMES

What if your child's birthday falls on or around Bastille Day (July 14), or Cinco de Mayo, or Earth Day (April 22), or the World Cup, or any number of significant days in countries around the world? When you're ready to move beyond the

Princess, Cars, Power Ranger, or Pony party theme, these can supply an offbeat alternative. Here are more ideas for a fun, nondidactic party:

- A Parisian theme has many possibilities for boys and girls, including creating a *parfumerie* game to guess various scents, playing a game of recovering stolen art for the Louvre museum (e.g., a scavenger hunt), and staging a tricycle race à la *Tour de France.* Fashionistas can do activities with dress-up and stage a design contest with various fabrics and household items. Print pictures of the Eiffel Tower or other favorite Paris destinations to make postcard invitations or for craft activities during the party.
- An Egyptian theme can include a "tomb raider" game, similar to the stolen art scavenger hunt from the Parisian theme. Dance to popular Egyptian disco music. Make crafts to simulate hieroglyphics of guests' names or make pharaohs, pyramids, or jewelry to imitate the ancient culture. Many elementary schools study ancient Egypt extensively. Ask teachers what resources they know about.
- Olympics parties can include flag-making for random countries that each child picks from a hat. Have a ready "cool" fact available about that country that the child could identify with or get excited about (e.g., which sport they are strongest in, profile a famous local athlete, how many athletes from that country participated in the last Olympics, or a famous landmark from that country). Relay and group games can be played at the party, followed by random ribbon award ceremonies (e.g., for the fastest or most creative finishers, best teamwork, loudest team spirit, most authentic flag, etc.). Snacks can revolve around a Greek theme or a recently past or upcoming Olympics' host location.

Invest in a huge world map.

If you haven't gotten around to getting your big world map yet, before a party is a good time to do so. Mark the places you'll "visit" during your global party, and this can serve as your main decoration. When the festivities are over, hang it where daydreaming young eyes can fix upon it. National Geographic's World Mural Map, 110 inches wide, is the classic oversized map; there are also Peters and Universal maps and many online outlets for purchasing them.

United States or international? Not an either-or choice!

As I've emphasized throughout *Growing Up Global,* there's no need to choose between patriotism for one's country and a love of the world. At your Around the World party, you can include a U.S. table or a station based on a favorite part of the United States, tucked among your other countries. New Orleans/Mardi Gras, Wild West, New York, Hawaiian luau—the possibilities are virtually endless for themes. When we have hosted "international" parties I always make clear that hot dogs, apple pie, and other all-American fare are welcome—they reflect our guests' culture, too.

BETTER TO GIVE THAN TO RECEIVE?

A *New York* magazine feature writer asked actress Natalie Portman, just before the release of her movie about a magical toy store, *Mr. Magorium's Wonder Emporium,* "What's the best gift you've been given?" She replied, "My family and friends have been doing FINCA (Foundation for International Community Assistance) donations. It's a nonprofit microfinance organization. It gives loans to women who earn under $3 a day to start businesses in developing countries. So that's nice, because, you know, I don't really need anything."[2] When we stop to think about it, how many of us or our children really *need* many gifts each birthday, and couldn't we instill a sense of giving to others alongside the birthday gifts our children will receive? This issue of give versus receive, or "presence" versus presents for birthdays and holidays, has recently caused considerable debate.

On one side, a growing number of families include charity as one of their family values and are finding creative ways to engage in philanthropy. Starting kids young in giving while getting is like developing your child's muscle for sharing and compassion.

It is possible to both give and receive at the party. This practice might work particularly well when your family throws a large bash. Rather than pile up twenty or so wrapped presents that overwhelm the child, fewer than half of which are remembered or played with, you can send a note along with the invitation requesting that the gift cost under $10 or $5, so they can also donate to a favorite charity on behalf of the party. You could follow a program like Echoage.com or Birthday partygameslady.com where guests pool money to get one big, cherished gift for the celebrant and make one donation all together for a good cause.

On the other side of the debate, some argue directing birthday gifts to charities can create children that grow up resentful of philanthropy, feeling forced to give when they really didn't feel like it or weren't ready for it. Charity should not be reserved for special occasions, and it should be done more quietly and humbly and not as a display that goes with a party. If it's done out of political correctness, the kids can usually smell it from a mile away and will grow up resisting your charitable efforts. If it's a sincere desire on the part of the parents but still resisted by kids, then you might look for other outlets for giving as a family.

There isn't a right or wrong answer to this debate. The most important step in this process, I think, is to discuss the idea first with your children: Maybe they don't even remember half the gifts from last year's party; or they might want to do their part to cut down on generating waste; or they might be moved by a need that they have seen, from earthquake or hurricane victims on TV, to animals left alone at a nearby shelter, to homeless and hungry families in your town or in another country—these personal experiences could lead them to make a conscious decision to "do good" while celebrating their birthday. A birthday celebration that involves giving back works best when it's well planned. A child needs time to let the concept sink in. And more, they need to become invested in the cause they'll give to.

Making a difference through a birthday doesn't need to be confined to giving away one's birthday presents or making cash donations. If your party involves craft-making, make a card, jewelry, paper flowers, wall-hangings, posters, and so on, to give others, like children at the local hospital, seniors at a nursing home, or families in a shelter. Make time that day or another day to deliver the gifts (with anyone from the party who wants to and can go). Respectfully visiting those for whom you have made a gift can create an active connection between your child, that cause, and the recipient.

Theme parties—so you can "have your cake and eat it too!" There's nothing wrong with having a fun theme party and also making a difference in the world. Here are a few themes you can try:

• A party at the zoo can raise awareness of and donations for global climate or wildlife issues. Guests and host can donate supplies for the zoo (talk to administrators about their needs, first) as part of the "gift" and the group can deliver them together.
• Some animal shelters or humane societies will allow birthday parties on premises

and friends can contribute to the shelter. You can make accessories for the pets or the shelter as a party activity.

- Hold a "literacy party," asking for a book donation to a favorite local or international charity; invite a storyteller and give books in lieu of goody bags. Guests can dress up as a favorite book character.
- At a dress-up or princess party, ask friends to bring dress-up gifts to cheer up boys and girls at a children's hospital cancer unit. Gifts also could be brought for a play corner at an area emergency room, particularly in the inner city, where there might be heavy traffic and few distractions for children.
- A "water" theme party can take place in the summer at a pool (or indoor pool anytime of year) or in the backyard with sprinklers and spray guns. Acknowledge the global water crisis by curbing the sprinkler use to a specific number of minutes and share with the kids why you are doing that. Games with water-filled balloons emphasize water conservation—try not to pop the balloon! Serve a brand of water (like Earth-Water or Ethos) that benefits global water projects, or just serve filtered tap water as the most environmentally sound choice. Direct donations to an organization that supports clean water like waterforpeople.org or www.globalgreen.org. Watch a DVD like *Planet Earth, Volume 1* or the IMAX film *Deep Sea* when you need a break from the water play.
- At a pottery party, donate "clay" to an organization like Aid to Artisans directly or through www.changingthepresent.org. Learn why this will make a difference in an artisan's life.
- Have a picnic party at a local farm. Talk to the farmer about how you could co-operate to make this mutually beneficial. They might allow you donkey rides or a chance to feed some of the animals and talk to the kids about how a working farm works. Could the guests perform some kind of service for the farm? Then, guests can donate to an organization like Heifer International or a local CSA (Community Supported Agriculture).
- For the international theme parties listed previously, you can include a donation from the party to related organizations. For example, Médecins Sans Frontières (Doctors Without Borders) was founded by French volunteers (for the Parisian party); Seeds of Peace brings together Arab and Israeli youth (for the Egyptian party); and some of the sports charities listed in Chapter 4—games can benefit from an Olympics-themed party.

Internet resources to help advance your charitable goal. Learning to Give, at Learning togive.org and the Youth in Philanthropy page at the Foundation Center's website (youth.foundationcenter.org) have curricula giving ideas and many links to teach children about philanthropy; once you get into it, you can apply these ideals to your birthday party.

To create cool electronic invitations use pingg.com, which directly links to Changing the Present (changingthepresent.org), from which you choose up to six of your favorite causes for your optional electronic gift registry. It also links to amazon.com for a more "traditional" gift registry, so you can give and get. You can give a gift of charity through Justgive.org and give charity gift cards through sites like networkforgood.org, charitygiftcertificates.org, and tisbest.org.

After the party: Once the party festivities are over, you can reinforce the "giving back" message to your child. If you chose a local charity, go together to drop off donations, so they can see the place and catch the spirit of their service. In communication with the nonprofit's staff, see what follow-up you can do. Consider taking along a few of your child's friends on the return trip.

If possible, have your child and interested party guests maintain a pen pal relationship with children from the area for which they did service or collected a donation. For example, if you gave to a wildlife, water, or other environmental program, with some thoughtful advance planning you might be able to obtain a P.O. box or email address for children who live in the affected area and begin a correspondence with them. If your donation targeted sports, literacy, refugees, or health this also might be feasible. Don't expect an instant response to your offer, however. Often you will need to persist or get creative in contacting the overworked administrative office as this adds one more thing for them to do. Nonetheless, there's a chance they will welcome your desire to make a sincere connection with the children they see every day, who are often forgotten by those more fortunate.

Remember to send thank-you notes to everyone who came. Share one or two positive outcomes from the party in your cards. This could be the smile on the face of one of the kids you took a gift for, or how cuddly one of the animals was, or a quote from an international charity indicating the impact the group's donation made. If you collected funds, mention how much you gathered for which charity and possibly include the organization's website. If your child is too young to write the card themselves, ask them how they felt about a "meaningful" aspect of the party and quote them directly in the card—put it in their words, not yours.

———

Like laughter and music and games and good food, celebrations can serve as a universal language for bringing people together. Indeed, they involve each of those elements that are fun or revered—and don't require too much translation. Every culture celebrates. And every celebration brings people together with ample hospitality, joy, and usually, tradition. Among our most memorable celebrations have been those that we opened up to include friends from backgrounds that might not celebrate the same holidays as we do, or the times that we welcomed students or friends that were new to the country. Their "fresh" eyes gave new meaning to our usual get-togethers. They also involved more "giving" of ourselves. Your children can be involved in explaining why you do what you do, and in the process they might get excited about your family customs that they could have taken for granted previously.

Birthday celebrations—the most universal of all festivities—also can serve as a way to connect with the world. Through globally minded themes, trying customs from other places, or remembering those less fortunate, a birthday can serve as an annual reminder of reaching out personally to the world. In a way, it's like showing gratitude for being born. Don't choose between having fun or making an impact. Do both. Have your cake (or *bon bon* or *torta* or *baklava*), eat it, and share it, too!

RESOURCE BOOKS CITED IN CHAPTER 7—THAT YOU MAY FIND HELPFUL, TOO

Children Just Like Me: Celebrations! Barnabas and Anabel Kindersley (New York: DK Publishing, 1997).

Barron's Educational Festival Time! series by Jonny Zucker and Jan Barger Cohen: *Lighting a Lamp: A Diwali Story* (2004); *Apples and Honey: A Rosh Hashanah Story* (2001); *It's Party Time! A Purim Story* (2004); *Lanterns and Firecrackers: A Chinese New Year Story* (2003); *Hope and New Life! An Easter Story* (2004); and *Fasting and Dates: A Ramadan and Eid Story* (2004).

Kids Around the World Celebrate! The Best Feasts and Festivals from Many Lands, Lynda Jones (New York: Wiley, 1999).

National Geographic's *Holidays Around the World* (2006–2008) series by Debra Heiligman, featuring titles around Ramadan, Rosh Hashanah, Yom Kippur, Easter, Christmas, Hanukkah, Diwali, Kwanzaa, and Thanksgiving.

The *Rookie Read-About Holidays* series (Children's Press, Scholastic)—twenty titles in the series, with the major cultural holidays, as well as *Cinco de Mayo, El Dia de los Muertos,* Holi, Earth Day, and Veterans' Day.

Celebrating Ramadan and Celebrating Chinese New Year by Diane Hoyt-Goldsmith and Lawrence Migdale (photographs) (New York: Holiday House, 2002 and 1999).

The Islamic Year: Surahs, Stories and Celebrations by Noorah Al-Gailani and Chris Smith (United Kingdom: Hawthorn Press, May 2003).

Muslim Child: Understanding Islam through Stories and Poems, Rukhsana Khan (author) and Patty Gallinger (illustrator) (Morton Grove, IL: Albert Whitman and Company, 2002).

How to Be a Perfect Stranger: The Essential Religious Etiquette Handbook, Fourth Edition, mentioned in Chapter 6.

There's No Such Thing as a Chanukah Bush, Sandy Goldstein, Susan Sussman (Morton Grove, IL: Albert Whitman & Company, 1983).

Get Ahead by Going Abroad, Perry Yeatman and Stacey Nevadomski Berdan (New York: Collins Living, 2007).

The Runaway Rice Cake, Ying Chang Compestine (author) and Tungwai Chau (illustrator) (New York: Simon & Schuster Children's Publishing, 2001).

Musubi Man: Hawaii's Gingerbread Man, Sandi Takayama (author) and Pat Hall (illustrator) (Honolulu: Bess Press, 1997).

The Runaway Latkes, Leslie Kimmelman (author) and Paul Yalowitz (illustrator) (Morton Grove, IL: Albert Whitman & Company, 2000).

The Runaway Tortilla, Eric A. Kimmel (author) and Randy Cecil (illustrator) (New York: Winslow Press, 2000).

The Cajun Gingerbread Boy, Berthe Amoss (New Orleans, LA: Cocodrie Press, 2004).

Throw Your Tooth on the Roof: Tooth Traditions from Around the World, Selby Beeler (author) and Brian Karas (illustrator) (New York: Houghton Mifflin, 1998).

Welcome Dede! An African Naming Ceremony; Here Comes Our Bride! An African Wedding Story, and *Saying Good-Bye: A Special Farewell to Mama Nkwelle,* Ifeoma Onyefulu (London: Frances Lincoln Children's, 2004, 2004, and 2003).

Family Pictures/Cuadros de Familia and *In My Family/En Mi Familia,* Carmen Lomas Garza (San Francisco: Children's Book Press, 1992 and 1996).

Kinaaldá: A Navajo Girl Grows Up (We Are Still Here: Native Americans Today series), Monty Roessel (Minneapolis, MN: Lerner, 1993).

Weddings, Ann Morris (New York: Harper Collins, 1995).

Now We Can Have a Wedding! Judy Cox (New York: Holiday House, 1998).

Uncle Peter's Amazing Chinese Wedding, Lenore Look (author), Yumi Heo (illustrator) (New York: Atheneum/Anne Schwartz Books, 2006).

Beni's First Wedding, Jane Breskin Zalben (New York: Henry Holt, 1998).

Navajo Wedding Day: A Diné Marriage Ceremony, Eleanor Schick (Tarrytown, NY: Cavendish Children's Books,1999).

La Boda: A Mexican Wedding Celebration, Nancy Van Laan (author) and Andrea Arroyo (illustrator) (New York: Little Brown and Company, 1995).

The Road to Mumbai, Ruth Jeyaveeran (Boston: Houghton Mifflin, 2004).

Joining Hands and Hearts: Interfaith, Intercultural Wedding Celebrations, Susanna Stefanachi Macomb (New York: Fireside, 2003).

Sadako and a Thousand Paper Cranes, Eleanor Coerr (New York: Penguin Group USA, 1999. First edition, 1997).

Lifetimes: The Beautiful Way to Explain Death to Children, Bryan Mellonie (New York: Bantom Books, 1983).

The Fall of Freddy the Leaf: A Story of Life for All Ages, Dr. Leo Buscaglia (New York: Henry Holt, 1982).

Water Boy, David McPhail (New York: Abrams Books for Young Readers, 2007).

A Drop Around the World, Barbara McKinney (author) and Michael Maydak (illustrator) (Nevada City, CA: DAWN Publications, 1998).

ADDITIONAL RESOURCE BOOKS RELATED TO CHAPTER 7

The Great Race: Story of the Chinese Zodiac, Dawn Casey (author) and Anne Wilson (illustrator) (Cambridge, MA: Barefoot Books, 2006).

The White Nights of Ramadan, Maha Addasi (author) and Ned Gannon (illustrator) (Honesdale, PA: Boyds Mill Press, 2005).

The Latke Who Couldn't Stop Screaming: A Christmas Story, Lemony Snicket (author), Lisa Brown (illustrator) (San Francisco: McSweeney's, 2007).

Chapter 8

Watch the World—Read a Movie

Film is one of three universal languages.
The other two: mathematics and music.

FRANK CAPRA

My father describes his ideal childhood weekends in the late 1940s in Iran. "They started on Thursday nights [Friday is the day off in predominantly Muslim countries] and the highlight was going to the Cinema Mayak or the U.S. Cultural Center in Isfahan—if you had a good connection at the U.S. consulate or embassy to get you in—to watch American swashbucklers like Errol Flynn fight the bad guys. Early on, the movies were all in English and we couldn't understand a word, but it didn't matter; we loved the gunfights and sword duels. By the 1950s, local cinemas got more sophisticated: We watched John Wayne speaking Persian. . . . I can almost hear the crackling of the roasted pumpkin and watermelon seeds the audience chewed during the movie—our Iranian popcorn."

After watching the 2007 film *The Kite Runner* set in Afghanistan, I remembered my father's story when one of the boys in the film had to be told that he couldn't go to Iran to meet his hero, Charles Bronson, who spoke Farsi (Persian) in the movies they watched. The boy in the movie identified so closely with the 1970s action star that he couldn't fathom him coming from anywhere but the neighboring country. Little could the Afghani child imagine that Charles Bronson actually was the son of Lithuanians who emigrated to work in Pennsylvania coal mines.

Going to the movies is a universal experience. Hollywood still reigns, but the movie industry outside the United States is growing in size and popularity. Some of the best family movies—both serious and whimsical—come from countries like New Zealand, France, China, and even Iran and Mongolia. Kids all over the world still enjoy the characters American kids love, from Harry Potter (English) to Spongebob Squarepants and the Rugrats (both developed by Hungarians). Like my father's generation, the world is watching "us"; but what do we know about *them*?

Dinner and a movie and a journey

Cable TV movie nights with zany hosts make watching classic or cheesy favorite movies more fun by accompanying segments of the films with similarly themed foods. Try this with foreign movies. Have a meal—or just snacks—that go with the country in the movie. Crepes, noodles and dumplings, kabobs, hummus and pita, wasabi peas, mango lassi and samosas—get creative! Particularly when starting to watch new genres, the food angle can help to increase anticipation for a fun experience and also allows more opportunities to pause the film and talk about what you just saw.

My friend Hanh, who grew up in Vietnam, recalled one of her happiest childhood memories: watching *The Sound of Music* (dubbed into Vietnamese) and acting and singing the parts with her own siblings. Similarly, my mother saw it dubbed into Persian while she was pregnant with me in Tehran ("They even sang in Persian!" she recalls). I first saw and loved *The Sound of Music* as a young child in Indiana, and recently my own daughter downloaded the songs onto her iPod for singing along on long car rides. Who would imagine that the story and songs depicting a 1940s family in the Austrian Alps could have such an impact upon multiple generations living in such different circumstances?

Good movies in any language transport audiences to places and experiences they might never have imagined. Watching a foreign film creates a vicarious travel experience, taking us anywhere we want to go. We start to care about other cultures when we see them. The less we see, the less likely we are to care. The movies help us to "see."

To enjoy foreign films takes some getting used to and repeated exposure. Like learning a new language, the sooner you start, the easier it is to accustom your children to diverse cinematic styles. Thanks to vast film databases like Netflix.com, Blockbuster.com, and more resources described later in this chapter, the best foreign films ever made are now easily accessible.

GETTING STARTED: PICK MOVIES FOR ENTERTAINMENT, NOT AS EDUCATION

With few exceptions, I rarely buy movie DVDs, as I don't expect to see them more than once. I thought I was buying something we'd all want to see multiple times when I purchased *An Inconvenient Truth*, Al Gore's presentation on climate change. At the time, my middle-school-aged daughters already were interested in environmental conservation and the movie had garnered much attention. What was I thinking? It's an important project, but my kids don't want to spend their precious free time watching a PowerPoint presentation given by a middle-aged, former vice president—again and again. Family movie night should be fun, not "academic," and I've been working hard ever since to regain my reputation for movie picking.

My top foreign family film picks: The Essential 7

There are so many to choose from, but don't miss these Essential 7. The content on all of these is quite innocent, and depending on each family's preferences, suitable for children over six:

• *Beauty and the Beast.* See the original French version, made in 1946, where Disney's inspiration came from.

• *My Neighbor Totoro* and, for slightly older audiences, *Spirited Away.* Discover mystical, magical worlds that are uniquely Japanese.

• *The Cave of the Yellow Dog* and *The Story of the Weeping Camel.* These films show life in Mongolia that is innocent, real, and contemporary, yet worlds away from what we know.

• *Lagaan.* The best elements of India's "Bollywood": catchy song and dance, love triangle, good guys versus bad guys, and a little bit corny.

• *The Legend of Roan Inish.* The real Irish countryside is infused with elements of legend to captivating effect.

• *Children of Heaven.* A brother's love and care for his little sister as they seek her lost pair of shoes humanizes Iran's children in a universal story.

• *Winged Migration.* Follow familiar and rare bird species to and from all corners of the globe with keen cinematography that awakens the senses while it calms the soul.

My husband did much better when he chose *Fiddler on the Roof,* which became one of our daughters' favorite movies. This classic was at times fun, romantic, silly, and ultimately heart-wrenching to watch. At the same time it taught about the rural Jewish community before the Russian revolution, gave insights to an important immigrant experience, portrayed the strength of a people's belief systems, and many other lessons, without getting preachy or didactic. These songs also found their way onto my daughter's iPod. A good movie is just that: It speaks or sings for itself. There are so many good titles—including funny, silly, light movies—that choosing where to start might be the most difficult step.

Gaining a global vision is not exclusive of having fun and being entertained, and it doesn't need to become a family's one-track agenda. Even if your family enjoys foreign films, you probably shouldn't watch them exclusively. I'm not opposed to pop culture (in moderation). I hope my kids will never feel the need to escape home to watch a movie that's cool or enjoyable because Mom and Dad are intent on feeding them a diet of movies that are "good for them."

Where does the story from the kids' movie come from? There are many ways to gain exposure to "foreign" films or themes—without planning to, you already may have. If you or your kids grew up watching Disney cartoons, you got a small glimpse from another culture. Of course, the movies have taken substantial creative license (i.e., they stretched historical truth), but they are often American children's first exposure to other cultures. Examples to point out to your children:

- *Beauty and the Beast* is set in rural France, *Pinocchio* in an Italian village.
- *Peter Pan* and *Mary Poppins* are set in London.

Revisit Peter and the Wolf.

The world's greatest symphony orchestras have recorded their versions of Prokofiev's *Peter and the Wolf*—a now-classic Russian story—since the 1940s. In 2008, a modern version won the Academy Award for Best Animated Short and in 2006, a CD featuring Sophia Loren, Bill Clinton, and Mikhail Gorbachev won a Grammy Award. Both depict concern for modern environmental degradation not seen in older versions. Listen to the music and the story on CD before watching the Disney adaptation—there's something for everyone in any of the versions.

- *Jungle Book* was inspired by Rudyard Kipling's stories from India.
- *Mulan,* loosely based on a famous Chinese legend and poem from the sixth century, came from the central plains of China.
- *Pocahontas,* born around 1595, was from the Powhatan confederacy of tribes of the Algonquians in Virginia's Tidewater region. The Disney movie takes liberties with history, but her significance is reflected in a painting depicting her Christian baptism, which hangs in the U.S. capitol building rotunda.
- *The Prince of Thieves* tells the story of Moses in the Bible.
- *Aladdin* is loosely based on the stories of Scheherazade's *1001 Arabian Nights.*
- *Lion King* takes place in the Masai Mara of Kenya.
- *Ratatouille* is set in modern Paris.

If you are aware of the international settings in these popular movies, you can use the opportunity for learning. For example, before watching the movie, ask the kids to listen for a phrase in a foreign language (from French to Swahili to Chinese and Hindi) or for hints that reflect the setting (e.g., accents, slang, references to locations). For foreign phrases, try to write the words you hear in the movie phonetically, then look up the exact definition. Could you have guessed the meaning based on the context of the film? How does the different cultural setting show in the architecture, landscape, food, clothes, names of characters, and other details of the movie? Are the characters' names typical of the cultures that are being depicted? Are there features of the movie that are unrealistic for that culture or playing to stereotypes that Americans might have of that culture? Disney's *Lion King* movie, for example, uses real Swahili expressions like *"hakuna matata"* (no problem, no worries), words (many of the animal names, like Simba, are actually the Swahili word for that animal), and re-creates the actual landscape of the East African plains around the Masai Mara. Unfortunately, it also reinforces the notion of the rich animal life in Africa without depicting anything about the human culture of that region.

CINDERELLA'S GLOBAL ROOTS

A popular topic in American elementary- through high-school curricula traces the global nature of the Cinderella story. Some elementary-school curricula teach kids that the beloved 1950 Disney movie (based on the French story *Cendrillon,* which dates from about 1700) finds its roots as a legend in China that is over one thousand years old. (Some say it goes back thousands of years to a Greek story.) The Chinese story of Yeh-Shen introduces an evil stepmother who prefers her unattractive biological daughter over her beautiful stepdaughter, culminating when a handsome prince locates his mystery love after considerable conflict, and matches a unique and unusually small slipper to the foot of his true beloved, Yeh-Shen. A version of this story is found in the 2004 book *Bound,* for readers ages eleven and up, and in multiple picture books for younger children.

Picture books of the Cinderella legend are readily available in a vast array of cultures (a quick amazon.com search can show you): Egyptian, Persian, Hungarian, Hmong and Cambodian, Vietnamese, Indian, Mexican, Irish, Caribbean, Korean, Zuni (Native American), and even the Smoky Mountains. Modern takes on the traditional tale can be found in books like *Prince Cinders* and *The Paper-Bag Princess.*

Cinderella film adaptations date back to silent picture versions from England and France, Julie Andrews's 1957 made-for-TV pic, Happily Ever After's multicultural take of the story, popular adaptations with Drew Barrymore, Brandy, or Hilary Duff, and a 1989 shorter film, *Ashpet: An American Cinderella,* about a girl who lives in the American South circa WWII. After you read or watch versions of the Cinderella story from other cultures, discuss the differences. If the movie was about the Chinese or Irish or Caribbean Cinderella, what elements would be different from the Disney interpretation? Could you think of a new version yourself?

SEE THE OLD AND THE NEW

If your family enjoys comparing Cinderella from different eras and cultures, try it with other films, like:

- *Beauty and the Beast:* The 1946 classic by French director Jean Cocteau (available on DVD) ranks high on many film lovers' lists of favorites. This doesn't particularly depict real French culture, and the lives of Belle's sisters are comical, but it fascinated my family to see candelabras and statuettes come to life, as inspiration for the Disney version. My kids thought the cover of the DVD suggested a scary movie, but I eventually let my five-year-old watch and she was captivated (and unscarred).
- *Wild Child:* This 1969 classic from another French director, François Truffaut (who also plays the protagonist doctor), is based on the true story from 1806, where a boy who has grown up in the forest is captured and educated outside of Paris—it's like an original *Tarzan,* but also has elements of the *Miracle Worker,* about Helen Keller.
- *The Jungle Book:* In addition to the classic Disney version of 1967, live-action interpretations of Rudyard Kipling's stories were made in 1942 and 1997. The same year Disney's cartoon came out, the former Soviet Union released an ani-

Process what you watch.

The American Academy of Pediatrics recommends no more than one to two hours of TV viewing per day, but American kids on average watch at least double this—translating into more hours of TV watching than going to school over the course of a year. For the most part, no one is talking to the kids to help them process all this information. Here are some guidelines for a discussion, whether it's a foreign art house film or a TV cartoon:

• Mention that you would like to talk about the movie or show once it's finished. In other words, *talk about what you're going to talk about* to prepare for this new process and make the watching less passive.

• Notice (aloud) a few subtle (age-appropriate) differences that reflect the era or culture from the film.

• Is there a sallent difference between the roles of men and women that reflect the times or the culture? Are other stereotypes perpetuated? If some part of it offends you, mention it.

• How does the film soundtrack reflect the film's cultural influences? What about other artistic elements (photography, set design, costume) that tell about the setting?

• What did you like most or least about what you just saw? What do you think about the particular characters?

• Can you find books and other media that can lead to deeper learning on that topic?

• Finally, don't expect too much from the discussion. For example, it's probably not realistic to cover more than a few of these points per movie or show. Like other concepts throughout this book, the experience will be *theirs,* not yours—and kids may not be ready to converse about it. Particularly if this type of discussion is new, things won't change quickly. Allow time and space for a transition to this new method of "watching."

mated interpretation closer to Kipling's original work. In the dubbed version, American icon Charlton Heston narrates.

- *The Thief of Bagdad:* The 1940 live-action movie won Academy Awards for cinematography, art direction, and special effects, but seems almost comical to today's tech-savvy kids. Don't watch it for a view of the real Baghdad, either. It was clearly made on a Hollywood set, and actors portray stereotypes of Arabs, with plenty of historic and cultural inaccuracies. If you like a swashbuckling pirate adventure, though, you might enjoy seeing where Disney's 1992 *Aladdin* got much of its inspiration. It also was striking to me to notice the romanticized view of the palaces, markets, and public life of Baghdad (and Basra, also depicted in the film) compared with what its image and reality have become today, particularly as viewed on the news. For another take on this story, see *Old Khottabych,* made in the Soviet Union in 1956 (available through Netflix and other sources). Russians from that era compare it to the fame and fantasy of Harry Potter, but inserted with Leninist propaganda.

- *Romeo and Juliet:* Shakespeare's star-crossed lovers were depicted by Hollywood in 1968 and in numerous remakes from the 1990s and later. They are joined by Caucasian and Puerto Rican youth of New York in *West Side Story,* released in 1961, and then Bollywood's 2004 *Veer-Zaara,* a tale of love between an Indian and a Pakistani (in Hindi). In 2005, the short comedy-musical *West Bank Story* cast Israelis and Palestinians in competing falafel stands (available at westbankstory.com). There are so many literary interpretations, too. Probably the most famous globally are the classic stories of Majnun and his beloved Layli in Middle Eastern literature.

- *Other Shakespeare* (for more mature audiences): Japan's celebrated Akira Kurosawa adapted *Macbeth, King Lear,* and *Othello* to Japanese cultural realities and Indian Bollywood productions also have taken on a number of Shakespeare's works, like *Maqbool* (from MacBeth) and *Omkara* (from Othello). The Chinese version of *Hamlet* is portrayed in *The Banquet.* These can be watched with English subtitles.

- *Superman* and superheroes: In addition to numerous U.S. interpretations of the superhero, there are low-budget knockoffs and virtual cult-pulp classics, *The Indian Superman* and *Turkish Superman* (preview them on YouTube). One that's newer, more widely available, and a better production is India's *Krrish.* Originally named Krishna, Krrish is a homegrown hero who relies on his high IQ but also breaks out in Bollywood-style song in Hindi. Some observers note that the superhero genre has been light in Indian pop culture because there already is a strong reliance on Hindu gods (such as Hanuman, the flying monkey god, who some believe is the inspiration for the original Superman).

- *Shall We Dance?* The 1997 original from Japan got better reviews than the U.S. version with Richard Gere from 2004, and Australia's *Strictly Ballroom* (1993) comes somewhere in between.

ATTEND A CHILDREN'S FILM FESTIVAL—PHYSICALLY OR VIRTUALLY

Experience an international children's film festival to see the creative talent directed toward family audiences by independent filmmakers all over the world. These festivals demonstrate how varied films for and about kids can be and have begun to set an example for the big Hollywood studios.

If your children love watching or making movies, look for a festival within an easy drive from your home. Major festivals take place in Chicago, Toronto, and New York. But you can also find them in East Lansing, Michigan; Rafael (Mill Valley), California; Homer, Alaska; as well as Seattle; Dallas; Los Angeles; and San Diego. These are strictly film festivals; international children's music and arts festivals take place annually in many more places, a few of which are mentioned under the section A Weekend in a Continent in Chapter 5.

By global standards, our North American film festivals seem small. The Brazilian Kids' Film Festival draws close to 100,000 visitors annually, and similar festivals in Italy and the Czech Republic had 82,000 and 58,000 attendees, respectively, in 2005. The biggest U.S. festival, in Chicago, had about 24,000 attendees (thanks to local schools bringing their students for a unique field trip), and was ranked number nine in size worldwide—reflecting, in part, other countries' greater receptivity, more ready audience and government funding to support independent films for children.

If you can't make a trip for a festival, visit one virtually. A website like filmfestivalworld.com includes most of the festivals in the world, organized by genre (e.g., children's, drama, science fiction, documentary, etc.), country of origin, and awards won. After reading descriptions of recent award-winners, I got new ideas for more films I'd like to watch with my family.

Start your own film festival. You can start a mini film festival at your kids' school, at church, in your neighborhood, or to benefit a charity. Facets.org has a "Best of Fest" DVD, which is pretty much a "film festival in a box" for kids through age ten (ages five to eight are most responsive; and a few films in the package suit ages two to five years). For older kids, explore the full library of films at Facets, Janus films, or other outlets. A festival sets a standard for your mission, morals, and respect for your audience (e.g., not exposing prematurely to highly sexual content). This also offers an opportunity to watch new genres with your community, like short films that often turn out to be the most popular offering at the festivals. Nicole Dreiske, Chicago International Film Fest and Facets founder, shared these insights and also told me, "One element that contributed to Chicago's success is the inclusion of young voices in the film selection committee—kids gave immediate feedback, which helped ensure audiences will like what they go to see." Involve kids in your process, too.

Before embarking on your own film festival, check into public performance rights. This is essential if you're going to charge admission or a "membership contribution," even if all the proceeds go to charity. Learn how organizers of other cities' small festivals dealt with licensing and permits, or see if there's an intellectual property attorney in your community who can help you. It might sound glamorous for Johnny Depp, but you don't want to be accused of "piracy" with your great new initiative.

Choose subtitles to increase foreign language accessibility. All over the world, people have learned English by watching television or movies. I know plenty of people who learned to speak in the style of *Days of Our Lives* and *Dynasty,* or more recently, *Oprah.* Similar principles can apply for English-speakers wanting to learn a new language. If you have a choice of renting or watching a movie that is dubbed versus in subtitles, pick the subtitled movie if everyone watching is a strong reader, and particularly if the movie is in a language that you (or a family member) have an interest in learning. This way the ear listens to one to two hours of a particular language and you don't have to endure watching actors' mouths appear distorted as English words are superimposed over the original language.

In Finland, the government advises the use of subtitles instead of dubbing foreign-language TV programs to accustom its population to multilingualism. Officials point to the success of Finnish students in international tests as proof of the effort's effectiveness, together with other factors. After getting used to this style of movie watching, I have often forgotten that I "read" the movie and didn't listen to it. It doesn't feel like work. I don't expect kids younger than about fifth grade to be able to absorb subtitles and enjoy the movie—you will know if they get it and like it. If they become accustomed at a younger age, then it won't be such a stretch as adults. For younger children, try reading the movie to them; as an added benefit, you will be able to censor language or concepts you're not ready for them to hear.

WATCHING YOUR FAMILY VALUES

Every year, brilliant foreign films covering subject matter that span the global experience are released to critical acclaim. But it's difficult to find many that are appropriate to watch with anyone under sixteen—especially when we're used to American values of "appropriate" viewing. I'm alarmed by how much questionable content seems targeted to younger children. So it's almost eye-popping to see what is considered okay abroad for family-viewing. In Europe, and increasingly, in Asia and Latin America, it's common to see nudity in a TV commercial after eight P.M. Seductive dancing, lewd touching and language, relations between younger and younger children, or content that puts serious issues of life and death squarely front-and-center seem to be part of the acceptable viewing diet for most ages in many countries. Channel-surfing on U.S. cable TV shows that even seemingly innocent programs, from game shows in Spanish to Punjabi music videos featuring girls wearing saris (albeit skimpy ones), might slide into territory we would readily classify as "R-rated."

If TV content from overseas sources might cause American audiences to squirm, the movies can be more dangerous. Some films are made for their artistic value, with less of an eye to commercial returns, and therefore less guidance by a big movie studio of what will be appropriate for the widest possible viewing audience. Then, when these films reach the U.S. market, they are unrated, making it doubly difficult to gauge their suitability for young people. The best route is to watch it yourself first, then make a judgment based on your family's own value system. I find this is particularly true for films about children. So many of the acclaimed foreign movies see the world through the eyes of children and these are exactly the movies I want to see with my adolescent and preadolescent daughters. But on some occasions, one or two scenes that I am uncomfortable with their viewing will give me pause about the entire film.

Visit parental guidance sites. Websites like commonsensemedia.org or kids-in-mind .com help parents decide what they'll allow their children to watch, and include more mainstream films but fewer movies made abroad. Netflix film listings also include the Common Sense Media rating, if there is one. The Internet Movie Database (imdb.com) is populated with just about every commercially released movie. For some titles made abroad—but certainly not for all—it includes parental advisory information, as well as the ratings and reviews in various countries. So, something rated PG-13 in the United States might be for eleven and up anywhere from Chile to Switzerland. The more difficult case—and typical of most foreign-made movies—is the nonrated film, so there is nothing "official" to help guide parents in their choice of appropriate film matter.

To find more movies than I have listed here throughout this chapter, see the kids' section and catalogue at the facets.org website and browse netflix.com. The website 1worldfilms.com sells foreign films and describes them generally, but does not include favorite lists or reviews. If you are interested in films from a particular culture—perhaps you are traveling to that place or it reflects your heritage—look up sites that serve as "storefronts" for that ethnic community, like yesasia.com (Japanese, Korean, Chinese), iranian.com, africanfilm.com, tulumba.com (Turkish), russiandvd.com, and webmallindia.com.

Now for the best foreign movies to see with children of varying ages, based on my own experience and that of parents I polled around the world. While I cannot provide a scientific rating of appropriate content for varying ages, I can offer a general guideline for parents. With a few exceptions, I try to avoid American movies, even if they're set abroad. For example, it excludes my daughter's recommendation of Disney Channel's *The Cheetah Girls: One World,* where the girls go to India—but if your child wants to see that, use it as an opportunity to talk about big issues, like globalization and immigration; or little things, like the Indian-style fashion accessories, the names of the Indian costars, and other differences from a movie that is set entirely in the United States.

In the sections to follow, I start with various categories of documentaries and move on to feature films, organized by age, genre, and in some cases, country of origin.

REALITY CHECK—OR, DON'T SHY AWAY FROM DOCUMENTARIES

If movies open a window to life around the world, the clearest view might come from an excellent documentary. To get the kids hooked, describe it as a "reality" show and not an "educational" or "documentary" film. Like *Survivor* or *American Idol* (both of which are takeoffs from British TV shows) or *The Amazing Race,* many of the foreign documentaries will draw you into real life with scenarios that wouldn't be as compelling if they were dreamed up. The documentary films listed following are safe for family viewing and fall into three categories: the planet, music-related, and "harsh realities." If you have teens and older, you can broaden the range of subjects and choices considerably to thrill, shock, or fascinate.

Get to know the planet we all share. Countless nature documentaries and television shows—like those played on National Geographic, PBS, and the Discovery Channel—carry an underlying message of wonderment and interconnectedness with all forms of life on earth. The Planet Earth series, made by BBC with an unprecedented budget of $25 million over five years, shows us we're all on one planet and what a remarkable place it is. The British version is narrated by Sir David Attenborough, Britain's face and voice of natural history shows, and actress Sigourney Weaver hosts the American version. The Discovery Channel ran the series in parts, and it is available in a box set of eleven discs as one of the best nature documentaries ever made. So, record it on Tivo or DVR, buy the box set, or check it out from the library—but don't miss it to get a sense of place on our shared planet.

The other recent stand-out portraying the big picture of our globe alongside the tiny details of nature's wonders is *Winged Migration,* included in the Essential 7. This quiet film has been requested over and over by my youngest daughter, and it manages to captivate everyone else in the family who happens to walk by when the DVD is playing.

Though great productions like these are released on DVD and more people can see them at home on high-definition TVs, watching the wonders of the planet at an IMAX theater remains a singular, sensory experience. If you can, attend the IMAX movie at a nearby museum—even if you can't spend time at the museum before each film, you'll get to walk through a bit and support the institution while you're going to see the movie. Surviving the Mount Everest climb, chasing a wild animal in an African jungle, or experiencing the wonders of the deep sea come alive on the larger-than-life screen.

See the world through music and musicmakers. Just as music is a universal language, films depicting the people and places behind the music can serve as a powerful unifier, showing unique aspects of a culture or way of life. Each of the following titles takes us on a journey that the diverse music and musicians bring alive. The greater your child's interest in the topic, the younger they can be to appreciate these films.

- *East Side Story*—*L.A. Times* film critic Kenneth Turan included this recommendation to me as one of his favorite foreign films: a quirky look into the world of Communist musicals as propaganda. For kids who have a vague knowledge about the Cold War, this is a fun way to introduce an important aspect of modern history.
- *Genghis Blues*—A blind San Francisco blues singer on a musical journey to Mongolia.
- *Buena Vista Social Club*—The legends behind Cuban music and a bit of the country that's been off-limits to American visitors.
- *The Komediant*—The Yiddish theater seen through the life of one of its legends and the legacy that lives on in musical comedy. If your family loves Broadway, look for connections with this almost-gone genre.
- *Romantico*—The life of Mexican mariachi singers in the United States and how they eke out a living.

- *Ballet Russes*—The best ballerinas in history tell the backstory, mixed with gorgeous dance footage.
- *Crossing the Bridge: The Sound of Istanbul*—See the musical culture in Istanbul, Turkey.

Harsh realities: I've said that watching foreign films should be fun and entertaining. Yet, there are times when you want to see what life is really like somewhere else—and this often involves witnessing hardship or suffering. To see a civil war, life as a refugee, a public health crisis, or the liberation of a nation through the eyes of children adds perspective the news cannot. The following are available through public libraries or major online outlets and are just a beginning:

Going to School in India—Different school environments—like going to school in the dark, or on a boat or a bus—are shared by child narrators who each love their school. Any child getting ready for elementary school (ages five and up) can partake in what is shared as a happy gift of learning, despite the hardships implied in each of the bite-sized chapters. As the child on a wheelchair declares, *"If I was able to walk or fly anywhere, I would fly to school."*

God Grew Tired of Us—This film follows the travels of the lost boys of Sudan. Their painful journey and values from home are vividly contrasted with new experiences in America. My adolescent daughters and their friends found humor in parts where, for example, a square of butter was eaten whole on the airplane ride and considered an odd soap-like food, or the boys were explaining where they came from to a group of suburban American girls at a community pool.

Beat the Drum and *Angels in the Dust*—Both from South Africa, about children with AIDS. These are children's stories, but be aware that they can be extremely upsetting and uncomfortable. Young girls who have been raped, people dying of AIDS, and the effects of extreme poverty are all part of the story, so the reality of life for the young lives shown contains plenty of R-rated material, but is worth watching for those who are ready.

Sierra Leone's Refugee All-Stars—Six musicians who escape the civil war meet in a refugee camp, form a band, and take their music to the world. Signs of the brutality of the long civil war—like the hacked off limbs of the innocent—are not hidden from the audience. But the central characters show the power of hope and resilience in trying to build a better future for themselves and their country.

Amandla! A Revolution in Four-Part Harmony—If your children are learning about civil rights struggles in the United States, expose them to the system of forced racial separation in South Africa known as apartheid. *Amandla!* shows the struggle for freedom from apartheid closely intertwined with the people's music.

The film carries a PG-13 rating for "some images of violence and for momentary language," which are relevant to the ugliness of racial division and ensuing brutality, but are not used gratuitously.

War Dance—Beautifully shot, about children of the war in northern Uganda. Their displacement is told through the eyes of the youth who have suffered unimaginable horrors. Intermittent stories recounting man's inhumanity to man are almost unbearable (particularly if you are watching with your own children at your side), but then after each horrific vignette things turn to tell a story of resiliency and then, hope. (If the orphans' experiences are too painful to hear, you can skip ahead on the DVD to the group dance and song segments.) Descriptions of the savagery of war give it a PG-13 rating. But the rest is a story of children and the music competition in the city that gives so much hope. Some viewers called it "life-changing."

Rize—Like *War Dance,* this is another PG-13 documentary. It chronicles how music and dance (in this case, Hip-Hop Krumping and Clowning) can transform and channel the energy of youth in an intensely dangerous environment. The "civil war" in this case, comes from drug- and gang-related violence in South-Central L.A., which for some readers might be as foreign as another country.

Promises—This film chronicles Palestinian and Israeli children who live twenty minutes apart, but are worlds away from each other. Although the film shows the perspective of kids, the content is not "light" (e.g., close friends from both sides have been killed during the *Intifada*) and it leaves no illusions that because they are young they will be easy to bring together.

FEATURE FILMS BY CATEGORY AND FOR VARIOUS AGES

For ages four and up: Here are some of the best foreign films for the youngest viewers.

The Red Balloon—France, 1956. Once you adjust to the fact that this film isn't punctuated by cataclysmic action, you can enjoy the view from a young boy and his beloved red balloon in Paris in the 1950s. This is a favorite of preschools with a French language program. The DVD is now available with a second feature that's also a French children's classic, *White Mane,* an "arty" film in black-and-white. This film is also slow-paced. Though generally harmless, it contains some fighting among the wild horses.

The Children of Noisy Village—Sweden, 1986. Directed by Sweden's Lasse Hallström, who also made the classic *Pippi Longstocking* and *My Life as a Dog.* This film depicts the summer vacation of a small band of children enjoying the simple life in the prewar era: running barefoot in fields, climbing fences, playing pranks, fishing, camping, taming a dog. It's the antidote to too much structured, indoor activity, modeling how kids can connect with free play and nature, without TV, video games, and shopping malls. It offers a snapshot of rural life in northern Europe and it's a model for environmentalists: Clothes are hung out to dry, groceries are carried home in reusable baskets, and walking is the most-used mode of transportation. It's probably most interesting for ages three to six, but if you give an "assignment" like looking for clues to living an environmentally sound life or finding new things to do outside, older kids (once they get over the dubbed voices) can enjoy this calm classic, too.

Cave of the Yellow Dog—Mongolia, 2005. (Included in my Essential 7.) If you miss watching Lassie or Old Yeller, take in this story of a girl and a beloved dog living in a yurt in western Mongolia, with glimpses of real family life.

For elementary schoolers and up: These films also are lovely, and family friendly. They're for slightly more mature audiences than the four and up list because of content ranging from the mystical and magical in *Roan Inish* and *Totoro* to the baby camel's rejection by his mother in *Weeping Camel,* to difficult life circumstances in *Children of Heaven. The Butterfly* contains a short scene with strong language, but otherwise it's a feel-good, family film.

My Neighbor Totoro—Japan, 1988. (Included in my Essential 7.) Realism and fantasy enter the lives of two sisters who move to the Japanese countryside with their father in this critically acclaimed movie and cartoon. The ways of Japanese life come out in subtle movements and customs.

The Secret of Roan Inish—Ireland, 1994. (Included in my Essential 7.) The magic in a little girl's family tree becomes real on the mystical Irish island where she stays with her grandparents.

The Story of the Weeping Camel—Mongolia, 2003. (Included in my Essential 7.) Predecessor to *Cave of the Yellow Dog,* this meditative story of four generations of nomadic shepherds in the Gobi desert shows their traditional way of life, some of the impact of the modern world on their ancient ways, and their connection with the earth and the animals.

Vitus—Switzerland, 2007. A musical prodigy just wants to be a "normal" kid, with the help of his eccentric grandfather. Watch how easily some of the characters switch between languages. Note similarities or differences of modern European life with the life that you know.

The Butterfly—France, 2003. The search for a rare butterfly reveals an intergenerational friendship and life lessons in the French countryside. Other good intergenerational "buddy" films, *Monsieur Ibrahim* (also France, 2003, costarring an aged Omar Sharif) about the friendship of an elderly Muslim and an adolescent Jewish boy in the 1960s, and *Kolya* (Czech, 1997 Academy Award Best Foreign Language film), about a middle-aged classical musician and a young Russian boy he's left to care for on the eve of Communism's fall, deliver on the theme, but sexual situations leave both of these for teen and up audiences.

The Way Home—Korea, 2002. This simple film became a box-office blockbuster in Korea, showing an intergenerational, city-country friendship unfold. The manners of a modern, disrespectful boy serve as an extreme model of how *not* to treat others, especially elders. Do you see this film differently, knowing that the grandmother in the film had never seen a movie before costarring in this one?

Cartoons: Nickelodeon's *Dora* and *Diego* expose little ones to Spanish-speaking protagonists and pass along excellent accents to young viewers who repeat the words. *Ni Hao, Kai-lan* tries this with a bit of Mandarin Chinese. But there are other internationally influenced cartoons and animated films, and when they are made in other countries the animation styles differ substantially from the fare on Nick and Disney. Children can get a sense of the influence of Japanese animation through *Totoro* and *Spirited Away,* without being exposed to some of the raunchier content of manga and anime. Here are a few other examples:

Kirikou and the Sorceress—France, 2000. This animated film of life in a West African village takes a combination of African folktales and artistic styles, set to music by iconic Senegalese Youssou N'Dour, and puts them together in one movie about an endearing and brilliant hero-baby, Kirikou. The sorceress and suspense can be scary, but there is little that most kids, ages seven and up, haven't seen. The film reached limited North American audiences because the French director refused to cover the bare-chested (cartoon) village women, insisting they be portrayed authentically, with only skirts on, and little Kirikou and the children run around in birthday suits. I saw this in eight episodes on YouTube, but you can also order it via Netflix, amazon, facets, or specialty sites like Africanfilm.com. Prior to watching, prepare the kids for minimally clad characters—this is how they "dress" in everyday village life in that part of the world.

The Man Who Planted Trees—Canada, 1987. This dreamy animated short film set in the Alps changed the way I looked at a grove of trees and made me want to go out to plant trees. In telling the story, the film contains a brief scene of World War I and World War II battles as well as reference to depression and suicide in the village (which is overcome when the village becomes verdant); otherwise, it's a message of hope and the power of individual action. Ages eight and up can probably handle it. This won the Academy Award for Animated Short Film in 1987. Look for more winners in this category.

Mafalda La Pelicula—Argentina, 1982. Mafalda, like "Lucy" from *Peanuts,* is a favorite in Latin American popular media and Spanish classes. Also see *Bal Ganesh* from India and Britain's popular *Wallace and Gromit* films.

Road movies: A classic film genre chronicles adventures of characters on the road, where getting from Point A to Point B is secondary to the process of the journey that ensues. In the case of foreign films, the geography can be as interesting as a character in the story. Ages ten and up.

Viva Cuba—Cuba, 2005. Two endearing children run away from Havana. Their innocence seems to mirror Cuba's as they travel the length of the island. This might be the closest many of us get to visiting Cuba.

Intimate Stories—Argentina, 2002. An old man, a single mother, and a traveling salesman journey through Patagonia to each fulfill a personal yet simple goal.

Le Grand Voyage—France, 2004. A French teen and his traditional Moroccan father drive from southern France to Mecca for the father's "hajj" or duty of pilgrimage in Islam. The road trip takes them through numerous countries and cultures, challenging their relationship. This is a rare look at Muslim piety without falling into preachiness or stereotypes.

Riding Alone for Thousands of Miles—China, 2005. The film takes us to Japan and China, propelled by a father's love for his estranged and dying son. A theme of serious communication obstacles stands alongside gorgeous views of rural China. Rated PG for "mild thematic elements," it's a gentle and enjoyable film.

The Middle of the World—Brazil, 2004. Based on a true story, a family of seven rides four jalopy bicycles from northeast Brazil to Rio—a difficult journey that takes six months—in search of a better life. The film is unrated, but probably would get a PG-13 due to a few scenes, and the treatment of the children can get very rough.

Growing up and coming-of-age: For those going through adolescence or confused about their identity, it helps to know they're not alone in their journey. Here are a few films portraying that process. Generally, these are appropriate for about ages twelve or thirteen and up.

The 400 Blows—France, 1959. This classic of the French "New Wave" practically created the coming-of-age genre. It's loved by film students and critics, though it may seem too boring to a modern adolescent—my ninth grader fell asleep watching, but my eighteen-year-old nephew loved it.

Whale Rider—New Zealand, 2003. A Maori tribe must contend with a girl as its next leader. I was surprised to see this lovely family film carries a PG-13 rating "for brief language and a momentary drug reference," but Common Sense Media recommends this movie for ages eleven and up. Don't miss this one.

My Life as a Dog—Sweden, 1985. This outwardly simple film contains so much: sickness and health, loss and triumph, multigenerations, life in a Swedish town and a village, coming-of-age discovery, community—all seen through a pre-pubescent boy's eyes. Contains some bawdy jokes and a scene of the village sweetheart modeling nude for the sake of art. Whereas so many critically acclaimed foreign films center on tragedy, this one touches on tragedy but ultimately is pure joy.

The Year My Parents Went on Vacation—Brazil, 2006. Brazil's 1970 World Cup final and a quirky Jewish neighborhood in São Paolo serve as the lighter backdrop for a twelve-year-old boy who is dropped off at his dead grandfather's apartment while his parents seek safety away from the military dictatorship.

The Education of Little Tree—United States, 1997. A young boy learns the Cherokee "way" from his grandparents in the 1930s. The author may have manufactured what he claimed to be truth, but its value as entertainment remains.

Tito and Me—Yugoslavia, 1992. This lighthearted tale of a ten-year-old boy who reveres Yugoslavian leader Tito gives a glimpse of a nation that no longer exists. Another take on the closing stages of Communist rule is *The Way I Spent the End of the World* (2006), about the end of the Ceaușescu dictatorship in Romania, from the perspective of youth and their antics.

Himalaya—France/Nepal, 1999. This film combines the beauty of the rugged Tibetan Dolpo region of Nepal, which few outsiders have seen up close, with a story of power transferred to a new generation. The film crew spent seven months without electricity or running water, showing conditions that are both current and ancient. Look for small things, like how affection is shown (foreheads touch, not lips) among family members. Contains a brief, implied sexual scene, no nudity.

Immigration films: We're all immigrants, but the experiences—depending on the times, the culture, the economic conditions, and the politics—vary wildly. Films with immigration themes often depict intense hardship, sometimes as experienced by the children. I mentioned *Fiddler on the Roof* and *God Grew Tired of Us,* which can go in this category. Here are a few more:

Golden Door—Italy, 2007. A depiction for ages thirteen and up, of departing the old country and arriving at Ellis Island.

La Misma Luna ("Under the Same Moon")—Mexico, 2008. This tale of the life of an undocumented immigrant woman who works as a domestic in L.A., with her son back in Mexico, gives glimpses into the hardships of so many invisible workers around us. Rated PG-13 for its emotional and difficult themes.

The Syrian Bride—Israel, 2006. Once the bride leaves the Golan Heights in Israel to marry in Syria, she can never return home. The conflict in the Middle East gets personal through this family caught in the web of international border rules. Some background on the issues is helpful to know before watching, but do watch it.

Journey of Hope—Switzerland, Turkey, 1990, winner of the Academy Award for Best Foreign Film, about the ordeal of a Kurdish family from Turkey illegally immigrating to Switzerland. I saw this film many years ago and still remember how hard I wept at the family's hardships. Be aware of the highly emotional content.

Pelle the Conqueror—Sweden, 1988. An impoverished Swedish father and son emigrate to Denmark in the nineteenth century, essentially laboring as slaves on a farm (yes, there are blond-haired, blue-eyed slaves). They yearn to go to "Amerika" for a better life, and this film brings alive the hardships in the old country of many of our forefathers. Like many other great foreign films, some of the sexual themes make this inappropriate for ages under fourteen. That's too bad, because the rest of the movie contains so much depth, beauty, reality, and humanity.

So many life lessons: Most of the movies listed in this chapter contain a moral or life lesson. Here are a few more:

Pather Panchali—India, 1955. This Bengali classic makes it to Top Movies of all Time lists of critics in the United States, United Kingdom, and India. India has changed very much in fifty years, so it won't give an accurate view of the modern side of the nation, and there's none of the glitz of a typical Bollywood flick. It does, however, show the human face of poverty and the struggle of a family to survive on virtually no financial resources—issues that remain very real today. Despite their hardship, the children are endearing and playful. The film score by maestro Ravi Shankar offers a taste of classical Indian music.

Ushpizin—Israel, 2005. The rituals of Orthodox Jewish life are challenged by unexpected houseguests and the hosts' faith is displayed along the way.

Millions—England, 2005. Seven-year-old and nine-year-old brothers find a sack of British pounds the week before the euro becomes official currency. They have to decide quickly: Invest or give it to the needy? Enjoyable for ages nine and up.

Waking Ned Devine—Ireland, 1998. A lottery story in a quaint village that's more about generosity than greed; endearing and humorous.

Cyrano de Bergerac—France, 1990 (starring Gerard Depardieu), but also, versions made in 1922 and 1950. This romantic classic takes on the age-old question: Looks or personality?

Chak De India!—India, 2007. A modern, Bollywood take on classic sports movies that transform ragtag teams into winners, featuring Indian women's field hockey.

War and occupation seen from a child's perspective: I am not a fan of war movies, but it seems so many acclaimed foreign films, like the classics, take place during war. World War II in particular has provided fodder for the foreign film industry, and this is understandable because just about every country experienced it in their own way. The list of Academy Award nominations in the Best Foreign Film category over the years includes Russian, Polish, British, French, Japanese, German, Italian, Belgian, Chinese, and Algerian war films. If you are interested in World War II history, make sure to see some of the excellent non-U.S. perspectives.

Another angle is the child's take on war and occupation, which has fascinated moviemakers. Naïveté can turn an intense and painful experience into something more watchable, innocent, and sometimes even funny. In the end, a "war" film portrays the ultimate loss of innocence—a theme running through so many films with children. Here are a few, probably suitable for ages eleven and up, unless otherwise noted:

Empire of the Sun—United States, 1987. Steven Spielberg's epic of a British boy taken prisoner by the Japanese in Shanghai during World War II.

Au Revoir Les Enfants—France, 1987. Louis Malle's tale of a French Catholic school that hides several Jewish boys during the Nazi occupation of World War II.

Life Is Beautiful—Italy, 1997. A fable of the human spirit in which an Italian Jewish father in a Nazi concentration camp creates a game and humor for his young son to help him survive the ordeal. This winner of three Academy Awards in 1999 is rated PG-13, but Common Sense Media rates it as an excellent family film for ages twelve and up.

The Diary of Anne Frank—Multiple versions of this classic book about a girl and her family hiding from the Nazis during the occupation of Amsterdam have been adapted for the screen.

Hope and Glory—United Kingdom, 1987. A boy's antics in the London suburbs during the blitz of World War II.

Machuca—Chile, 2004. Adolescents experience life under Socialist President Allende and then Pinochet's military coup on September 11, 1973 (Chile's own "9/11"). The characters reflect the country's intense class divisions and competing social values. The excellent film is unrated, but probably deserves a PG-13 or R rating for some sexuality, language, and military violence.

A calm European vacation: If you need a movie with adrenaline, don't go here. These "quiet" films shot in Europe hark back to slower, simpler times. Viewers who do enjoy these find themselves settling comfortably into the peace and the small details of the films.

My Father's Glory and *My Mother's Castle*—France, 1991. These linked stories by writer and filmmaker Pagnol tell the story of his idyllic childhood at the turn of the century in the French countryside. They carry a G and PG rating, respectively, but may not be enjoyed by the youngest audiences. Pagnol's films *Jean de Florette* and *Manon of the Spring* (PG-13) also rank highly among critics, but offer a more tragic and epic scale.

Babette's Feast—Denmark, 1987. From a story by Isak Dinesen, writer of *Out of Africa*. A French woman takes refuge in a fishing village in Denmark for a classic "foodie" movie. It carries a rare G rating and won the 1988 Academy Award for Best Foreign Language Film, but the slower pace and story also might appeal to older viewers, not that you can't try . . .

Other films set in Europe but for slightly older audiences—The 1948 Italian tragedy, *The Bicycle Thief*; *The Chorus*, France 2004; and *Cinema Paradiso*, Italy 1988; which received an R rating at its release but is quite innocent by today's standards (i.e., the sexual content is for on-screen kissing and the violence is when one character is burned—not graphically—in a fire).

Glimpses of China: Chinese films like *Ju Dou, Raise the Red Lantern,* and *Farewell My Concubine* have attracted a large adult following. Expose your children to the nuances of Chinese art and culture through these titles:

Not One Less—China, 1999. A thirteen-year-old girl in rural China becomes the substitute teacher in the village school. Note the city and country life, as well as a glimpse at educational deficiencies in the world. The film's prolific director, Zhang Yimou, also made *The Road Home,* set in rural China, and *Riding Alone for Thousands of Miles,* set between China and Japan, all appropriate for ages ten and up.

King of Masks—China, 1999. Set in the 1930s, the mastery of Chinese and "change-face" opera forms the backdrop of a sentimental story demonstrating the strict social boundaries of a traditional culture.

Finally, if you've never seen Kung Fu genre films, rent at least one. You might prefer a classic starring Jet Li or Jackie Chan, or, for ages twelve or thirteen and up,

Crouching Tiger, Hidden Dragon and *Hero* are more sublime than the usuals, with something for everyone.

Out of Africa and into Africa: There's Hollywood, Bollywood (India), and even Nollywood, referring to the prolific movie industry in Nigeria. Senegal, Algeria, and South Africa also have churned out significant films. Possibly due to the hardship of life in many of these communities, African-made films often are inappropriate for audiences under fifteen. A few you might try, rated PG and for about ages eight and up:

The Gods Must Be Crazy (I & II)—South Africa, 1980, 1989. Somewhere in the Kalahari Desert, a bushman, whose real name is N!Xau, finds a Coke bottle—his village's first encounter with Western culture—and this launches a surreal, anthropological, and humorous story for all ages that's become a cult classic. (The "!" in the name represents the clicking sound used in some Southern African languages; try re-creating a word you hear in the film, with that sound in it.) A similar story line set in the faraway Gobi desert is found in the film *Mongolian Ping Pong,* from 2005.

Duma—South Africa, 2004. After his father's death, a boy befriends a cheetah and traverses southern Africa to return his friend to his rightful home.

A glimpse of Iran: Since the 1979 Islamic Revolution in Iran, few Americans have traveled to the country—formerly America's biggest ally in the region—but a film industry has flourished. This has given the millions of Iranians living abroad in exile a view of their country, and for many non-Iranians, it might be the only contact they have with this misconstrued land. The films usually express a national sense of melancholy. They also reflect strong government-imposed restrictions on showing sexuality, violence, and anything else that would give a movie a PG-13 or R rating. As a result, movies from Iran often use children as their main subjects and are among the most family-friendly of any country's films. To begin, see:

Children of Heaven—1999. (Included among the Essential 7.) A brother loses his sister's only shoes and goes through Tehran figuring out how to get a new pair for her.

The Color of Paradise—1999. From Majid Majidi, the director of *Children of Heaven,* this time we travel to the countryside with a blind child contending with his widower father's lack of love. Also by this director, *Baran,* or *Rain,* 2001, about the difficulties of illegal workers (in this case, Afghanis in Iran) and a girl who must pose as a boy in order to help support her family.

Gabbeh—1997. Two elderly people, who, while washing their rug, tell a folk-tale about a forbidden love that turns out to be their own story.

In *Offside,* a 2006 film still banned in Iran, we meet girl soccer fans who try to get into their country's World Cup qualifying match by posing as boys. Also, *Osama,* set in Afghanistan, is about a girl disguised as a boy (whom she calls Osama) in order to go to school.

The Australian outback: The aborigine culture of Australia baffles me—possibly because I have never known an Australian aborigine personally. These films help shed light on their culture and some of the difficulties they have faced.

Rabbit-Proof Fence—2001. Three girls escape the 1930s government program that separated mixed-race, aborigine-white children from their families at a young age to prepare them for a life of deprivation as domestic or factory workers. The 1,500-mile trek back home shows the strong resolve of these children amid extreme racism, hunger, and other intense obstacles. Rated PG and suitable for ages around eleven and up.

Where the Red Ants Dream—1984. Set in the Australian desert, made by iconic German director Werner Herzog. The differences in worldviews of white-Australian and aboriginal cultures stand in stark contrast when a mining company wants to blow up parts of the native peoples' sacred land. An almost documentary look at a little-understood culture, with environmental themes way ahead of its time. A few scenes include cursing by white people; otherwise, no other objectionable content. Probably ages eleven and up.

Walkabout—1971. This film has become almost a cult classic that's loved or hated for its surrealism and stark juxtaposition of conceptions of "civilized" versus "savage." The opening scene is bizarre and disturbing. A teenage British schoolgirl and her little brother are abandoned in the desert. Only with the help and "primitive" ways of an aborigine boy can they survive the severe conditions. Includes a father's suicide that might be hard for a viewer of any age to watch, even though the filmmakers treated it as almost an aside to the real adventure that was to follow. Also, the teenage girl swims naked and is shown full-frontal, but this is not in an overtly sexual situation. Screen this before deciding who you'd allow to see it. In the United States, it got an R rating; in the United Kingdom and Germany, it was rated for ages twelve and up.

Learn about specific episodes in world history: Sweeping epic films like *The Ten Commandments* and *Ben Hur* make for good family viewing and learning. Also of note:

If you want more

I couldn't include every good family film from abroad or with international content. There are so many; more are made every year, and different families have different sensibilities. My teenagers weren't ready for film school favorites by Japanese director Akira Kurasawa, like *The Seven Samurai,* or documentaries on subjects in which they had no interest in the first place, but yours might love Kurasawa and others.

If you have a suggestion that's not included in the chapter, or an experience to add about a movie I have listed, please share, via www.growingupglobal.net. Also, on the website you'll find more resources to help you decide which movie to watch this weekend.

Gandhi—(Set in India), 1982—Depicts India's fight for independence from England in the early twentieth century through the life of its hero of nonviolent resistance.

Amadeus—(Set in Austria), 1984—The eighteenth-century royal court of the Austrian emperor and the life of composer Mozart—combining intrigue and genius—create a compelling story.

Lawrence of Arabia—(Set in the Arabian desert), 1962—T. E. Lawrence is the British officer who unites the Arabs against the Turks in World War I; their actions create the foundation for modern-day politics of the region today.

Films featuring children but not necessarily for children: As you embark on your quest to discover great foreign films to watch with your family, you will come upon many that are not appropriate for viewing with children under fifteen that are great films. Just a few examples include: *Water*—an eight-year-old Hindu girl becomes the widow of a man she hasn't met and as a widow must live in isolation from her family. *Salaam Bombay*—considered by some as the Oliver Twist of India, but amid brothels on the gritty Bombay streets. *Born into Brothels*—a documentary chronicling the view of children living in Calcutta's brothels. *The Kite Runner*—a story of two boys' lives before and during the Taliban reign in Afghanistan. *Central Station*—a woman and a child journey through Brazil together in search of his father. *Nowhere in Africa*—a Jewish family flees the Nazis by moving to East Africa. *The Fast Runner*—a rare look into Inuit culture, seen through the lives of two brothers.

———

Three generations of my family spent a summer that morphed into a fall, screening dozens of foreign films to inform this chapter. What started as homework turned into a fondness for offbeat interpretations of life on our planet; these connected us as much to one another as to the characters on the screen. When our neighborhood librarians, school teachers, and baristas joined us on a quest for great world films, the global issues and characters gave us a reason to pause and listen to one another. When we switched to canvas bags for bringing home our groceries, we recalled the precocious children of a Swedish village who walked home from the market with their baskets in hand; practicing piano daily evoked a young prodigy in an Austrian conservatory; cheering for our team at the World Series reminded us of a circle of neighbors in São Paolo rooting for their heroes' dream-come-true at the World Cup; and losing a shoe recalled a little girl in Tehran who had to get her only pair back. These scenes were filmed thousands of miles away, mostly in places we've never been, with people speaking languages we don't understand, but none of that mattered—we were hooked and we were transported.

Thanks to a range of flourishing technologies, just about any foreign-made film I want to see is instantly available to me. I can download one legally off a website, have another delivered to my mailbox, record a feature film or documentary onto my TV set, rent a DVD while I'm picking up a loaf of bread, or order a film with a click from a shop in Mumbai. Specialty theaters across the country are reviving showings of classics and "art-house" films, as well as screening brilliant movies made outside Hollywood. Film festivals showcase refreshing works from around the world for family viewing and are more accessible than ever. All this combines to show us that we don't need a plane ticket to start to "see" the world.

My dad still tunes in to the classic movies channel on TV, and my daughters tease him, "Are you watching *Bridge on the River Kwai* again?!" But then they might sit down and join him—again. By mid-August, they reached a saturation point on "helping Mommy research movies." When a new stack of DVDs from the library was greeted with groans at home, I knew it was time to feed them something different. If the foreign films were a treat, like ice cream, I realized I couldn't feed it to them all day. Nonetheless, after a month without ice cream, they missed it.

RESOURCE BOOKS CITED IN CHAPTER 8—THAT YOU MAY FIND HELPFUL, TOO

The Egyptian, Korean and Persian Cinderella and *The Irish Cinderlad,* Shirley Climo with
   various illustrators (New York: HarperCollins Children's, 1989, 1996, 1999, 2000).
Yeh-Shen: A Cinderella Story from China, Ai-Ling Louie (author), Ed Young (illustrator)
   (New York: Penguin Putnam, 1996).

The Rough-Face Girl, Rafe Martin (New York: Penguin Putnam, 1998).

Cendrillon: A Caribbean Cinderella, Robert D. San Souci (author), Brian Pinkney (illustrator) (New York: Simon and Schuster, 1998).

The Turkey Girl: A Zuni Cinderella Story, Penny Pollock (author), Ed Young (illustrator) (New York: Little Brown and Company, 1996).

The Paper Bag Princess, Robert N. Munsch (author), Michael Martchenko (illustrator) (Buffalo, New York: Annick Press, 2002).

Shen's Books, a publisher of multicultural children's books in Walnut Creek, CA, has released various Cinderellas: Mexican, Hmong, Cambodian, Indian, Philippine, and a guide for multicultural Cinderella curriculum.

ADDITIONAL RESOURCE BOOKS RELATED TO CHAPTER 8

The Best Old Movies for Families: A Guide to Watching Together, Ty Burr (New York: Anchor, 2007).

Chapter 9

❦

Sustain Your Friendship—
Service and Giving

How wonderful is it that nobody need wait a
single moment before starting to improve the world.

ANNE FRANK

Once you and your children feel a closer connection to what is going on in the world and how others live, play, study, eat, worship, and celebrate, it is natural that you will care about the health and survival of the planet and its inhabitants—whom you regard as your family and friends. What can you do to help ensure a more environmentally, socially, and economically sustainable future for the planet? What impact do your daily choices make on the earth and its inhabitants?

Without incorporating the next level of awareness—action—into a global mind-set, the effort and insights you have achieved remain theoretical and superficial. You and your children might gain advantages from global knowledge and fluency, but how does "growing up global" make you a person who makes a positive impact?

THINK GLOBALLY, ACT LOCALLY *AND* GLOBALLY AS A FAMILY

Service and action at a global level bring to life the concept of "world citizenship." Early in the book I discussed the idea that world citizenship can be adopted as a family value. Closely connected with this value is the ethic of service to humanity. Such service can be compatible with individual interests, and it need not be bounded by artificial borders—local community involvement is as valuable as is making a difference outside one's immediate sphere of activity. It goes back to the idea of "be a friend to the whole human race" and helping your new friends wherever they happen to live.

A Kid's Guide to Giving, written by fourteen-year-old Freddi Zeiler, is a handy little workbook-type resource to help kids figure out how to start giving back. The first half of the book helps kids think about the concept of giving and the second half lists information on organizations that help people, animals, and the environment. For more detail on creating an action plan, and lots of vignettes of regular kids' activism, see *The Kids' Guide to Social Action* by Barbara Lewis. To focus your service on poverty alleviation, see Daley-Harris, et al., *Our Day to End Poverty: 24 Ways You Can Make a Difference.*

From the time my daughters were only about three, we talked about how the world of humanity is like the human body, and from a young age they could relate this knowledge, empathizing with the needs of those unlike them. The body is composed of millions of diverse cells. The parts are so different from one another, but when someone is afflicted with pain, even if it's at the tip of the pinky—a relatively "insignificant" or nonvital body part—the entire body suffers. I was raised with this metaphor from the teachings of the Baha'i Faith, as a way of seeing my connection with others in the world. After our girls cried from a splinter in their hand, they could remember that such a tiny thing disrupted their whole body. Ongoing pain disrupts one's life routine; similarly, pain experienced by humanity disrupts peace and prosperity on the planet—the business of collective living. These tangible examples bring home the reality of our closeness with all the members of the human body. Displaced children from a massive hurricane, tsunami, or civil war far away feel relevant to children who are conscious of their existence, just as the splinter that prevents the child from running out to play.

Because you are reading this book, you are way ahead in helping your family think globally and adopt the idea of world citizenship as one of your family values. Before patting your enlightened back, however, take a closer look at how you live your life. Do your actions unwittingly contradict your words and philosophy?

Like a financial budget, take an inventory of how you and your children spend your time, probably the most precious resource of busy families. Step back and see if this reflects the values that are important to you. Do you feel you have any control of how to prioritize your time? And for children, does every hour seem programmed with sports, music, or academics?

Channel your search for a good cause.

In 2007, Google had nearly $17 billion in revenue. It's estimated that extending universal primary-school education to every child in the world would cost $10–15 billion dollars per year. So why not channel some of the searches to benefit good causes? Your help is just a click away. Try:

• Goodsearch.com—With this Yahoo! powered search engine, 50 percent of revenues go to charities you designate.

• Ripple.org—100 percent of your click revenues go to specific causes tackling urgent global issues.

• SearchKindly.org—100 percent of revenues go to a long list of causes.

I've been using Goodsearch.com and it reminds me of my designated cause every time I search the Net. Then my teens started using it after borrowing my computer, so my example exposed them to this idea.

Filling the schedule with these worthy activities poses a challenge on two levels. First, you simply may not have much time or energy to devote to new activities that look beyond your own circumstances. Service-oriented endeavors require your imagination and good energy, not the tired, spent energy left over after so many other priorities have been completed—which means they might never take place at all. Second, when sports, music, or academics occupy all your children's time (and a parents' time with their children, either in driving, waiting, practicing, drilling, or assisting), a subtle signal is sent that our valuable time needs to be devoted to self-oriented, competitive activities. There is nothing wrong with excelling in any of these areas, but make sure your time reflects your values and vision. This ethic can be instilled from the time kids are old enough for peewee baseball and ballet, and continue to inform sincere considerations of volunteer activities for college applications.

GET STARTED—CREATE A PLAN

Creating a plan for service and giving helps your family consider its interests and priorities. Close your eyes and see yourself doing something that makes a difference in the world. What inspires you to take action? How is each family member's inspiration different or similar? How much in financial resources would you like to set aside per month in "giving," and how much time per week or month can you carve out? Hold a family meeting to discuss a few of these points—you'll learn so much about everyone's thinking while having a very important discussion.

Start with information. The facts (from UN statistics):

- 1.2 billion people—or one out of every six people—live on less than $1 per day.
- Every day, 800 million people go to bed hungry.
- Every day, 28,000 children die from poverty-related causes.
- Carbon dioxide emissions globally grew 30 percent over the past decade, and despite conservation efforts, emissions production is accelerating worldwide, impacting the planet's climate change.
- About eighteen million acres of forest area are lost per year.

It's not easy to take in the facts—they're mind-boggling, unsettling, or maybe totally unfamiliar—but try anyway. Start to learn more about these numbers with the annual United Nation's *Millennium Development Goals Report,* available free online. The annual report synthesizes complicated country-by-country data into regional summaries that are easier to follow and comes up with straightforward conclusions. For further rigorous analysis and data, see England's Institute for Development Studies and its Eldis "knowledge service." Get facts and updates through respected nongovernmental organizations (NGOs) working in the

Small gifts add up!

Individual giving—most commonly $5 to $50 donations—to the victims of the 2004 Asian tsunami passed $1.8 *billion* from the United States. Private giving to Hurricane Katrina and Rita victims surpassed $3.5 billion (From Indiana University Center on Philanthropy).

Raise kids who care.

A few ways to nurture compassion in children at home:

• *Caring kids come from caring homes.* Beginning in infancy, children who've consistently been loved and nurtured are more comfortable showing a healthy compassion to others because they know what it looks like.

• *You aren't what you buy.* Buying stuff doesn't bring happiness and the accumulation will never end or be enough. Be an example yourself. Appreciate nice things, but don't treat shopping as an antidote to your shortcomings.

• *Limit screen time.* Passive experiences behind a screen limit kids' active connection with the world.

• *Discuss* issues and causes you care about, people who inspire you, and ways you've been touched by others' kindness. Give words to meaningful experiences in age-appropriate ways, recognizing the issues your child cares about—from their social life to cleaning up the planet.

• *Encourage real conversations,* not just text- and instant messages.

trenches. For example, sites for Bread for the World, Save the Children, Environmental Defense Fund, and many others serve as good locations for synthesized information on their issues of concern. Additional information sites targeted to kids are included following.

Determine priorities. Before reacting to any cause, determine your family's interests and priority issues. Are you moved by the story statistics tell—like the fact that 2.5 billion people, almost half the developing world's population—live without improved sanitation, or that over 500,000 prospective mothers in the world die in childbirth or during pregnancy each year? Perhaps you have a long-standing interest in a topic, like environmental conservation or women's leadership opportunities, or your child was moved by a presentation at school? You also can base your decision on Millennium Development Goals (described in the following sections). Some websites that help you learn about a worthy cause or evaluate an organization's effectiveness include:

- Dosomething.org—Gets teens mobilized, informed, and maybe excited enough to take action. Young people are starting "Do Something" clubs all over the country.
- Networkforgood.org—Your giving record is available on their secure website to review, manage, share with friends, or to refer to at tax time.
- Charitynavigator.org—Charities are independently evaluated with the famous star rating system. Site design allows readers to get a quick sense of the organization.
- Guidestar.org—After free member sign-in, obtain financial and organizational information on all 1.5 million nonprofit organizations registered in the United States. Also see Razoo.com, which uses the Guidestar database, to give, get informed, and manage your giving.

Young children familiarize themselves with myriad brands and consumer products. If you think in those terms, learning the good works of some charity "brands" might not be so hard. It can take some time to get to know the lingo and navigate the information, but good organizations have learned to speak plainly to their audience, to convey the dedication and inspiration they feel toward their cause.

Another great resource for getting to know charitable causes might be through your house of worship. Your church may support a clean water program in a particular village where it sends missionaries. Its national arm might collaborate with the United Nations and other global players, including faith-based NGOs, some of the biggest fundraisers and most active international relief organizations worldwide. If a group from your church is traveling to help build a school or orphanage, join them and learn from the seasoned group members. This may be an ideal opportunity to travel somewhere new with your child (if they are old enough to participate). The months in between signing up and taking the trip can be spent learning about the area you'll be visiting, the people, and their culture. Even if all the members of your family are not going (or none of you are), pinpoint a particular project or mission and learn about it, assist in any aspect of preparation, host a fundraiser, organize a donation drive for supplies, or enlist other friends in support. Your efforts will create a personal connection to the cause, resulting in a more profound experience. Some early preparation for younger travelers helps dispel a bit of the insecurity of the unknown.

Get a taste of some of the inspiring projects worldwide where even a small

Give thanks. Give.

After the Thanksgiving meal with our big extended family, we might play games like *Scatter-gories* or watch a classic movie. A new tradition we started—with anyone who wants, there's no pressure to "play"—is a Giving Thanks Gathering. We plug in a laptop to the big TV and go on the GlobalGiving.com website. We consult about what issue area we would like to support. Then we navigate the site, choose our top favorite projects, discuss them briefly, and vote on our choice. After making the difficult decision of which project to support, whoever wants puts their anonymous donation in a hat. It's exciting to count the total from our group effort. This isn't meant to replace personal philanthropic giving nor to put anyone on the spot, but it's a great activity to share across generations. It works best when the parents of the younger kids orient them in advance in language they can grasp. This way they learn about a need in the world and bring some of their own savings to contribute.

financial gift can make a big difference. GlobalGiving.com has created a dynamic marketplace and community to connect givers with real people and projects around the world. Choose your issue and place of interest, then scroll through to learn about the projects you can support. Donors get updates on the project's progress, they can have direct contact with the people they are giving to, and this has led to visits to the project and sharing further ideas to help the local community, creating a new model of dynamic interaction—strangers become friends!

THE MILLENNIUM DEVELOPMENT GOALS CAN GUIDE YOUR SERVICE

"We are six billion voices and this world will do what we say."
(Campaign slogan for the Millennium Development Goals
reiterated by celebrity spokespeople from around the world.)

All the nations of the world, including the United States, adopted The Millennium Development Goals in the Year 2000 *to stamp out poverty from the earth by 2015.* The amazing worldwide effort is presented in a straightforward way so the complex goals and targets translate into tangible targets. It's a sort of strategic plan for the world, outlining our marching orders for making the world a better place—the campaign of our lifetimes.

A focus of the campaign is to take the effort beyond government officials and the United Nations, whose track record of keeping their promises for collective, peaceful action is less than stellar, and engage everyone. Children and youth have a special role to play: to get involved and make a difference for the world they will inherit.

While the expectation is out there for all of us to get involved, my informal sampling of friends, parents at my kids' schools, and assorted acquaintances revealed that 99 percent of the good people I talked to had no idea about the Millennium Development Goals. If we don't know what they are, how are we going to get involved? Nonetheless, it's a great concept, and it's not too late to get involved and make a difference.

EIGHT GOALS AT A GLANCE—TAKE THEM TOGETHER OR ONE AT A TIME

Look at these eight icons with your children. Can you guess what they are meant to represent? Given what you've learned about the world, would you have thought that these would have been chosen as the priority goals for the nations to work on together to halt poverty? The eight goals are:

1. Eradicate extreme poverty and hunger.
2. Achieve universal primary education.
3. Promote gender equality and empower women.
4. Reduce child mortality.
5. Improve maternal health.
6. Combat HIV/AIDS, malaria and other diseases.
7. Ensure environmental sustainability.
8. Develop a global partnership for development.

Channel the concern of a sleepless night.

So many creative initiatives, like Free the Children, Ryan's Well, and Wheels for Africa, began as a result of a caring child who was agitated after learning about an injustice perpetrated somewhere in the world. Their compassionate parents didn't tell them to forget about those thoughts or that it's "all okay." Instead, they helped the children develop a plan of action, find creative avenues for service, fundraise, and even engage in policy advocacy. This way, kids felt empowered to right a wrong and not stand helplessly or anxiously on the sidelines. These successful organizations all started because of a young child who was deeply affected by a situation they learned about in the world.

In subsequent sections you will find each of the eight goals broken down into various levels of discussion and a quick list of ideas for action. Even though all the goals are listed along with ways your family can get involved, this is meant to give an overall sense of a very big picture. No one should feel they have to know it all and do it all. Just take one step and get started with that.

We're more than halfway through the ambitious campaign, marked so far by some accomplishments as well as serious setbacks. Learn about the goals and targets starting with kid-friendly education sites like www.nick2015.com, Nickelodeon Channel's commitment to raising awareness and getting kids involved in the fight against poverty worldwide, the kid-oriented U.N. Cyber School Bus portal, UNICEF (the United Nation's Children's Fund dedicated to saving, protecting, and improving children's lives worldwide and supported largely by private donations), and Oxfam.

If there is any doubt that getting involved in stamping out global poverty is cool, look at the supporters of the One Campaign, which is about "uniting as One to make poverty history." From actors Brad Pitt and Cameron Diaz to rappers Mos Def and P Diddy, campaign leader Bono, and more, these stars come out to implore the world's leaders and regular citizens to get involved. The focus at One.org is on taking action, not rhetoric.

The possibilities for getting involved in the MDGs are boundless and many ideas for families to choose from are listed in the following pages—undoubtedly there are more ideas every day; please share them at www.GrowingUpGlobal.net.

MILLENNIUM DEVELOPMENT GOAL 1: ERADICATE EXTREME POVERTY AND HUNGER

The Good News: As of mid-2008, the goal of reducing absolute poverty by half is "within reach for the world as a whole."

The Not-Good News: This goal is unlikely to be met in sub-Saharan Africa, especially considering that higher food prices may move one hundred million more people into poverty and exacerbate malnutrition. Ongoing wars and conflicts displace families and push millions more people into poverty. These conditions combine to make decent jobs unattainable for those who need them most.

Talk to your kids about eradicating extreme poverty and hunger:

With elementary schoolers: Look at pictures of various children from Africa (in a magazine like *National Geographic,* on websites of the organizations listed in this chapter, or in books like *Material World* and *Children Just Like Me*). Discuss how your daily life is similar and how it's different, but start with similarities. What are you most grateful for in your own life? Have you ever been hungry for several hours or more? What was that like?

With tweens: In addition to the points listed previously, if you have been hungry for a few hours—or forgot to bring your lunch money to school and had to skip a meal that day—how did it affect your ability to do schoolwork, sports, or a job? How did it affect your mood and outlook?

With teens and up: How do you feel about the statement: "We are the first generation that can end poverty"? What do you think about celebrities getting involved in supporting these charitable campaigns? Can you try to get your friends excited about making a difference in the world?

Warning: Following any of the steps in the eight "Make a Difference!" sections will cause you to stumble on lots of fascinating websites and videos that introduce you to a community of people determined to change the world. . . . You might want to join them!

MAKE A DIFFERENCE!

If you'd like to make a difference in the campaign to eradicate extreme poverty and hunger, choose an action item. Then get more details on each of these points in the appendix in the back of this book:

- Invest in microfinance and support small businesses worldwide.
- Participate in feeding programs, with as little as $1, that sponsor a child's meal.
- Give a goat or other livestock to nourish and help a poor family become self-reliant.
- Play "Free Rice," a vocabulary game online that donates to hunger programs.
- Host a "world meal" or fast to feel hunger.
- Volunteer at a food pantry and start a local food drive.
- Advocate for the poor by writing to your elected officials.
- Put your savings in a bank that gives back to the community.
- Research a scientific innovation that benefits many for a school project or science fair.
- Buy fair trade products and shop with philanthropy-oriented e-commerce sites.

Now, go to the appendix for ideas on how to implement any of these points.

Take a look at what it's like.

Watch the PBS Wide Angle film *Back to School*—available through pbs.org—tracing the multi-year struggle for education of particular kids in Afghanistan, Kenya, Benin, India, Japan, Romania, and Brazil. Notice the advantages a child from Japan has and how this impacts his potential for success. Compare the difference in expectations and conditions for a child living in stark poverty. What should be done to help? What can you do? Which of the stories impacted you the most?

MILLENNIUM DEVELOPMENT GOAL 2: ACHIEVE UNIVERSAL PRIMARY EDUCATION

The Good News: In almost all regions of the world, primary-school enrollment exceeds 90 percent of national populations, and in some areas receiving humanitarian assistance, it's 100 percent, or universal. Quality education is a key to any country's security and development.

The Not-Good News: Children in the poorest 20 percent of the world's population are still less likely to attend school, which is probably of inferior quality.

Talk to your kids about achieving universal primary education:

With elementary schoolers: Talk about the words: Achieve. Universal. Primary. Education. Find pictures of diverse classrooms (use *National Geographic,* a Google Images search, or the images from the PBS film *Back to School*) and compare what they look like and contain inside them. Think about the things you've learned and have access to now that you can read (like reading the signs on the highway or in a store, and experiencing an adventure through a good book); imagine what your life would be like if your parents didn't know how to read and you never learned, either.

With tweens: Does knowing that many children don't have access to education influence your motivation to go to school? How can you use your benefit of education to help others learn? Spend about ten minutes looking at a website or a book in a language you don't speak. This is sort of what it's like for people who remain illiterate—they see signs and books and receive mail that they cannot make sense of. How did that feel to you? Imagine what your job prospects would be if all writing looked so foreign to you. Now imagine how that impacts a country when so many people in it can't read.

With teens and up: In most places in the world, elementary school is available for free. Then why do so many children still not attend school? Why are so many kids who do go to school (even in the United States) still functionally illiterate? How does becoming literate affect poverty, hunger, and preventable diseases, help preserve the environment, or build a peaceful democracy?

Sponsor a child—create many lasting impressions.

My friend Monette grew up in Holland and now works for UNICEF. An early memory from her childhood is the framed picture her father kept on his desk, of a child from Africa whose education he personally sponsored. As she grew up, her parents always encouraged her international experiences, but the frame on his work desk lovingly demonstrated her parents' values. She recalled this simple gesture when her daughter Sophie's second-grade class took on the sponsorship of a child in Uganda. Each child in the class committed to bringing $1 per month to support a child through Plan USA. The children were encouraged to take on an added responsibility at home to "earn" the $1. In the classroom, the picture of the child—named Subaiya, which they all learned and spoke about her by name—occupied an important place, as a virtual classmate. This effort also cemented the ties between the children, as they had a mission to support Subaiya's education.

"It was quite easy for each child to bring $1 and it offered many teachable moments," according to teacher Karen Ager. She adds, "I have committed to Subaiya's education so that when the school year ends, the next class and I [will] keep the sponsorship going." Imagine the millions who could benefit if more classrooms across the country would support just one child.

MAKE A DIFFERENCE!

If you'd like to make a difference to achieve universal primary education, choose an action item. Then get more details on each of these points in the appendix at the back of this book:

- Tutor someone in your own community.
- Raise a reader; adopt a "reading buddy."
- Support urban after-school programs that also help schools abroad.
- Raise awareness in your community on global literacy issues.
- Advocate for our government to support the United Nation's convention for children's rights.
- Sponsor a child's education.
- Get inspired by how others' lives have been changed through service and education.
- Initiate a partner school and a pen pal program.

- Fulfill a U.S. classroom's wishes for improving a school.
- Buy a book that funds literacy elsewhere.
- Donate a computer to a needy child.
- Teach English as a Second Language.
- Support Sesame Workshop and see its impact on kids worldwide.
- Devote your vacation to tutoring or performing service for a school somewhere in the world.

Now, go to the appendix for ideas on how to implement any of these points.

MILLENNIUM DEVELOPMENT GOAL 3:
PROMOTE GENDER EQUALITY AND EMPOWER WOMEN

The Good News: Girls' primary enrollment increased more than boys' in all developing regions between 2000 and 2006. As a result, two out of three countries have achieved gender parity at the primary level (i.e., equal numbers of boys and girls in elementary school). Women are gaining ground in the workforce and in political decision making worldwide.

The Not-Good News: Despite impressive gains, girls account for 55 percent of the out-of-school population. Women worldwide disproportionately hold jobs that are more insecure and lower paying.

Talk to your kids about promoting gender equality and empowering women:

With elementary schoolers and up: This goal is about girls, so why should boys care? Were you ever treated unfairly by a teacher, by kids on the playground, or elsewhere because you were a girl (or a boy)? How did you feel after that?

With tweens: Everyone's education is important; why focus particularly on girls? Do you know a woman who has overcome the odds to succeed in something? What circumstances was she faced with? How are things different now? What's the difference between being "equal" and being "the same"?

With teens and up: Do you think the United States has achieved gender equality? What does a society with gender equality look like? What doesn't it look like? The 2008 Global Gender Gap report from the World Economic Forum found Norway, Finland, and Sweden as the countries with the greatest degree of gender equality, and Saudi Arabia, Chad, and Yemen as having the least. How may social, political, and economic life differ in these countries?

MAKE A DIFFERENCE!

If you'd like to make a difference to promote gender equality and empower women, choose an action item. Then get more details on each of these points in the appendix at the back of this book:

• Be informed about how investments in women disproportionately, positively impact society.

Start with a single day.

The United Nations has designated particular days throughout the year to commemorate important issues. Mark your calendar in advance to do something special with the family that day, or get more ambitious and organize an event at school or your place of worship.

January 20: World Religion Day
March 8: International Women's Day
March 22: World Water Day
April 3: International Day for Mine Awareness
April 22: Earth Day
June 20: World Refugee Day
September 21: International Day of Peace
October 16: World Food Day
October 17: International Day for the Eradication of Poverty
November 16: International Day of Tolerance
November 20: Universal Children's Day
December 1: World AIDS Day
December 10: Human Rights Day

- Spend two minutes watching *The Girl Effect.*
- Educate a girl.
- Say no to violence against women and girls.
- Connect with women worldwide and locally through a women's fund.
- Invest in women's enterprises.
- Purchase beautiful and useful pieces made by women worldwide for your home.
- Support women and girls in sports.
- Empower adolescent girls.
- Encourage girls in your local community to aim high.
- Honor those who care for your own children and children far away.
- Ensure Afghan girls and other girls will never again be deprived of their right to education.

Now, go to the appendix for ideas on how to implement any of these points.

MILLENNIUM DEVELOPMENT GOAL 4: REDUCE CHILD MORTALITY

The Good News: In 2006, for the first time since mortality data have been gathered, annual deaths among children under five fell below ten million.

The Not-Good News: A child born in a developing country is over thirteen times more likely to die within the first five years of life than a child born in an industrialized country. Between 1990 and 2006, about twenty-seven countries—the large majority in sub-Saharan Africa—made no progress in reducing childhood deaths. The leading causes of childhood deaths—pneumonia, diarrhea, malaria, and measles—are easily prevented through simple improvements in basic health services and proven interventions like vaccinations and clean drinking water, but these are often unavailable to the needy.

Talk to your kids about reducing child mortality:

With elementary schoolers: If your youngsters are terrified of getting vaccinated, talk about how it has saved millions of lives and that some diseases have been vir-

At the 2007 Harvard commencement, Bill Gates said, *"If you believe that every life has equal value, it's revolting to learn that some lives are seen as worth saving and others are not. . . . a conscious effort to answer this challenge will change the world."* What can your family do in a "conscious effort?"

tually eliminated from the planet. Try to have the conversation in advance, not right before going to the doctor's. Give yourself a little pinch and demonstrate how that little bit of discomfort is preferred over weeks of illness. (If you are opposed to vaccinations, talk about other interventions for child health.)

With tweens: Can you imagine, when you look at a picture of one of those children from far away, needing medical care, that they could be your friend? How could you build this friendship? What would you want to do for them? With them? Say to them? This is the age where a sense of justice can be instilled; the unnecessary loss of young children's lives is certainly something to be outraged about.

With teens: Why do so many children die of preventable diseases like diarrhea? Why do so many poor families have so many children? What are some of the social, cultural, and economic considerations they probably make?

MAKE A DIFFERENCE!

If you'd like to make a difference to reduce child mortality, choose an action item. Then get more details on each of these points in the appendix at the back of this book:

- Collect change—as little as $.06 can buy life-saving solutions for children.
- Put your artwork to good use, through UNICEF cards or your own creations.
- Conserve water use and pass along your savings to those who need it most.
- Help children without access to clean water get low-cost remedies to their unsafe water supply.
- Get involved in Kiwanis Clubs for adults and youth of all ages.
- Buy multicultural books, films, and photography to support children worldwide.

Having trouble choosing which goal to focus on?

If it's difficult to choose one priority area, get involved with the Millennium Villages. These are designated villages throughout Africa that receive infusions of resources to implement comprehensive plans focused on all eight goals simultaneously. The Millennium Promise campaign has developed a "toolkit" for getting involved, shares how schools and others are making a difference, and welcomes your input.

- Support a surrogate family environment for displaced children.
- Sponsor a child whose family cannot provide their necessities.
- Assemble care packages to get items like grooming supplies and toys to millions of displaced children.
- Send your shoes to a future track star (or teacher, surgeon, diplomat, artist . . .) in Africa.
- Invite an international health professional to speak at your school.
- Set up an "investment fund" for your children's charitable giving.

Now, go to the appendix for ideas on how to implement any of these points.

MILLENNIUM DEVELOPMENT GOAL 5: IMPROVE MATERNAL HEALTH

The Good News: Where mothers are educated, fewer children die of preventable causes. The solutions to saving mothers' lives are known.

The Not-Good News: In thirty years little actual progress has been made to save mothers' lives: Where conditions were good, with skilled health workers and facilities, preventive care remains good and where poor, remains poor. A woman's risk of dying from treatable or preventable complications of pregnancy and childbirth over the course of her lifetime is 1 in 22 in sub-Saharan Africa and almost as much in South Asia, compared to 1 in 7,300 in wealthier countries.

Talk to your kids about improving maternal health:

With elementary schoolers: When they see their mommy or an auntie or family friend who is pregnant, do they want to try to treat them especially well? Maybe carry some of their groceries, or make sure they sit in a comfortable space, or help them with work around the house. Many women around the world aren't able to take special care of themselves or their baby while they are pregnant, so let's care for those around us. It's nice to know that treatments are out there to help solve this problem; the world just needs to try harder to get them to those who need it.

Nobel Peace Prize Heroes.

Winners of the Nobel Peace Prize—especially more recently—are individuals and groups that have toiled for decades without fanfare to make a positive impact on the world. Each has a heroic story that you can learn about with your children.

• Muhammad Yunus, 2006—Founder of microlending model Grameen Bank of Bangladesh.

• Wangari Maathai, 2004—First African woman to win and founder of Kenya's Greenbelt environmental movement.

• Shirin Ebadi, 2003—Iranian women's and human rights lawyer/activist.

• Doctors Without Borders, 1999—French organization serving impoverished and violent regions of the world.

• And so many others, like Rigoberta Menchú, Aung San Suu Kyi, John Hume, and David Trimble.

Working together makes a huge difference.

The Global Fund to Fight AIDS, Tuberculosis, and Malaria is a global partnership that dramatically increases the resources to fight three of the world's most devastating diseases. After less than six years in existence, it had raised and committed over $11 billion for 136 countries, and saved millions of lives. In 2008, *American Idol* audiences gave $10 million to the Global Fund. The Product (RED) campaign contributed over $110 million in three years—and these are just a start. Your donations or purchases might have been pooled with commitments from the biggest governments, foundations, and corporations to make a big impact.

With tweens: In many parts of the world, girls around your own age are expected to get married and have children soon after. Can you imagine what that life would be like? Why do you think those circumstances improve when a girl is educated?

With teens and up: There already are specific goals around gender equality and improving children's health, why is there a separate maternal health goal? When mothers are unhealthy and uneducated, what are some of the effects on the people, society and environment around them?

MAKE A DIFFERENCE!

If you'd like to make a difference to improve maternal health, choose an action item. Then get more details on each of these points in the appendix at the back of this book:

- Learn why maternal health hasn't improved for poor women in three decades.
- Dedicate baby shower and Mother's Day gifts: Honor those you love by supporting women's health worldwide.
- Add your name and voice to a global campaign for maternal and child health.
- Help mothers feed their families and themselves.
- If you're nursing, share your breast milk with babies worldwide.

- Print coupons, deliver diapers and formula to social service agencies in your community.
- Invest in socially responsible funds.
- Imagine and learn about a refugee's life.
- Donate supplies to women's hospitals treating the poorest patients.

Now, go to the appendix for ideas on how to implement any of these points.

MILLENNIUM DEVELOPMENT GOAL 6:
COMBAT HIV/AIDS, MALARIA, AND OTHER DISEASES

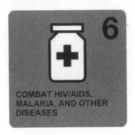

The Good News: HIV prevention programs are yielding results, reducing risky sexual behavior among youth, and antiretroviral drugs are adding years to people's lives. More countries are creating provisions to care for children orphaned by AIDS. Use of insecticide-treated mosquito nets and malaria treatments has grown substantially.

The Not-Good News: Poverty, ignorance, and inequality—not lack of known treatments—prevent care for those in need. By the end of 2007, about 70 percent of the estimated 9.7 million people in need of AIDS treatment in developing countries were not receiving the drugs, and by 2020 it's estimated there will be twenty million children orphaned due to AIDS. Malaria and tuberculosis, though treatable, continue to afflict millions.

Talk to your kids about combating HIV/AIDS, malaria, and other diseases:

With elementary schoolers: Diseases like malaria and tuberculosis have been pretty much wiped out in North America and Europe. Do you know if one of your grandparents or great-grandparents ever contracted one of these? Do you know why these diseases persist in some countries? Talk about some of the simple preventive means, like insecticide-treated bed nets to fight malaria, ten-cent water purifying packs to create safe drinking water, and vaccines that cost just a few

Subscribe to good ideas.

Magazines geared to kids can raise awareness of global issues and action and still entertain. These are for ages nine to fourteen unless otherwise noted.

• *Skipping Stones*—For twenty years, this nonprofit publication has showcased diverse input of multicultural stories, poems, and issues.

• *Faces* magazine introduces kids to diverse cultures of the world in a fun, smart format.

• *Cricket* is the classic kids' magazine—dedicated to instilling a love of learning, free from advertising—from the same publisher (Carus) as *Faces* and twelve other quality kids' magazines including *Muse* (Science) and *Calliope* (dedicated to world history).

• *National Geographic Kids* entertains and educates while getting kids "excited about their world."

• *Time for Kids* has a regular "Around the World" piece, featuring a country and many aspects of life in that nation.

• *Your Big Backyard* is published monthly by the National Wildlife Federation, for ages three to seven; for seven and up, see *Ranger Rick* magazine.

cents. Younger children can feel reassured that the know-how is out there, but it just needs to get to the right people and places. Turn this into an empowering discussion—we can pitch in to get the solutions to where they are most needed.

With tweens: If the resources have been invented and are plentiful, why don't they get to those who need them?

With teens and up: Over fifteen million children in Africa have lost one or more parents to AIDS, and millions more children are made vulnerable by its impact. Even if a child in sub-Saharan Africa never gets the virus, how is she affected by

Small Changes at Home

The total world cost of meeting all water and sanitation needs is $10 billion per year. According to *The Green Book,* $10 billion equals the savings when each home in America sets the thermostat one degree higher for air-conditioning and for heaters a degree lower. Change your home temperature, and pass the savings along to support clean drinking water or toilet (sanitation) facilities for the poor.

AIDS in her community? This age group is most vulnerable to contracting HIV; how can this be reversed?

MAKE A DIFFERENCE!

If you'd like to make a difference to combat HIV/AIDS, malaria, and other diseases, choose an action item. Then, get more details on each of these points in the appendix at the back of this book:

- Get informed with ready-to-use, free, quality curricular materials.
- Support culturally relevant solutions to health challenges.
- Choose (RED) T-shirts, iPods, laptops, sneakers, greeting cards, and more.
- Watch a movie chronicling life with AIDS and poverty.
- Lend a hand to AIDS patients and other shut-ins in your home community.
- Join your local Rotary Club's efforts to eradicate polio and partner with its clubs worldwide to help advance health and other initiatives.
- Mobilize nets—basketball, tennis, volleyball . . . mosquito nets!

Now, go to the appendix for ideas on how to implement any of these points.

MILLENNIUM DEVELOPMENT GOAL 7: ENSURE ENVIRONMENTAL SUSTAINABILITY

The Good News: Leaders worldwide recognize the earth's warming and know they must take action. The net loss of forest area remains high but is slowing down, and the use of ozone-depleting substances has been successfully halted. Simple, proven, low-cost interventions can significantly improve the lives of all people, particularly the poorest—who are affected most severely by environmental degradation.

The Not-Good News: Just 0.7 percent of the earth's oceans are protected from biodiversity loss. Carbon dioxide emissions released by the burning of fossil fuels continue to increase every year, as are the number of animal species threatened with extinction. Almost half the world's population faces a scarcity of water. Nearly one in four people in developing countries use no form of sanitation, resulting in a high incidence of disease.

Talk to your kids about ensuring environmental sustainability:

With elementary schoolers: Of all the Millennium Development Goals, our children can probably relate to this one the best and have probably heard the most about it. Nonetheless, the immediate impact on us so far is limited—we don't need to collect dirty water to drink, we probably don't live on a sinking island, our home may not be located near a hazardous waste site, our trash is dutifully picked up every week, and so on. Talk about the services available to your family that limit your environmental vulnerability, as well as the risks that your living conditions can't control. What is an aspect of your environment that you appreciate the most?

With tweens: What are some of the links between poverty and environmental sustainability? How does fighting poverty and supporting education help the earth?

With teens and up: How might environmental problems more adversely affect women and children than men in poor communities? All the world's religions contain teachings about man's stewardship of the planet. How could this common

Stew·ard·ship (ˈstü-ərd-ship)—*noun.* The conducting, supervising, or managing of something; especially: the careful and responsible management entrusted to one's care <*stewardship* of our natural resources>. (From *Merriam-Webster's Online Dictionary.*)

When you go out of your way to recycle or consume less energy, you are taking responsibility for stewardship of the planet. Consider and discuss your family's active role in environmental stewardship.

teaching across faiths help to bring people together? What does this concept of "stewardship" mean to you?

MAKE A DIFFERENCE!

If you'd like to make a difference to ensure environmental sustainability, choose an action item. Then get more details on each of these points in the appendix at the back of this book:

- Learn more about reduce, reuse, recycle—and how so many in the world practiced these principles before environmentalists popularized them.
- Replace plastic water bottles with your own reusable water bottles.
- Consume less energy and keep the change.
- Bring Jane Goodall's organization and global environmental awareness and activism to your school.
- Turn your trash into cash, and take a field trip to the local dump.
- Cause a ripple effect with your activism.
- Plant your own vegetables.
- Advocate for an environmentally friendly school.
- Watch *Running the Sahara* and learn about man's quest for water.
- Recycle your bicycle.
- Use your birthday to make the world better.
- Stop the junk mail.
- Travel green—pack light, use less, stay in a "green" destination, meet and eat local, purchase carbon offset credits—or "voluntour."

Now, go to the appendix for ideas on how to implement any of these points.

MILLENNIUM DEVELOPMENT GOAL 8:
BUILD A GLOBAL PARTNERSHIP FOR DEVELOPMENT

The Good News: Official bilateral aid to Africa (i.e., from one country to another, like the United States to Kenya) increased 9 percent in 2007, though governments have not met overall pledged assistance targets. Not waiting for governments to fix the problems, nongovernmental organizations, the private sector, and a number of developing countries are stepping up involvement. Internet and cell phone use are expanding in developing countries, easing the "digital divide."

The Not-Good News: Official development assistance from wealthy nations to poorer ones has fallen at a time when it is most needed. The United States gives less than 0.2 percent of its national budget in aid, but has pledged 0.7 percent. Developed countries spend over $370 billion subsidizing their own farmers—more than triple all the assistance that governments send in foreign aid to the entire world. Just the cows in Europe receive $2 per day in subsidies. This is more than the income of half the world's population at a time when poorer nations are being told to halt their own government support to agriculture. Such contradictions contribute to the global food crisis and make it difficult for governments of poor nations to remain faithful allies to the wealthy.

Talk to your kids about developing a global partnership for development:

With elementary schoolers: More and more people around the world use cell phones and the Internet. How might these help the lives of poor people? What is a "partnership"? What does peace look like?

With tweens: Why do you think more money is spent on weapons than on development aid? Getting the nations of the world to agree on policies—like fighting poverty, saving the environment, and creating peace—is a little like getting a group of stubborn friends to get along. What are some of the ways to resolve conflicts between friends that might also work for countries? How could you become a peacemaker (at school and in the world)?

With teens and up: Billions of dollars have been spent over decades on programs for the poor. Why might these not have solved the problems? If Americans are the most generous people on earth, then why is our country the second-smallest per capita donor of official development assistance (ODA) (e.g., aid dollars from the government)?

MAKE A DIFFERENCE!

If you'd like to make a difference to build a global partnership for development, choose an action item. Then get more details on each of these points in the appendix at the back of this book:

- Encourage your county or town to adopt a sister-city.
- Start a "giving circle"—Pool donations with friends to make an impactful gift.
- Get informed about the real story on U.S. foreign assistance.
- Find your hero from among so many who are changing the world.
- Let your elected leaders and media know about the issues you care about.
- Offer your technology and Web-designing savvy to your favorite cause.
- Advocate for peace and human rights.
- Donate or recycle your old cell phones and computers, with proceeds benefiting your favorite causes or your local school.
- Join a network for global youth action.
- Use your Facebook and MySpace pages to proclaim your causes.

Now, go to the appendix for ideas on how to implement any of these points from the final Millennium Development Goal.

DON'T WAIT FOR FINANCIAL WEALTH TO START GIVING GENEROUSLY

"I have nothing and what I give is just a drop. But added to the others will fill a cup."
(Betty, of Acholi quarters slum in Kampala, Uganda, cited in a report
from the Association for Volunteers in International Service.[1])

Betty is one of the hundreds of thousands of refugees from the gruesome, nineteen-year civil war in northern Uganda. She and her fellow Acholi tribeswomen committed themselves to earning funds to send to the victims of Hurricane Katrina for their basic necessities, which resulted in over $1,000 being sent to Gulf Coast families. This act of generosity is mind-boggling when you consider that the women's income is less than $1 per day, and it is earned by pounding stones from the nearby quarry—by hand—that will be used in smaller pieces for road and housing construction. The income barely supports their families, but these young and old women knew what it was like to lose their homes and were reaching out to help others who had lost theirs. They didn't doubt this was something they needed to do, and they didn't question if their contribution would make a difference.

Their astonishing generosity embodies the idea that one doesn't need to be wealthy in order to help others. When Americans have experienced true need and crises, the world community has pitched in to help us, just as Americans give abundantly to benefit countless causes around the world. It's important to share these lessons with our children—everyone can find some way to give, and people around the world have cared for Americans in need, just as Americans have reached out to the world. Dixie Duncan, a mom who helped start Wheels for Africa with her son Winston, says, "I grew up poor in South Carolina and I'm a single mom working full time. I knew I couldn't *not* afford to show my son the world. When I heard there was a direct flight to South Africa, costing $600 for Winston and $800 for me, I started saving for it. I always wanted to go to Africa. . . . After our trip we started collecting bikes and running the organization. It isn't easy, but it's changed our lives."

Real heroes—from Me to We

When Craig Kielburger was twelve years old, while scanning for the newspaper's comics' page, his eye caught a story about the murder of a twelve-year-old who had escaped slavery and a life as a child laborer in Pakistan. Learning about this grave injustice and the life conditions of millions of other children, Craig organized his classmates, researched the issues, took advantage of an offer to travel to Asia to see conditions of child laborers, and wasn't afraid to speak up on their behalf, at the highest levels of decision making. He founded Free the Children, which has grown into "the world's largest organization of children helping children through education." He also co-authored with his brother, Marc, *Me to We: Finding Meaning in a Material World*. This book is for anyone wanting to "be the change" and one of my favorite resources for sharing with all ages, on getting active and inspired.

ME to WE, through the Leaders Today program, runs an active summer ambassadorship program for young people, involving travel and service in developing countries, if your teen is ready to take the next step.

My daughters and I witnessed acts of great generosity during our stay in West Africa. On one occasion we had gone to visit family friends, the Tambas, who lived in a decent hut off a long dirt path. We stayed about an hour, discussing everything from our children to world events. Early in the visit I had commented on the strikingly beautiful rooster in their yard—full-bodied, black, with turquoise feathers in its tail. As we were leaving, Mrs. Tamba held the rooster by its feet and offered it to me. She said that she had wanted to find us an adequate gift and now that she knew I liked the proud rooster, the family insisted that we take it. I held back a shriek when the bird was thrust toward me, and once I regained composure, I was overwhelmed by their generosity. This family relies on the eggs, chicks, and even the droppings for fertilizer for their daily existence. The closest analogy to our life might be to offer your car to a visitor who compliments you on it. My brother-in-law explained in Wolof to Mrs. Tamba that we were honored by their gift, but we would be out all day and couldn't keep the bird; perhaps we could take a picture of their family with the rooster to keep the memory? They agreed, and that picture is a precious reminder of our days in The Gambia.

I have shared this story in presentations about our stay in West Africa to try to illustrate some of the values of their culture. Think about it—under what circumstances would you be willing to hand over your car keys to a mere acquaintance, with nothing in return? Even for children who have not earned the funds to buy a car, this act of giving was beyond belief; but the reality is that people all over the world engage in sacrificial levels of generosity every day, each time making the world a better place.

———

When we acknowledge that humanity is one, and we share a common destiny, then our actions to better the world cease to be "charity," or a handout. We're no longer looking from the outside in.

Giving and serving make us whole. If we never give, we're deprived of something almost as vital as our five senses. The world's religions all teach this, and wise people have known this forever, it seems. Public relations experts seem to have come on board, too. The websites and messages of so many organizations doing good works are attractive, straightforward, and so compelling as to draw the reader in to their cause. But writing a check isn't enough, and we can't simply be content as Facebook friends of the poor and needy. Personal contact touches our hearts and creates a tangible but almost unexplainable connection, the way true friendship does.

Technology and new media serve as a means, but not the end: They can open doors for regular people to make a difference. We learn about kids organizing lemonade stands that raise millions of dollars for cancer research, mobilizing thousands of volunteers for literacy or environmental campaigns, forming a group to lend their allowance money to an entrepreneur in Mali, refusing to purchase T-shirts made under slavery-like child labor conditions across the planet, and preferring items whose profits will benefit "good causes," from salad dressing to sneakers. When our children become aware of these examples, they may aspire to them. Indeed, many have blazed trails with creative initiatives that have raised millions of dollars and touched many thousands of lives.

At the same time, parents need to be content when their children are aware of good examples but don't seem moved to action. Not every child wants to be an activist or get involved, at least not right now. Like a seed that's been planted, they might do something years from now, when no one is looking. They could be watching and waiting to get involved in a club in high school, or when presented with the right cause by a friend, mentor, or TV show. There is no set formula for when or how the fruit will show itself. And, it's important that you not feel disappointed that you, the passionate activist you've been since you can remember, have borne a child who seems unmoved. That's probably one of the most difficult struggles of not judging another individual—to not judge the effectiveness or inaction of your own child. Maintain a loving, non-guilt-inducing attitude so your relationship can grow in the long run. If you authentically infuse the ideas of service, connection, and compassion into your family's values, your children will surely benefit and live out those values, but in their own way. And your world will be a better place for it.

Don't wait for your child to create a plan that moves mountains. But don't underestimate them, either. We live in an amazing time where regular people can impact the world profoundly. Your family can choose a cause you all care about and begin something small. It might just change the world.

Resource Books Cited in Chapter 9—That You May Find Helpful, Too

A Kid's Guide to Giving, Freddi Zeiler (Norwalk, CT: Innovative Kids, 2006).

The Kids' Guide to Social Action, Barbara Lewis (Minneapolis, MN: Free Spirit Publishing, 1998).

Our Day to End Poverty: 24 Ways You Can Make a Difference, Shannon Daley-Harris, Jeffrey Keenan with Karen Speerstra (San Francisco: Berrett Koehler, 2007).

The Green Book: The Everyday Guide to Saving the Planet One Step at a Time, Elizabeth Rogers and Thomas Kostigan (New York: Three Rivers Press, 2007).

Me to We: Finding Meaning in a Material World, Craig Kielburger and Marc Kielburger (New York: Fireside, 2008).

ADDITIONAL RESOURCE BOOKS RELATED TO CHAPTER 9

Planting the Trees of Kenya: The Story of Wangari Maathai, Claire A. Nivola (New York: Frances Foster Books, 2008).

One Hen: How One Small Loan Made a Big Difference, Katie Smith Milway (author), Eugenia Fernandes (illustrator) (Toronto: Kids Can Press, 2008).

Beatrice's Goat, Page McBrier (author), Lori Lohstoeter (illustrator) (New York: Atheneum, 2001).

Paths to Peace: People Who Changed the World, Jane Breskin Zalben (New York: Dutton Juvenile, 2006).

MORE RESOURCE BOOKS RELEVANT TO CHAPTER 9, CITED IN APPENDIX

Leaving Microsoft to Change the World: An Entrepreneur's Odyssey to Educate the World's Children, John Wood (New York: Collins Business, 2007).

WorldChanging: User's Guide for the 21st Century, edited by Alex Steffen (New York: Abrams, 2008).

Ryan and Jimmy and the Well in Africa that Brought them Together, Herb Shoveller (Toronto: Kids Can Press, 2006).

Three Cups of Tea: One Man's Mission to Promote Peace . . . One School at a Time; Three Cups of Tea: One Man's Journey to Change the World . . . One Child at a Time (for young readers), Greg Mortenson and David Oliver Relin (New York: Penguin, 2006, 2009).

Giving, Bill Clinton (New York: Alfred A. Knopf, 2007).

How to Change the World: Social Entrepreneurs and the Power of New Ideas, David Bornstein (New York: Oxford University Press USA, 2007).

Widening Our Circle of Compassion

A human being is a part of the whole, called by us "universe," a part limited in time and space. He experiences himself, his thoughts and feelings as something separated from the rest, a kind of optical delusion of his consciousness. This delusion is a kind of prison for us, restricting us to our personal desires and to affection for a few persons nearest to us. Our task must be to free ourselves from this prison by widening our circle of compassion to embrace all living creatures and the whole of nature in its beauty.

ALBERT EINSTEIN

An individual has not started living until he can rise above the narrow confines of his individualistic concerns to the broader concerns of all humanity.

MARTIN LUTHER KING, JR.

Albert Einstein and Martin Luther King, Jr. embody diversity: agnostic Jewish and religious Christian. White and Black. German-born and Georgia-born. Scientist and clergyman. Yet, their vision converges around an idea: We are liberated when we rise above our limited selves, and reach a consciousness that embraces all of humanity. Taken together, their statements help us understand what it means to be a human being—a globally minded human being.

If you ponder deeply enough on their quotations, you may not need the preceding nine chapters of this book. You will have attained an evolved state of consciousness that accepts no barriers between you and others—the ultimate expression of "growing up global." As a parent you will know how to free yourself from the "prison" that separates you from others and impart this to your children over the course of the eighteen or so years they remain under your care. Your compassion toward all beings would be boundless. Your own process of "widening [your] circle of compassion" would already guide you to do what was necessary to connect with the world.

Alas, that's not how it works for most of us. As I was reflecting on "the whole of nature in its beauty," my daughter called to reprimand me for being late for the carpool pickup and a pot of water on the stove boiled over. So, for all of us who would love to widen our circle of compassion, but need to get through the obligations of daily life, it's okay to get a little help from bullet points, checklists, and website suggestions. What's important is that in our overcommitted and harried lives, we start with something, anything, to connect us with the larger world out there.

Choosing between our country and the rest of the world should be a nonissue. We are local *and* global, and we're never too young (or old) to get started. Without the baggage of so many experiences that might prejudice their thoughts, our children can often lead us. Think of three "global" activities you'd like to try as a family in the next month, write them down, and post them in a visible spot. Then just do them. Every family's expression of how they go global will vary with their internal dynamics, interests, and circumstances. Do what works for you.

Just about everyone I canvassed for this book agreed in one form or another that becoming a world citizen is a lifelong process, not an end in itself. All the various ideas and approaches scattered throughout these pages help fuel the journey and make it real. It's a long road, so we might as well enjoy the ride.

Professor Einstein and Dr. King used terms like *compassion* and *broader concerns of all humanity.* These concepts, and the higher aspirations expressed by so many visionaries can be looked at like the various facets of a shining gem. Viewed together they describe what's known universally as *love.* Practicing universal virtues like empathy, humility, effort, respect, unity, and many more will make the process of "growing up global" more profound and lasting—like an expression of love, not a forced assignment.

I think back to one of our last days in West Africa. I had dropped off Sophia at preschool, and as I approached our home, I waved hello to what seemed like a hundred children on their way to the neighborhood school where we had volunteered. After three months, my daughters and I knew most of these kids, and I heard them call out my name: "Hello Homa" or "Meess Homa, Meess Homa." No more "two-bob, two-bob" ("white person, white person") to which we had become accustomed. These children recognized me as their friend, and in that exchange something profound united us. We had a relationship.

It felt like a going-away present.

Action Steps to Advance the Millennium Development Goals

The United Nations Millennium Development Goals campaign to end extreme poverty on our planet needs us. It needs our imagination—to get creative with our actions and not limit ourselves to what's listed or what's been done; our elbow grease—to get off our chairs and do something; and our voices—to share the situation and ideas with our friends, and to tell our elected officials and media leaders that we know about it, and that we care. Unimaginable suffering around the world stands alongside the bright potential for millions (billions!) of us to do something big to alleviate it, and it is not flying by us or our families unnoticed.

Trying to decide on a specific way to get involved and make a difference can feel daunting. It doesn't have to. The eight goals are meant to clarify and break down the big issues. As difficult as it may be, pick one goal. Then pick one activity. Stick to it. Give it a try before setting out on a second one. But do try at least one. Along with some of the strategies listed in Chapter 9 for how to choose which area of focus you'd like to take, the key may be to listen to your family. Your children's thoughts on solutions to the world's problems may be naïve, but they also might be the clearest. If they are excited about an endeavor, all of you can be.

Following is a list of the eight goals followed by ideas, organizations, and action steps you can take to do your part in achieving one of the goals. This resource is meant to closely follow the discussion points in Chapter 9, as well as give a bit more detail to the bulleted Make a Difference! lists in that chapter. Add more suggestions or share your experiences with making a difference toward the goals, at www.growingupglobal.net.

MILLENNIUM DEVELOPMENT GOAL 1:
THIRTEEN WAYS TO HELP ERADICATE EXTREME POVERTY AND HUNGER

1. *Become an investor.* Kiva ("agreement" or "unity" in Swahili) lets you lend as little as twenty-five dollars to an entrepreneur to help lift him/her out of poverty. Families can fund a project together or have each individual choose one, like a sewing machine to a seamstress in Bangladesh or a supply of seed to a farmer in Mali. Pool your funds with others, like your Girl Scout troop, soccer team, or book club, or find a like-minded group in the site's "Community" section. Your business loan can be paid back or donated to Kiva for job training of its entrepreneurs. When you search the Kiva.org website and learn about the individuals applying for loans, the program really comes alive. The organization FINCA, whose site is VillageBanking.org, also facilitates involvement through lending to microbusinesses in poor communities. TrickleUp.org gives small grants to micro-entrepreneurs globally, and microloan funds serving the United States are growing. You might not be ready to become an actual $10,000 (and up) investor in the Acumen Fund, but check out its mission and innovative programs for "building transformative businesses to solve the problems of poverty" at www.acumenfund.org.

2. *Feed a child.* A one dollar donation through the World Food Program's "From Hunger to Hope" campaign delivers a meal to four children through its global school feeding program. As an effort with your children, sacrifice the snack you were going to buy, then go to fromhungertohope.com and see how good it feels to make a gift! Save a month's snack money, or $50, to feed a child for an entire academic year.

3. *A goat—the gift that keeps giving.* Heifer International and others let you donate a llama, a goat, a flock of chicks, and more to help poor families get out of hunger and become self-reliant. Browse the Heifer homepage or catalogue with your children so they can visualize the positive impact a single animal can make on one family's livelihood. When your younger child contributes toward the purchase of a sheep, chicks, or a cow, give them a beanie baby or hand puppet of that animal to commemorate the gift from your family. If your

The big, good, global, nonprofit organizations that do it all

Throughout this resource list I could repeat some organizations under just about every heading. They are *big*—with budgets running in the hundreds of millions of dollars, *good*—demonstrating a proven track record of reliable service and management, and *global*—their reach extends to all continents. Some familiarity with the big relief agencies becomes part of the literacy of a globally engaged person.

Organizations with a Christian mission are the biggest fundraisers in the relief and development community. In *US News & World Report*'s recent ranking of the largest international charities, Christ-centered World Vision ranked number one in revenue and the U.S. Fund for UNICEF was the only secular organization in the top five. The big secular organizations active in relief and development are:

• U.S. Fund for UNICEF

• Care International

• Save the Children

• Children International

• The Carter Center

• MercyCorps (and its youth program, NetAid)

• Oxfam (grouped with its large U.K. arm, it's much bigger than U.S. revenue would indicate)

I refer to these organizations collectively later in the appendix as the "big, good, global . . ."

family contributes toward the planting of trees for a community, plant a sapling of your own to connect with that gift. World Neighbors's (wn.org) gift catalogue lets you choose a symbolic gift like a herd of guinea pigs to advance long-term solutions in communities in poverty.

4. *Test your vocabulary.* At Freerice.com, twenty grains of rice are donated to hunger relief for every word you get right on their quiz. This is a fun online game for ages ten and up—and you can play it together with your kids.

5. *Host a world meal or a hunger meal.* Invite your children's friends (around ages eight and up) and their parents; each family will donate what they would have spent at a restaurant to a charity of choice. See "Break Bread" in chapter 5 for details on the meal.

6. *Fast. Feel hunger.* World Vision hosts a "thirty-hour famine" that raises funds and awareness, particularly among youth in church groups across North America. Some youth groups might spend the weekend together, sleeping outside in boxes in the cold and performing service activities. The experience of feeling hunger for a prolonged, but specific period might be one that stays with the person for the rest of their lives. Similar programs are promoted by Catholic Relief Services, Action Against Hunger, Oxfam, and others. If you fast or give up a meal as part of your religious observance, dedicate your sacrifice to helping the hungry. You don't need to be part of an organized group to consciously experience hunger; the important thing is to be aware of the effect of poverty in the world, and nothing makes it more immediate than your own empty belly.

7. *Volunteer at a local food pantry.* Kids and their parents will learn much about the needs of their local community by performing service at an area food shelter. Feedingamerica.org, formerly America's Second Harvest, can help you locate a food bank near you. Before telling the food bank what you'd like to do, ask about their needs and see if you can help to fill a need.

8. *Organize a food drive during the off-season.* When it's not Thanksgiving or Christmas season, around February to March or summer (when kids don't have access to school lunches), local food banks are usually the neediest. Distribute a letter from your family describing the needs of the local food charity and your inspiration to work locally and globally toward eradicating hunger, a Millennium Development Goal (this will help spread the word on the MDGs). Accompany the kids as they give out the letter to neighbors along with a brown paper grocery bag for donations. Designate a time you'll stop by to pick up the bag and thank them for working with you to eradicate hunger.

9. *Pick up your pen and write a letter.* Kids may not be old enough to vote, but they can practice their penmanship and writing skills to convey important messages to their elected representatives and speak on behalf of their parents, who do vote. Individually written letters do make a difference in policymaking. Kids' earnest desire to help will stand out from among the form letters members of Congress get.

10. *Work on a science project that benefits many.* Some of the world's best innovators are applying their smarts to helping solve global inequities. Perhaps your son or daughter comes up with an energy, agriculture, education, or other tech solution for their next science fair project. Examples of useful innovations to show budding scientists include the merry-go-round that pumps water when kids play on it, from PlayPumps International; the Network Relief Kit by NetHope that supplies an Internet connection where there is none; and "energy from dirt" batteries by Lebone Solutions.

11. *Put your bank savings to work to make a difference.* When you put your money in the bank, it's supposed to start working on wealth creation throughout the economy. During the 2008 financial meltdown, we saw how interconnected banks and investors were and how susceptible the whole system was to mismanagement. Through a trusted organization like Shorebank (www.sbk.com), you can open an FDIC-insured savings account for the kids that earns a competitive return as well as a "social return." The deposits help fund the bank's sustainable and environmentally friendly developments, including its mortgage rescue program. Search the Internet for Community Development Banks to find more banks near you.

12. *Buy fair trade products.* When you buy products labeled "certified fair trade" (like fashion accessories, coffee, chocolate, and more), you know that more of your dollars will go back to those who need them most. Costco, Trader Joe's, and some supermarket chains are beginning to mainstream fair trade products, making it easier to make fair purchase, and Ten Thousand Villages shops and others dedicate their entire inventory to fair products. When you do pay extra for coffee or gifts in order to benefit the farmworkers, craftspeople, and their families, point this out to your children. Read them the story of the producers, usually found on the product label.

13. *Make an e-commerce difference.* If you're a devoted eBay shopper, check out their www.WorldofGood.com division, dedicated to social change.

MILLENNIUM DEVELOPMENT GOAL 2:
FOURTEEN WAYS TO HELP ACHIEVE UNIVERSAL PRIMARY EDUCATION

1. *Tutor.* Our daughters' first experience tutoring readers during middle school showed them the potential impact on another young person's life and it boosted their motivation to improve their own verbal skills. You don't have to travel far in the United States to find a community where children struggle to read. And while reading specialists and other professional educators are crucial, kids as young as nine or ten can offer to help a neighbor or classmate to read.

2. *Raise a reader and a reading buddy.* Children who grow up around their parents' example of reading in their spare time will love to read themselves. They are more interested and likely to engage—in whatever way—with the world. Kids can help start or volunteer with an after-school "reading buddy" program to encourage children who love to read and those who struggle to share the experience together.

3. *Help schools near and far.* Building With Books conducts after-school programs for urban American youth who mobilize to improve their own communities while also wanting to help poor communities abroad. In this model, those facing the greatest challenge in America and abroad are empowered to make a difference in the world, and there is lots of room to accept new volunteers—so your whole family might get involved.

4. *Participate in the Global Campaign for Education's Annual Action Week.* Through the organization's website, Campaignforeducation.org, you can learn about international progress on the literacy goals, participate in the international campaigns, and raise awareness in your own community.

5. *Tell your government to support the Rights of the Child—and celebrate.* Only the United States and Somalia have not ratified the UN Convention on the Rights of the Child. The "Child Convention" ensures basic human rights for all children, including the right to a home, food, clothing, education, health care, and protection from violence, neglect, and abuse. It was adopted on November 20, 1989, and every November 20 is International Children's Day. We

The Big Faith-Based Charities

Faith-based charities were the first to administer to the poor. They continue a legacy of serving those largely forgotten by society. As a group they are the biggest fundraisers for international relief efforts. Their programs may appeal to your family's values. Some of the larger organizations, grouped by faith affiliation, include:

• World Vision

• Salvation Army

• Christian Children's Fund

• Feed the Children

• Adventist Development and Relief Agency

• Catholic Relief Services

• Episcopal Relief and Development

• Samaritan's Purse

• American Friends Service Committee

• American Jewish World Service

• American Jewish Joint Distribution Committee

• Islamic Relief

• Aga Khan Foundation

• Tzu Chi Foundation

• Seva Foundation

• Sewa International

know about Mother's Day and Father's Day. This is Children's Day—but in this case, the children can give and make a difference in the world. Organize your own celebration in honor of the world's children. Kids can write to their congressional representatives to urge support for the world's children and U.S. ratification of the Child Convention.

6. *Read* John Wood's Leaving Microsoft to Change the World, the inspiration behind the organization Room to Read. Digest the story and share it with your children. Go to the organization's site, www.roomtoread.org to see the updates on how much impact Room to Read continues to make and how to get involved in this global movement.

7. *Initiate a partner school and pen pal program.* Instigate a personal relationship between your kid's school and a school abroad that could benefit from your resources. As part of the program, start a long-term pen pal program (perhaps lasting through the school career of each child), so kids from both sides benefit. Some, not all, of the pen pals will "stick" and create lasting friendships. iEARN, the International Education and Resource Network, and ePals are good sources for starting an online partnership with another school.

8. *Sponsor a child's education.* Even where primary education is offered for free, "hidden costs" prevent kids from attending school. These include the purchase of uniforms, shoes, school supplies like pencils, books, and paper, as well as daytime meals. They usually cost a fraction of what you'd pay in the United States, but any extra strain on a family's budget might be enough to prohibit a child's school attendance—especially a girl's. Many organizations sponsor children through school, including: Save the Children, Plan USA, Christian Children's Fund, and others, including those that are specific to a geographic location, like Tibet, South Africa, Cambodia, and in America. Through Invis ibleChildren.com sponsor a child from northern Uganda's war zone to pursue secondary school education. Invisible Children's documentary film exposes the horrors of war and its impact on children, then offers a youth-oriented outlet to take action.

9. *Fulfill a classroom's wishes.* Give through DonorsChoose.org, where U.S. public school teachers' requests are matched with donors on their friendly-to-navigate site. Go on the site with your kids and treat the "giving" as you would a shopping expedition—choose a request you like and get it. DonorsChoose gift cards make nice teacher gifts, too.

10. *Buy a book that funds literacy elsewhere.* Next time you're shopping for a book, try BetterWorldBooks.com, which donates the proceeds of your book purchase to literacy and other projects worldwide. Many schools hold book fairs, so kids get it: Think of this as a global book fair.

11. *Buy a laptop for $200.* Through One Laptop per Child, at laptop.org, you can purchase a low-cost, technologically appropriate laptop for a child in an impoverished school overseas, helping to open up educational opportunities and the world to them. When it's time to buy Junior a computer, you could challenge him to earn the $200 (through home responsibilities, a job in the neighborhood, or a more formal job) so that when you get him the new laptop, he's "buying" one for a child without that privilege elsewhere. Find organizations that can use your previous computer for educational purposes.

12. *Teach ESL.* Get trained in teaching English as a Second Language and volunteer to tutor newly resettled refugees in your community. Your local schools probably employ ESL teachers who could help you find resources for training and outlets for volunteering; or ask your local community college or public library. If your child is old enough, you might get trained together. Refugee resettlement groups like the International Rescue Committee, state and local government or religious organizations can connect you with local refugee families and other new immigrants. Share a meal with the family you tutor and involve your children in helping the kids practice their English.

13. *Support Sesame Workshop and watch their global programs.* I grew up watching Sesame Street and so did my kids; it turns out the children of the world have, too, thanks to the nonprofit efforts of Sesame Workshop and more recently, the original global programming, instilling positive learning for children in so many languages. Kids can watch Global Grover and the new characters of "Panwapa" online for a furry window to the world at www.sesameworshop.org (look up Initiatives and Around the World tabs on the homepage). For ages thirteen and up, the film *The World According to Sesame Street* shows how the Muppets make a social impact. This can be ordered on Netflix.

14. *Devote your vacation to teaching, tutoring, building a school, assisting teachers, or whatever you're asked to do.* You might not change the world by spending your vacation volunteering, but you and your family might be changed forever and gain a new insight on realities in different countries. Some organizations that can place you in a worthy community include: Cross-Cultural Solutions, GlobalVolunteers, Global Citizens Network, the Center for Cultural Interchange, and ProWorld Service Corps. See information clearinghouses at TransitionsAbroad.com, GoAbroad.com, and VolunteerInternational.org.

MILLENNIUM DEVELOPMENT GOAL 3:
TWELVE WAYS TO PROMOTE GENDER EQUALITY AND EMPOWER WOMEN

1. *Become informed.* Learn how investments in women disproportionately help the overall community, increasing the chances for peace and prosperity. Information from UNIFEM, UNICEF, Save the Children's Annual Mother's Index, Worldpulse.com, and the Girl Effect provide a snapshot of the particular challenges faced by women and girls.

2. *You Go Girl!* For ages ten and up; watch the two-minute video at Girleffect.org. Talk about your impressions of the message and how it's delivered.

3. *Educate a girl.* Educating a girl will impact her family, the community, and ultimately, the world in a positive way. Look up the "big, good, global . . ." organizations like monafoundation.org, as well as charity search websites to find opportunities for sponsoring a girl's education. This is probably the best bang for your buck to make a difference in the world. Involve the whole family—especially the boys—in choosing the organization and making a long-term commitment so that a promising girl can continue to pursue her dreams for a better life for herself, her community, and the world.

4. *Say no to violence against women.* Violence against women in its various forms is the world's most pervasive human rights violation, far too common, taking a devastating social and economic toll on communities and families, and becoming a fast-growing public health concern. Get informed at End Abuse.org or GlobalHealth.org. Your family can sign the global petition at UNIFEM.org, tell your friends about it, and contact your elected representatives to take action at the local and the global levels. Help women access justice with Tahirih.org. For teens and up, volunteer with a local women's shelter, hotline, or other support organization. Find one near you, anywhere in the world, at Hotpeachpages.net, the international directory of domestic violence agencies. If you are a man, show you care deeply about this issue—your voice will impact other men and shape the future of the boys around you.

5. *Connect with women worldwide, as well as in your backyard.* The Global Fund for Women is a member of the Women's Funding Network. With over one

hundred American member organizations, you probably have a local Women's Fund near you—and they want your participation. These charitable foundations invest in women and girl's opportunities locally and worldwide, and their work triggers a positive chain reaction for entire communities. You can throw a "house party" that benefits the Global Fund as well as your local women's funds.

Looking back, it's hard for me to believe I didn't realize there were serious needs in my suburban county; but with the help of the local Fund for Women and Girls, I soon found out about the hidden needs almost literally in my backyard. My daughters had a chance to help the local fund in elementary school by doing artwork for their annual holiday card, helping stuff envelopes for their fundraising appeals, volunteering as ushers at events, and in high school they are eligible to participate in the innovative Girls' Grantmaking program, where a committee of teens is given the responsibilities of philanthropy, deciding where a significant portion of real funds would best be used to effect positive change in their community. If your child would like to get involved in youth philanthropy initiatives, contact the Women's Funding Network, its local affiliate, or your local community foundation. Look for "Philanthropy" clubs forming in high schools.

6. *Invest in women.* Through Kiva.org, VillageBanking.org, Accion.org, and GlobalGiving.com you can advance women's training and entrepreneurship. It's been found over and over again that women invest much more of their incomes back into their families, and the positive impact on health, education, democracy, violence prevention, and the environment quickly follows.

7. *Display true beauty.* In the market for a carpet? Look for the RugMark label, the "AfghanMark: Made by Women in Afghanistan," Arzu brand, and others, for beautiful, fairly traded, and fairly made handwoven rugs. These organizations are working to end illegal child labor and offer education, healthy work environments, and medical assistance—impacting generations. I love the idea of putting one of these rugs in my daughter's room or our family room, so the spirit and the effort of those women is present and adds beauty to our lives. Discuss why you chose that particular rug brand with the family. Find other opportunities where your purchases have a ripple effect, like beaded jewelry gifts from TandaZulu that benefit AIDS orphans in South Africa, and countless others. Etsy.com is a vast online marketplace to explore handmade items, some of which benefit communities in need.

8. *Support women and girls in sports.* Mentor a girl. Coach a girls' team—and possibly connect them with a team across town or abroad. Contribute to the Women's Sports Foundation and visit the Billie Jean King International

Women's Sports Center in the Sports Museum of America in New York. Before traveling abroad find out how you can help a girls' or women's sports league in the area you are visiting. Do they need a coaching session? Some equipment? If traveling with your kids, take them along for the visit to create a lasting impression and possibly make new, global friends.

9. *Connect with adolescent girls.* The Nike Foundation asserts that investments in adolescent girls have the biggest ripple effect on a country's development. If you are the parent of adolescent girls *and* boys, empower them with this knowledge—they can be part of this Girl Effect, too. Our tweens and teens don't need to be treated simply as consumers or bystanders; they are at a unique place in their lives where their current choices and training can make a big impact on the world's future. Help them explore how they would like to make a difference.

10. *Encourage girls.* Girls Inc., Girl Scouts, and other local clubs reach out globally, help advocate for justice locally, and offer ways to help advance opportunities for girls. The University of Maryland's Center for Women and Information Technology maintains a rich "Girl-Related Resources" site for safe, smart, empowering websites at www.umbc.edu/cwit/girlres.html. If you are the parent of girls, you can use these resources to enhance your own daughters' extracurricular experiences.

11. *Honor the caring of children.* Every other democracy in the world has figured out a better way to balance work and family obligations, and provide quality, safe, nurturing child care situations. Look for and support solutions in the United States as well as for the poorest countries in the world, where women's burdens won't let them break out of the poverty trap. Give a special gift to your own child care provider. Together with your own kids, volunteer at a local Head Start center. Give to an organization that provides child care to low-income families. Offer to help someone in your community who lacks backup child care. If your children are younger, this could turn into a playdate; if they are a bit older, they can be the helpers and take age-appropriate responsibility.

12. *Ensure Afghan girls and other girls will never again be deprived of the right to education.* The 9/11 attacks on the United States opened many Americans' eyes to the horrors Afghans endured under the Taliban regime. Some 9/11 victims' family and friends channeled their grief by supporting opportunities for Afghan women for education and empowerment, which they had been denied for a generation. You can back their efforts by supporting the Goodrich Foundation, Americares, Help the Afghan Children, the Afghan Women's Mission, and the "big, good, global . . ." organizations.

MILLENNIUM DEVELOPMENT GOAL 4:
TWELVE WAYS TO REDUCE CHILD MORTALITY

1. *Collect change to buy lifesaving solutions for kids.* UNICEF estimates that it costs as little as $0.06 to treat life-threatening diarrhea with oral rehydration salts, $0.26 to $1.10 for measles vaccinations, pennies per dose of Vitamin A that prevents blindness, and a few cents for critical antibiotic treatments. Trick-or-treat for UNICEF or collect change year-round for children's lives. After going to the doctor for your annual visit and vaccinations, make a symbolic donation to UNICEF to "match" that care for a needy child.

2. *Put your artwork to good use.* Every year UNICEF's holiday cards are drawn by children around the world to benefit the world's children. Their website includes contact information where you can send your child's drawing for consideration on their global holiday cards. You don't have to wait for UNICEF's approval—you can print your own. Forgo commercial cards this year in favor of a card designed by your child. Include a message on the back of the card sharing with friends a cause or commitment your family has made to help your community and the world.

3. *Pass along your water conservation.* In middle school, a common science assignment is to track your family's home water use. Look at how much water your family uses every day, try to find ways to use less, and think of what you can do to help children with diseases caused by a lack of clean water.

4. *Share a clean glass of water.* The Children's Safe Drinking Water initiative, supported by PUR water filtration packets, hopes to share 3.5 billion gallons of clean water by 2012; by 2008, they'd surpassed 1 billion. Over four thousand children per day die because of lack of clean water—more than deaths from malaria and HIV/AIDS combined. Kids know dirty water is yucky, and the short videos on their website, csdw.org, are worth watching with kids of all ages, as I did with my five-year-old daughter and nephew. Sophia and Max were captivated by Dr. Greg's "science experiment" with a few kids around their own age, showing how the dirty water got clean; then they were ready to watch a few short clips from around the world showing people having their first glass of clean water ever. Simple arithmetic shows how much impact your

donation can make: ten cents buys one water filtration packet, each packet yields ten liters of clean water. One dollar gives a child clean water for *fifty* days; $7.50 gives a child clean water for a full year, and $30 provides clean water for the entire family for a year.

5. *Get involved with your local Kiwanis Club.* Kiwanis International consists of a network of volunteers dedicated to "changing the world one child and one community at a time." As well as adult groups, they operate a growing network of K-Kids Clubs for elementary-school ages, a Key Club at most high schools, and Circle K International in colleges. Circle K's *Saving Lives: The Six Cent Initiative* with UNICEF gets oral rehydration salts to children across the world. Kiwanis has come a long way since I was in high school, where the only girl allowed in the Key Club was the "sweetheart" elected by the boys. Today, clubs think globally, inclusively, and each local club initiates fundraisers and service activities its own members personally drive forward, similar to Rotary Clubs, described following.

6. *Buy multicultural books, movies, and photography to support children.* The Global Fund for Children produces picture books and other media depicting children from around the world, appropriate for toddlers on up. These celebrate our global family and help fund small grants for work with vulnerable children and youth.

7. *Support a surrogate family environment.* So many conflicts, natural disasters, and diseases have separated children from their parents. Where do they go when no one can care for them and the governments are too poor to provide an adequate safety net? One organization we saw in action in Africa was SOS Children's Villages. This is a vital network of long-term, family-based care environments in 132 countries for children who have lost their parents or have been separated from their families. Navigate their site with your children. The "big, good, global . . ." organizations highlighted earlier also assist orphaned children in the hardest environments with very little resources. The writer Pearl S. Buck was an early pioneer in crosscultural adoption. The foundation established in her name (psbi.org) offers overseas sponsorships as well as assistance adopting a child to join your family.

8. *Sponsor a child.* Children who continue to live with their families also might need sponsorship for their health, nutrition, education, and other basic expenses. Plan International and the "big, good, global . . ." organizations have well-developed child sponsorship programs. In some cases, the organization you work through might be too small or too big to foster a personal or long-term connection with the child. Make sure the program you support matches your personal values.

9. *Assemble "healthy kid kits"* to be sent through AmeriCares for children in

poverty in Afghanistan, Colombia, Guatemala, Iraq, and Mongolia. One-gallon Ziploc-type bags are filled with a new toothbrush, a large-tooth comb or small hairbrush, one travel-size bar of soap, one small facecloth, and one "fun" item—like a small handheld stuffed animal, handheld ball, Matchbox car, or a packet of stickers. The Americares.org site also includes ideas for how kids can fundraise to help victims of disasters.

10. *Pack up your shoes.* Shoes that your kids have grown out of, but have some good wear left in them, are valuable at Shoe4Africa.org. Children who get to wear shoes are less vulnerable to diseases, and some of them have gone on to be among Kenya's champion runners. Go to the post office with your kids, send a few pair at a time—this doesn't need to turn into a big "shoe drive" effort—and follow the shoes' route to Kenya on a map. Learn what a difference a pair of sneakers can make, as well as the other good works that have resulted from this simple idea.

11. *Invite a health professional to speak at your school.* Every year thousands of doctors, nurses, and other health professionals volunteer their vacations and expertise to assist humanitarian health projects at clinics and hospitals worldwide. Invite them to your school career fair or "heroes" day to share their insights.

12. *Set up an "investment fund" for your children's charitable giving.* Bill and Hillary Clinton agreed to give each of their nephews a set amount of money per month if they invested 25 percent of it in charitable causes and then could explain to their famous aunt and uncle what they supported and why. The boys took the responsibility seriously and became acquainted with diverse and important causes in America and abroad, which hopefully will launch their lifetime of giving.[1]

MILLENNIUM DEVELOPMENT GOAL 5:
NINE WAYS TO IMPROVE MATERNAL HEALTH

1. *Get informed.* With all the health care and communication breakthroughs over the past three decades, it's startling that the lives of mothers have not improved overall. The countries that have spent so much of their national budget on

warfare are the places where mothers have fared the worst. Learn more from the Global Health Council (GlobalHealth.org), UNIFEM, UNICEF, and the nonprofits active in women's health.

2. *Dedicate baby shower and Mother's Day gifts.* Honor a special mom with a gift of health to the world's mothers. For a baby shower, donate to an organization that provides sterile birthing kits to undersupplied hospitals in the world or special training to midwives and maternal health professionals. Contact your area's maternal and child health agency to identify a way to help low-income families locally. Children can make cards for grandmothers, aunts, and other special mothers in their lives with an enclosure about a maternal health program your family cares about.

3. *Add your name and voice to a global campaign for maternal and child health.* Global networks like Deliver Now and the White Ribbon Alliance for Safe Motherhood urgently aim to increase public awareness of maternal health worldwide. Middle school seems to be a time for petition writing—young activists can learn about these causes. Vocal organizers have mobilized for the rights of unborn children; couldn't we do at least as much for the mothers and the babies after they are born?

4. *Help mothers feed their families and themselves.* Young people can visualize how mothers everywhere are in charge of putting food on the table, and they seem to feed the men first, followed by the boys, then the girls, and what's left, themselves. Programs like the United Nation's Food and Agriculture Organization (FAO) TeleFood program, International Medical Corps, Self Help International, Bread for the World, and Winrock International work to help women adequately farm and nourish their families and themselves.

5. *Attention mothers of young children: Share your breast milk.* The International Breast Milk Project sends prequalified and screened frozen human breast milk—the best alternative to the biological mother's milk—to infants born prematurely and those affected by HIV/AIDS in Africa. Many young families may not be in a position to volunteer in Africa or adopt a baby, but this modern solution offers a direct and intimate connection between your baby and infants who you want to reach out to. The Human Milk Bank of North America, Milkin' Mamas, and the National Breast Milk Bank get breast milk to North American babies in need.

6. *Print coupons, deliver diapers and formula.* Social services agencies working in the United States often need donations of formula and diapers for the mothers of young children they assist. Take the kids to purchase and drop off the supplies (along with relevant coupons that your kids can find online and print out). The gift is tangible, and especially if repeated children are likely to remember it for a long time.

7. *Invest in a socially responsible fund.* Some of the funds to consider: Pax World Mutual Funds, Calvert Funds, Developing World Markets, and Domini Social Investments. Share this investment decision with your children if they are old enough to understand, especially if you are allocating a portion of their college fund.

8. *Try to imagine a refugee's life.* The U.S. affiliate of the French *Médecins Sans Frontières* (MSF), Doctors Without Borders, has slide shows on their website—www.msf.org—that offer a glimpse of life for the tens of millions of displaced citizens they care for—particularly the burden carried by the mothers. MSF's traveling exhibit, "A Refugee Camp in the Heart of the City," is available for viewing online. I watched some of the video demonstrations on my computer, including "Where Will I Go to the Bathroom?" This shows how difficult everyday realities of refugees can be. In 2006, more than three million individual donors worldwide contributed to MSF. Share this Nobel Peace Prize–winning, heroic, and truly global organization's work with tweens and up.

9. *Donate supplies to women's hospitals treating the poorest patients.* Hospitals working in the poorest areas continuously need medical supplies, ranging from antibiotics to tools, and even sterile gloves. Kids can picture these tangible needs. Makeshift medical facilities in refugee camps as well as those in areas recovering from conflict are often the most in need. If you'd like to help, the UN High Commission for Refugees and the medical organizations serving crisis areas can direct your donations to the right places. Specialized programs, like the Fistula Foundation, use small sums of money to save the poorest women's lives, efficiently and with love.

MILLENNIUM DEVELOPMENT GOAL 6:
SEVEN WAYS TO COMBAT HIV/AIDS, MALARIA, AND OTHER DISEASES

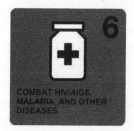

1. *Get informed using quality curricular materials.* For high school and possibly advanced middle schoolers, the Global Concerns Classroom, a program of Concern Worldwide, has developed curriculum guides on key issues related to

the global fight against poverty, including understanding the HIV/AIDS crisis. The guide poses various perspectives on difficult questions like the dilemma of spending limited resources on preventing HIV/AIDS versus treating it, and suggests where to look for more information.

2. *Support culturally relevant solutions.* If this is the issue that moves you and you'd like to give funds, find an organization that is sensitive to creating sustainable and culture-specific solutions. Explore with your family how some approaches might involve issues that don't seem relevant to disease treatment. For example, the children might need shoes to fight infections they get from the sores after so much walking in their bare feet; the community needs a road for medicines to reach them, or literacy programs for adults to follow treatment directions, or better quality roofs for their homes in order to fight certain diseases borne by the bugs that hatch in the grass-thatch roofs, or a sports program, cash, or a meal to serve as an incentive for young people to participate and stay in a training course. A few of the larger organizations known for this approach include Partners in Health, PATH, Doctors Without Borders, World Neighbors, and Africare. There are many others dedicated to working in a particular community, on a smaller level, that need support, too.

3. *Choose (RED).* With so many choices of iPod color or Dell Laptop exterior, Converse sneakers, Hallmark cards, GAP T-shirts, Armani accessories, Starbucks products, and even iTunes gift cards and Windows operating systems, choose the gift that gives back—with Product (RED). Kids buy these products and can proudly show they chose to help contribute over $110 million to fight AIDS through The Global Fund to Fight AIDS, TB, and Malaria. As Starbucks's tagline says, we do this for our *"Sha(RED) Planet."*

4. *Watch a movie chronicling life with AIDS and poverty. Angels in the Dust* and *Beat the Drum* put a human face on South Africa's children orphaned by AIDS. The films are tragic and emotional. In *Angels,* this is particularly so when relating the violence toward girls; both for viewers fifteen and up.

5. *Lend a hand to AIDS patients and others suffering in your community.* Meals on Wheels and other local initiatives regularly need volunteers. Families often own the perfect vehicle for delivering meals—a well-traveled minivan. Family vehicles might also work well to transport someone to a doctor's appointment, particularly if they use a wheelchair. Taking children along for the ride helps develop compassion and a level of understanding that a distant view can't. As sad as it might be to meet someone suffering from AIDS, it might also feel better to have reached out to help and made a difference in someone's day.

6. *Join your local Rotary Club to eradicate polio and support grassroots initiatives worldwide.* Rotary's motto is "service above self." It focuses on building good-

will and peace around the world and is determined to "eradicate polio." I have witnessed its members from U.S. clubs get behind worthy causes like youth leadership in Bolivia and solar power for a hospital in The Gambia. U.S. club members help guide these grant requests to fulfillment, the international foundation can match it, and an overseas club partners on it to multiply the impact. Together with your children, you can present a project for your local club to support. Another good resource is Rotary's youth program for ages fifteen and up, which provides international exchange opportunities for promising, globally minded young people around the world.

7. *Mobilize nets—basketball, tennis, volleyball . . . mosquito nets!* Malaria kills a child every thirty seconds. Mosquito nets serve as an effective, low-cost preventive tool. Kids get this: Without a net over their beds, people in some places are vulnerable to a mosquito bite that can make them very sick. *Sports Illustrated* writer Rick Reilly got a movement going with a May 2006 column challenging his readers to donate $10 for an antimalarial bed net that could save an entire family for four years of use. The overwhelming response led to the creation of NothingButNets.net and within a few months, over $1 million was raised, with much more since then. The website shows adults and kids creatively raising awareness and funds—these are the MVPs. Kids have instigated an outpouring of support, by organizing tennis, Ping-Pong, soccer, hockey, and basketball tournaments, juggling shows, bake sales, diorama dramatizations, and have given talks at churches, schools, and community groups explaining the devastating impact and simple solution. What could you do?

MILLENNIUM DEVELOPMENT GOAL 7:
FOURTEEN WAYS TO ENSURE ENVIRONMENTAL SUSTAINABILITY

1. *Recognize it's a privilege to discuss reduce, reuse, recycle.* In many parts of the world, electricity and clean water don't flow 24/7, and reusing water bottles, aluminum foil—anything—is just the way things are done. Cutting down water use (like taking a quick shower) or electricity use (like turning off the

lights) is a nonissue—they don't flow all day, every day. Not reusing something is unthinkable and the reminder to recycle is almost laughable—as I have learned when mentioning recycling among friends in Africa and they literally laughed at me. Recycling takes on a new meaning when everything is so creatively used until it's spent beyond recognition. When kids see living conditions among the world's poor, they can start to understand it's a privilege to choose to limit energy waste. It might actually be that *parents* need retraining to alter their resource consumption. We're the ones who grew up throwing everything away and leaving the lights on.

2. For ideas on "going green," see *The Green Book* by Elizabeth Rogers and Thomas Kostigan, or the six-hundred-page *WorldChanging: A User's Guide for the 21st Century*, edited by Alex Steffen along with its companion blog, *Plenty* magazine, and its blog, and more blogs, like Grist.org, Treehugger.com, and Idealbite.com.

3. *The privilege of drinking tap water.* Set an example to the kids—reduce use of bottled water to times you can't take your own container. We're fortunate to live in a country where tap water, for the most part, is safe and clean to drink. In fact, it's more regulated than bottled water and represents one of our nation's best infrastructure investments. Save money buying less bottled water, and reduce the energy costs associated with manufacturing, filling, and transporting the bottles. Buy safe refillable containers for sports and other on-the-go uses.

4. *Use less; keep the change.* Have a family meeting about energy consumption goals and track savings in terms of lower utility bills, gallons of water, kilowatt hours, gallons of gas, and other resources (like bottled water and lightbulbs) saved. Try to involve family members to keep track of different categories of resource use so everyone owns the process. Keep a chart—sort of like the old "chores" charts recommended to entice kids to make their bed, set the table, and so on. Then contribute to a favorite cause with the savings.

5. *Bring Jane Goodall and global environmental awareness to your school.* The Jane Goodall Institute's youth program, Roots & Shoots (Rootsandshoots.org), operates with schools and kids in about one hundred countries, with the motto "The Power of Youth is Global," encouraging informed and compassionate action. Famed primatologist and activist Jane Goodall and other global leaders serve as powerful role models and mentors to youth participants. These clubs seem to thrive in elementary and middle schools, but high schools and nearly one hundred universities also have Roots & Shoots Clubs. Local club activities can get as creative as their members wish, while the central organization can offer support, a global network, planning help, invitations to special events,

curriculum tie-ins, and ideas for further activities. If you'd like to start an environmental club at school, why not tap into a dynamic global network and make it a Roots & Shoots Club? The network also participates in global programs, like Roots & Shoots Day of Peace, in support of the United Nation's International Day of Peace. This reflects the experience Dr. Jane conveyed to me one day on a train ride in 2004, that "ultimately, my efforts to save animals and the environment are a way to work for peace." Roots & Shoots serves as an ideal vehicle to channel the energy of youth who are "Growing Up Global."

6. *Turn your trash into cash, a field trip—and more.* Take a trip to the local recycling center and landfill with the kids. Get a visual sense of the magnitude of solid waste disposal in your little corner of the planet. Offer to take your neighbor's hard-to-recycle-at-the-curb items with you.

7. *Cause a ripple effect.* Kids have succeeded wildly in raising funds for clean water and other environmental issues. Learn about www.Ryanswell.ca, where a first-grader set off to raise money for a well after hearing about global water needs from his teacher. His first $70 raised created a ripple effect, helping hundreds of thousands of people, and ballooning into a vibrant international organization. The Ryan's Well website also contains curriculum materials for water and advocacy issues. Read the children's book *Ryan and Jimmy: And the Well in Africa That Brought Them Together.*

8. *Plant vegetables.* The idea of tending the land, composting waste, and eating what you grow—local and organic—is new again. When kids witness their food production firsthand, a level of empathy, pride, and appreciation is cultivated that few other activities can bring.

9. *Advocate for an environmentally friendly school.* Kids spend a good chunk of their day at school and most schools remain big wasters of energy. How many times have you heard the classrooms are too warm in the winter, so kids go to school in a T-shirt? Food waste. Paper waste. Electricity waste. Electronics and gadgetry waste. Transportation waste (e.g., kids individually driven to/from school). Incomplete recycling programs. Fundraising that promotes further waste. Involve the kids in a schoolwide conservation effort and let them vote on how to dedicate the savings—possibly split between something that benefits the student body and support to your partner school or cause.

10. *Watch the film* Running the Sahara. Three men set off on a grueling journey, never done before, running about fifty miles a day for 111 days through the Sahara desert. Armchair travelers get a glimpse of the punishing terrain and human trials that come with it—particularly those caused by environmental degradation. A result of this project is H20 Africa, led by actor Matt Damon. Watch the film with family and friends and explore how you can get involved

in the quest for water. This is one of many high-quality documentaries supported by National Geographic. Explore National Geographic's website for more unique vistas of life on our planet.

11. *Recycle your bicycle.* When Winston Duncan was ten years old, he and his mother saved up to travel to southern Africa. He was struck by the lack of transportation: Everyone walked everywhere for everything. Duncan started a bike collection drive when he came home, which gathered 275 bikes just in the first weekend. In three years, he's attracted hundreds of volunteers and sent over 1,300 bikes with Wheels to Africa, which he started with his mom, Dixie's, help. Pedals for Progress (p4p.org) has collected about 120,000 bikes for poor communities worldwide. Watch p4p's video to learn about the impact bikes can make on a community. See ibike.org for a directory of bicycle recycling programs throughout the United States and Canada. Want to make your own town more bike-friendly? Get help from Bikesbelong.org.

12. *Birthday as opportunity.* In the previous chapter, there's a section on birthday party themes that make a difference—celebrate and share your commitment to the earth.

13. *Stop the junk mail.* Register with a service like the mailstopper.tonic.com, 41 pounds.org, StopTheJunkMail.com, or do it yourself through www .obviously.com/junkmail, and halt the waste of 1.5 trees lost per family's worth of junk mail, plus endless piles in a landfill. You also can request a halt to phone book delivery. Kids can help you complete the registration, and if they are the ones to check the mail, notice how much less paper you are throwing away.

14. *Travel green.* Tourism is a big perpetrator of waste and your family can make a conscious effort to put less strain on the environment. Pack light and smart, reuse (everything—linens, clothing, water bottles), choose your destination wisely (perhaps an eco-resort?), meet the local community, take advantage of local products and food, and have fun! Take a step further and purchase carbon offset credits, especially for air travel. Let the kids take the lead in calculating the offsets. Or plan a "voluntour" to combine tourism and volunteering.

MILLENNIUM DEVELOPMENT GOAL 8:
TEN WAYS TO DEVELOP A GLOBAL PARTNERSHIP FOR DEVELOPMENT

1. *Encourage your county or town to adopt a sister city.* When your local community links with a sister city, you gain a connection to specific places and issues across the globe. Perhaps the big employer in your town has operations abroad, or an immigrant population from a particular nationality lives in your community—these are possible locations for a sister city.
2. *Start a giving circle.* You and your kids will realize how difficult it is for different countries to act in a unified bloc when you try this with your friends. But you'll also see how much more impact you can make with pooled resources than acting on your own. Like an investment circle, all give funds and meet periodically to decide on where they should be donated, monitor progress, and plan for the next steps.
3. *Get the real story on U.S. foreign assistance.* Read Oxfam America's "Foreign Aid 101" on its website. Then decide how you want to get involved in making sure our tax dollars are spent wisely to help the world.
4. *Who's your hero?* The visionaries working "in the trenches" to better our world are some of today's heroes. Browsing through the sources recommended in this chapter you may have stumbled upon a few. Ashoka and its Changemakers initiative, as well as nominees of the World Children's Prize, United Nations' citizen "Ambassadors," stories on the JustCauseIt.com blog, and young people highlighted for making a difference in popular magazines like *Teen People, Time for Kids,* and even *CosmoGirl* can inspire heroic action. For heavier reading, see *How to Change the World: Social Entrepreneurs and the Power of New Ideas* by David Bornstein.
5. *Contact your elected leaders and media.* Opinion leaders and politicians might assume we're not interested in what's going on in the world. But if families and young people demonstrate their concern for people far away, then policies and rhetoric start to change. "You're with us or against us" is replaced by "We're all in this together." This will show itself in decisions of elected officials and media, such as in energy policy, foreign aid, education programs for local

school districts, television programming, and even library acquisitions and investments.

6. *Get to know your state and federal elected representatives' stances on issues you care about.* How they have voted, who they accept money from, and personal experiences, like a family member from another country or service in the Peace Corps. Write them about issues of concern (many organizations have sample letters for elected officials). With the media, comment on programming that you particularly enjoyed or might have been offensive. Make your voice and concerns heard.

7. *Offer your Web-designing savvy.* Kids can offer to build a cause's website. To help far away, Grassroots.org, committed to making cutting-edge technologies available around the world for free, can match your tech skills with your interests.

8. *Donate or recycle your old cell phones and computers.* Throwing used electronics in the trash—with all their toxic materials—poisons the environment and blocks their reuse by others who go without. Find local recycling centers (for anything) through Earth911.com or simply Google "computer (or cell phone, etc.) refurbishing and recycling." Gazelle.com will buy or recycle old gadgets and you can choose to get a check or donate the proceeds. Recycle and donate funds to various causes through CollectiveGood.com, PcsForSchools.org, WorldComputerExchange.org, and others. These recycling programs also make good school fundraisers.

9. *Join a positive network for global youth action.* TakingItGlobal.org, the Global Youth Action Network at Youthlink.org, New Global Citizens at Global Citizens.org, and UNICEF.org can connect like-minded young people.

10. *Use your Facebook and MySpace pages to proclaim your causes.* Link icons of your special causes on your Facebook and other pages to inform your friends and their friends about important work, link to a video or news story, network and share ideas among like-minded people, and invite large groups of people to real and virtual events.

Notes

For references to books cited in the chapters, please see the end of each individual chapter for "Resource Books Cited in Chapter—That You May Find Helpful, Too."

Introduction

1 Carlin Romano, "Parsing Putin," *The Philadelphia Inquirer,* September 28, 2003, p. H18.
2 Hara Estroff Marano, "The Dangers of Loneliness," *Psychology Today,* August 31, 2003.

Chapter 2: Greet Your Friend

1 Data source: *Ethnologue: Languages of the World,* 15th ed. (2005).
2 See Kidspace @ The Internet Public Library (http://www.ipl.org/div/hello/), "Say Hello to the World." Each of the language pages contains links for more information and pronunciation in each of the languages listed in the website, even though this site has removed its pronunciation files.
3 From various studies cited in "Research Points: Essential Information for Education Policy. Foreign Language Instruction: Implementing the Best Teaching Methods." Spring 2006, Volume 4, Issue 1. Published by the American Educational Research Association.
4 Ibid., AERA Research Points, p. 2.

Chapter 3: Play!

1 Renuka Rayasam, "Global Whiz Kids Rule Chess Boards," *The Atlanta Journal-Constitution,* July 30, 2003.
2 This game is included in *Mexico and Central America: A Fiesta of Cultures, Crafts and Activities for Ages 8–12,* by Mary C. Turck. (Chicago Review Press, 2004) p. 59.
3 "Global Strategies to Prevent Childhood Obesity: Forging a Societal Plan That Works," International Obesity Task Force, 2006. From http://www.iotf.org/documents/iotfsoc plan251006.pdf.
4 Richard J. Deckelbaum and Christine L. Williams, *Obesity Research* 9:S239-S243 (2001), Section I: Obesity, the Major Health Issue of the 21st Century, © 2001 *The North American Association for the Study of Obesity.*
5 "Sports and Physical Exercise in Finland" by Leena Nieminen, editor, *Finnish Society for Research in Sport and Physical Education.* From http://virtual.finland.fi/finfo/english/ sportexe.html.
6 These examples are cited in the Concept Paper for the United Nations International Year of Sport and Physical Education, 2005, which looks to sport "as a means to promote Ed-

ucation, Health, Development and Peace." The document can be accessed online at: http://www.un.org/sport2005/resources/concept.pdf.

Chapter 4: Go to School

1 Bob Herbert, Op-Ed "Our Schools Must Do Better," *New York Times,* October 7, 2007.

2 "A Stagnant Nation: Why American Schools Are Still at Risk," Strong American Schools, April 2008.

3 Caren Osten Gerszberg, "A Long Weekend? How About a Whole Year?" *New York Times,* Travel section, November 4, 2007.

4 *Starting Strong II: Early Childhood Education and Care,* p. 5. ISBN 92-64-03535-1, 2006. From http://www.oecd.org/dataoecd/15/35/37424318.pdf. OECD.

5 UNICEF, "State of the World's Children, 2005: Childhood Under Threat." Report found at http://www.unicef.org.

6 Wire side chat: Advancing the need for International, Global Studies. Article by Ellen R. Delisio, Education World®; Copyright © 2004 Education World; November 15, 2004. From http://www.educationworld.com/a_issues/chat/chat122.shtml.

7 From October 6, 2005, Intel Corporation News Release. "Washington and New Jersey Schools Named Top Winners at Intel and Scholastic Schools of Distinction Awards."

8 From http://www.nationalgeographic.com/roper2006/findings.html.

9 U.S. Supreme Court decision on June 28, 2007, in *Parents Involved in Community Schools v. Seattle Public Schools,* ruling five to four against school desegregation on the basis of race. When more than one in six African-American children attend schools that are 99 to 100 percent minority, it seems re-segregation is likely to get worse as a result of the court's ruling.

Chapter 5: Break Bread

1 Michael Pollan, Essay, "Food with a Face" in *Hungry Planet,* Peter Menzel and Faith D'Aluisio (California: Material World Books and Ten Speed Press, 2005), pp. 162–164.

2 From http://www.bbc.co.uk, School Lunch Survey, 2005.

3 For more information on this issue, see Yaroslav Trofimov's article in the *Wall Street Journal,* "It's White, Gloppy, Almost Tasteless and Malawi Loves It. But Nsima Stocks Are Low After Bad Maize Harvest; Yes, We Have Bananas," November 15, 2005, p. 1.

4 "Will Global Growth Help Starbucks?" by Carol Matlack, *Business Week,* July 2, 2008.

5 McDonald's, *2006 Annual Report to Shareholders.*

6 Najmieh Batmanglij, *New Food of Life:* Ancient Persian and Modern Iranian Cooking and Ceremonies (Washington, D.C.: MAGE, 1996), p. 417.

Chapter 6: What Do They Believe?

1 This concept is elucidated in the April 2002 letter "To the World's Religious Leaders" by the Universal House of Justice, Haifa, Israel. This message from the global governing council of the Baha'i Faith was delivered for the consideration of religious leaders from every faith background and on every continent.

2 Frederic and Mary Ann Brussat, *Spiritual Literacy: Reading the Sacred in Everyday Life* (New York: Scribner, 1996).

3 Huston Smith, *The Illustrated World's Religions: A Guide to Our Wisdom Traditions* (New York: Harper San Francisco, 1994), p. 245.

4 Huston Smith, *The Illustrated World's Religions,* p. 248.

5 Diana Eck, "From Diversity to Pluralism," found at: http://www.pluralism.org/plural ism/essays/from_diversity_to_pluralism.php. This is reprinted by permission from *On Common Ground: World Religions in America,* published by Columbia University Press. Revised 2006.

6 Huston Smith, *The Illustrated World's Religions,* p. 246.

7 Linda Kavelin Popov, Dan Popov, and John Kavelin, *The Family Virtues Guide: Simple Ways to Bring Out the Best in Our Children and Ourselves* (New York: Plume, 1997) or visit http://www.virtuesproject.com.

Chapter 7: Celebrate with the World

1 Swati Pandey, "Do you take this stranger?: For one American, a visit to India invites a fresh look at the notion of arranged marriages." *Los Angeles Times,* June 26, 2008, and subsequent email communication with the author.

2 Sarah Bernard, "The Tortoise and the Whoopee Cushion," *New York* magazine, November 26, 2007, p. 106.

Chapter 9: Sustain Your Friendship—Service and Giving

1 "Giving beyond limits: Women of Acholi Quarters Breaking Stones for Katrina Victims," October 17, 2005; from http://www.avsi-usa.org/news.

Appendix: Action Steps to Advance the Millennium Development Goals

1 Bill Clinton, *Giving: How Each of Us Can Change the World* (New York: Alfred A Knopf, 2007) pp. 30–31.

Acknowledgments

The long process of writing this book has felt akin to a spiritual search. It drove me to wake each morning at dawn to pray for clarity of heart and thought, then to find unexpected paths, and persevere, regardless of the bumps on the road. I am overwhelmed with gratitude to have experienced this journey.

I am blessed with an incredibly supportive family, a wide circle of friends, and their friends—my "posse"—who cheerfully shared their stories. They include Venus and Igor (Russia), Maryam (Germany), Jutta (Germany), Christele (France), Alejandra and Jorge (Mexico), Vijaya (India), Rohini (India), Nandini (India), Tao Tao (China), Dawn (China), Wei (China), Krista (China), Angie, Reyaz, Roya, Sarah (Saudi Arabia), Minou (Turkey and Saudi Arabia), Sammi (Thailand), Susan (Iowa and Yemen), Njuru (Kenya), Solange (Ecuador), Luz (Peru), Isabel, Kiko, Monica (Peru), Monica (Guatemala), Dominic (England), Mary (England), Kate (Hong Kong and New York), Johanna (Iceland), Shamim (Malawi, Israel), May (Israel), Martijn (Netherlands), Dennis (Netherlands), 'Alim (everywhere), Monette (everywhere), Helen (Singapore), Safia (Pakistan), Mehrnaz (Iran), Mehrdad (Australia), Michael (Denmark), Shirin (Greece), Renata (Poland), Ellen (all over Europe and New Jersey), Beth M-R (Jewish culture), Perry (Denmark and Chicago), Joanna (Cyprus), Makiko (Japan), Elhum (Japan), Pilar (Spain), Amaya (Spain), Bronwen (Australia), Gail and Zelalem (Ethiopia), Ashwin (India-USA), Jackie E. (USA), Victoria (USA), Tom T. (USA), Anne M-G (USA), David B. (USA), Cara (USA), Eric (L.A.), Hanh (Vietnam), Kathleen (Morocco and England), so many friends in The Gambia; the Veiths, the Johnsons, the Harastys, the Kitas, the Shamsy Rayes, the Clark Boldts, the Taherzadehs, the Millers. The parentheses associated with these wonderful people are inadequate or unwieldy, as few of them can be contained by one country. They live a global life, naturally, as do many more who contributed without being named.

Thanks for valuable insights from: Kenneth Turran, film critic for the *Los Angeles Times* and National Public Radio; Stephanie Stuve-Bodeen, children's author; Kavita Ramdas, Global Fund for Women; Anne Firth-Murray, author and changemaker; Anthony Zinni, retired General U.S. Marine Corps; Nicole Dreiske, Chicago International Film Festival and Facets founder; Dennis Whittle, GlobalGiving; Robert Orr, United Nations; Katherine Marshall, The World Bank; David Shear, Jane Goodall Institute and USAID pioneer; Kate Grant, Fistula Foundation; Harald Horgan, The York Group; Somaly Mam, author and human rights activist; and the diverse people faithfully engaged in the work of the Interfaith Center of Greater Philadelphia.

Stephanie Kip Rostan at Levine Greenberg Literary Agency embraced the concept instantly and helped to make this happen. Marnie Cochran, executive editor at Ballantine Books/Random House has been a joy to work with every step of the way. Thanks to the staff at the Easttown Library and Information Center, particularly Becky Sheridan, enthusiastic and dedicated children's librarian.

My longtime friend, through sickness and health, Elizabeth Nassau, gave a loving and careful eye to each page of the draft. Lorene Cary helped me find my voice. Liz Tankel, Dorothy Marcic, and Esther Sobel offered their boundless friendship and generously opened their quiet spaces to me (in the mountains, on Central Park, and across the street) when I needed to write. Friends from my book club, from the Chester County Fund for Women and Girls, from International House of Philadelphia, from the Baha'i community, as well as from many other corners of my life provided valuable feedback and support. Particular thanks go to Lisa Rapetti, Candyce Wilson, Darlene Tobin, Nancy Cleveland, Heidi McPherson, and Ken Bowers.

My family's unconditional support—emotional, logistical, intellectual, and nutritional—accompanied me from start to finish. My father, Zabih Sabet, gave me pep talks, reality checks, and constant encouragement. My mother, Sohie Sabet, was there for me selflessly, lovingly, and completely, as she always has been. My amazing siblings and their beloved families, Kevin and Shahrzad Sabet, and Mina Sabet, Christopher Bogan, and Juliet and Max—you each are a precious gift to me. My in-laws, starting with my esteemed and tender-loving parents in-law, Dr. Ali and Mrs. Rouha Tavangar; Sherry and Bozorg, Husayn, Varqa, and Amelia, who gave us a home and much more in Africa; Jahan, Nahal, Bobak, and Peymon; Nahid, Moujan, and Bayan—there are no "out-laws" among us!

Words fail to capture the depth of my gratitude and admiration for my beloved husband, Alexander Behrouz Tavangar. You believed in me and in *Growing Up Global* first, and unflinchingly assisted me each step along the way. To my beautiful sweetie-pies, Layla, Anisa, and Sophia: I learn from you, look to you, and love you—always.

Index

PHOTO: MICHAEL SPAIN SMITH

HOMA TAVANGAR has twenty years' experience working with governments, businesses, international organizations, and nonprofit agencies in global competitiveness, organizational and business development, and cross-cultural issues.

She has lived in the Middle East, East and West Africa, South America, and throughout the United States. In addition to English, she speaks Persian (Farsi), Spanish, Portuguese, and rudimentary French and Swahili. She holds undergraduate and graduate degrees in International Economics, and International Development and Public Affairs from UCLA and Princeton University. Her religious heritage includes four of the world's major faiths, and she has family living on every continent.

Homa has been researching *Growing Up Global* since spending the first anniversary of 9/11/01 in China, while she served as Special Advisor on International Business Development for the City of Philadelphia. From January through April 2007, she lived in West Africa with her children, where they spent a school term and she blogged their experience for the *Philadelphia Inquirer*. She is married and the mother of three girls, ranging in age from six to sixteen. She is active with their public schools in suburban Philadelphia and serves on the boards of several international organizations. This is her first book.